Up Society's Ass, Copper

Up Society's Ass, Copper

Copper

Rereading Philip Roth

Mark Shechner

THE UNIVERSITY OF WISCONSIN PRESS

The University of Wisconsin Press
1930 Monroe Street
Madison, Wisconsin 53711

www.wisc.edu/wisconsinpress/

3 Henrietta Street
London WC2E 8LU, England

1   3   5   4   2

Printed in the United States of America

Library of Congress Cataloging-in-Publication Data
Shechner, Mark.
Up society's ass, Copper: rereading Philip Roth / Mark Shechner.
p.   cm.
Includes bibliographical references.
ISBN 0-299-19350-0 (cloth: alk. paper)
ISBN 0-299-19354-3 (pbk.: alk. paper)
1. Roth, Philip—Criticism and interpretation.
2. Literature and society—United States—History—20th century.   I. Title.
PS3568.O855 Z89   2003
813′.54—dc21   2003006268

Publication of this book has been made possible in part by the generous support
of the Anonymous Fund of the University of Wisconsin–Madison.

For my father

Herbert Shechner

1914–2001

Updike and Bellow hold their flashlights out into the world, reveal the real world as it is *now*. I dig a hole and shine my flashlight into the hole.

—Philip Roth, interview with David Plante

The most basic formula of a highly developed culture— a formula which transcends all particular contents— may be suggested by designating it as a crisis constantly held back.

—Georg Simmel, "The War and the Spiritual Decision"

The road of excess leads to the palace of wisdom.

—William Blake, "Proverbs of Hell"

Up society's ass, Copper!

—Alexander Portnoy

Contents

Acknowledgments

The effort of writing a book may feel isolated, but in fact those us who do this sort of thing live in an echo chamber of voices. They infiltrate us and take up posts inside our heads. Ted Solotaroff once observed that he wrote for "a few good voices in my head," and it occurs to me that I do also and that moreover I am always talking to those voices, as if my lonely monologues were really flourishing dialogues. Writing, even in a cork-lined room, is like finding oneself in a morality play with angels at each shoulder, urging one to go left or go right, say it all or keep something back, write extravagantly or play it safe and observe the unspoken decorum of critical prose. It makes for extreme self-consciousness. I find it hard to write a sentence without calling to mind someone else's incomparably finer ones. But then, without those other voices, how do we discover our own? Over the years I've benefited immeasurably from conversations with Jeffrey Berman, Robert Boyers, Melvin Jules Bukiet, Sarah Blacher Cohen, Frederick Crews, Morris Dickstein, Leslie Fiedler, Andrew Furman, Mark Krupnick, Bonnie Lyons, Sanford Pinsker, Thane Rosenbaum, Jeff Rubin-Dorsky, Elaine Safer, Ted Solotaroff, Stephen Whitfield, and Hana Wirth-Nesher. In addition to these, countless critics and reviewers have chattered avidly and incessantly about Roth over the years, and I've profited from more of them than I can name. Those whom I might single out in particular include Robert Alter, James Atlas, Harold Bloom, Anatole Broyard, Robert Cohen, Richard Eder, Alain Finkielkraut, Richard Gilman, Eugene Goodheart, Jay Halio, Hermione Lee, John Leonard, Zöe Heller, J. Hoberman, Irving Howe, Frank Kermode, R. B. Kitaj, David Remnick, Richard Stern, John Updike, and James Wood. In addition, I never fail to find Michiko Kakutani and Norman Podhoretz entertaining on the subject of Roth. And Derek Royal, who keeps an online bibliography of Roth on the Web, has given me a running start on my own efforts in that direction.

Since I have been writing about Philip Roth virtually as long as I have been writing, most of these chapters were previewed and tested in newspapers and periodicals. Portions first saw light in *American Literary History, The Bookpress* (Ithaca, New York), *The Boston Book Review, The Buffalo News, The Nation,* and *Partisan Review,* as well as an anthology, *Contemporary American-Jewish Novelists,* edited by Joel Shatsky and Michael Taub. Parts of this book have appeared in somewhat different form in two previous books of my own, *After the Revolution: Studies in the Contemporary Jewish-American Imagination* and *The Conversion of the Jews and Other Essays.* With a few exceptions, all previous essays have been substantially edited to the point of being new essays.

My thanks too to the editors at the University of Wisconsin Press, for their patience and hard work. Bob Mandel and Tricia Brock have been model editors, and Adam Mehring has done Herculean work in cleaning out the Augean Stables of the original manuscript. My thanks to all. And to Nettie, *sine qua non.*

The cover drawing of Roth is by the artist R. B. Kitaj, from his book *First Diasporist Manifesto.* It appears here courtesy of the artist and Marlborough Fine Art, London.

Up Society's Ass, Copper

Introduction
"Because I Do What I Do"

Toward the end of *Operation Shylock,* the novel that marks the high point of Philip Roth's engagement with Israel, the book's lead character, one "Philip Roth," meets in a New York deli with a man code-named Smilesburger, a retired Mossad agent. "Roth" has asked Smilesburger to read the manuscript of a book recounting his adventures in Israel, where he engaged in some serious skullduggery for the Mossad. In the course of conversation, Smilesburger reveals to Roth that he is not, like him, a Jew of conscience and that he recognizes the Jews as the party at fault in the Middle East: "To make a Jewish state we have betrayed our history—we have done unto the Palestinians what the Christians have done unto us." He also makes a remarkable disclaimer about his reasons for taking part in this expropriation of Palestinian lands and suppression of rights. If one day, he says, there should be a Palestinian victory and he was brought up on war-crimes charges, he would offer no defense for himself. He would not plead the history of anti-Semitism; he would not plead the millennial Jewish claim to the land nor the horrors of the Holocaust. Nor would he even plead the simple truth: "I am a tribesman who stood with his tribe." He is prepared to say to his judges only that, "'I did what I did to you because I did what I did to you.' And if that is not the truth, it's as close as I know how to come to it. 'I do what I do because I do what I do.'"

It is a remarkable confession to find in fiction, where moral exculpation—being "redeemed" as the language of moral criticism has it—is

3

the norm, though such moral natures are hardly absent from political life. Whether there was ever an actual Smilesburger to say such a thing to the actual Philip Roth, we have no way of knowing, but his confession seems to stand as a statement of ultimate Realpolitik, that we do what we do because we do what we do, as it might be spoken with honesty by anyone whose hands are dirty from power politics, from Osama bin Laden to George Bush, from Yasser Arafat to Ariel Sharon. Although none would ever utter the sentiment so nakedly, we might indeed expect them to understand it: of themselves and of each other.

But might that not also stand as the novelist's ultimate defense of what he has written and whatever effect it might have on the world: "I do what I do because I do what I do"? Whatever else it does, it puts the writer beyond exculpation, beyond extenuation, beyond the need for any principled reasons to commit to the page whatever he or she finally commits to the page. It even puts the writer beyond psychology, to the extent that psychology provides sensible reasons and renders behavior morally palatable. And that I think is a happy place to be for a writer, finally, beyond having to justify, or to be justified: to be expected to be a moral agent of any kind. I'm certain that Roth would be no more at ease being mistaken for a moral agent than he ever was when mistaken, as he has sometimes been, for an immoral one, and while his books are brimful of ethical considerations—he is, after all, a Jewish writer—there is seldom a place where one can firmly place a finger on a moral issue and say for certain: "Here is where Roth comes down." Or, to isolate some particular psychological obsession and say, "Here is where Roth lives." That is not for reasons of postmodern indeterminacy, though Roth has sometimes taken refuge in it, but because it doesn't help any to do that. Roth's books don't become more available, nor do they take on new dimensions, when his hobbyhorses are put up in lights. We seldom if ever get closer to the heart of Roth's fiction by isolating the voice of responsibility. It's there, but no more important than the voices of terror, of loneliness, of mockery, of skepticism, of rage, of amazement, of comedy, of zealotry, of wild imagining. As for the voice of appetite, it is always on tap. Whatever else I undertake in this book, it is not an attempt to wrestle Roth to the mat and take his moral temperature: Roth does what he does because he does what he does, and in coming to grips with his books I find it helpful to respect that intention and follow the example. This book too will do what it does because it does what it does.

There is no choice: a book that has been written in bits and pieces, in the form of occasional essays and reviews, over a period of almost thirty years can't reflect a single intention or even a single state of mind or voice. Nor can it be rewritten as something more integrated, complete, or thematically consistent. That's a shortcut to transforming whatever was immediate about the reading experience and putting it under glass, where it becomes a museum exhibit even as I am doing it. What I find myself most enjoying, as I reread these essays, is the afterglow of the original adrenaline rush, which I could not possibly fake in a more coherent book written in a long sitting. The short reviews were written while the books were still white hot for me, and while they may not finally reflect my final assessment—how could they?—they do remind me of Roth's unending ability to get a rise out of me after all these years, which is why I've continued to write about him. I respond, and I don't ask of literature much more than this: to be provocative, to engage me, to make me want more. How rarely does that take place!

⤳

How did I get here? I never know such things for certain, but here is how I think it happened. While still a graduate student in California I had read and been wildly entertained by *Portnoy's Complaint,* and I assumed that my pleasure was widely shared. How could it not have been? In the terms that I might have used then, I had found the book's combustible and self-lacerating comedy "right on," and had heard in Alexander Portnoy's hysterical, insouciant, and self-dramatizing voice something so familiar and resonant that I had taken the book to be something of a secret cousin. It was no accident that my first eleven years were spent in Philip Roth's neighborhood of Newark, the predominantly Jewish (at the time) Weequahic section, so that its voices, though grown dim from decades away, could be reawakened by the book's free surges of language and crazed parabolas of laughter. Indeed, I lived just across the street from the grammar school that also served as the Weequahic High School Annex in those days. Although I had left that neighborhood at the age of eleven, winding up eventually in California, and had not had time to absorb the full culture of Jewish Newark, there was enough of it lodged dormant under my skin, like a sleeping virus, to be blasted into wakefulness by the book's careening and ironic comedy. What was not to like? I had no idea, and it took me a while to find out that the literary world is not built around my parochial enthusiasms. I was twenty-nine when *Portnoy's Complaint* was published, but to many things I was still sleepy.

By the time I became aware of the storm around the book I was an assistant professor, living and teaching in Buffalo, New York, and closer both geographically and in intellectual culture to what Harold Brodkey once called "the infinite oral thuggery" of New York City. For all I know, I was the only person in America who was taken by surprise by the double-barreled attack on Roth in the December 1972 issue of *Commentary*, which featured Norman Podhoretz's essay, "Laureate of the New Class" and Irving Howe's surly and agitated "Philip Roth Reconsidered." (Since this dustup will be discussed in detail later on, I'll simply allude to it here.) Even Roth, who had been taking blows for more than ten years, must have been on red alert for this. It certainly took me by surprise; the revelation that literary culture was a war zone was a wake-up call. I probably should not have been so surprised. I had spent the years from 1964 though 1970 in Berkeley and San Francisco and knew about cultural combat as a daily experience, one that exuded the pungent aroma of tear gas. But it was not easy in that time and that place to separate the spell of cultural revolution from the politics of antiwar and anti-what-have-you-got protest. It was something that took place in the streets, and it was not for many years that I learned that Lionel Trilling had called the cultural revolution "modernism in the streets" and looked upon it as a bad omen for Western Civilization. When it came to the academic side of life, the view from Berkeley was distinctly different from the view from Columbia: cultural warfare had not found a home in the west coast literary curriculum, not at least in any class that I ever attended. Things changed shortly afterwards. Someone said to me as I was leaving Berkeley for the east, "You're trading in Dickens for Dostoevsky." That sounded inviting. I couldn't wait. I was fast outgrowing California youth culture and was ready for some Russian soul and Dostoevskian strangeness, until I learned what it meant, the Kulturkampf around Roth being the Freshman Comp class of my unsentimental education. How could I know that lower depths I cherished would take the form of a live and desperate Nikolai Raskolnikov on my bookshelf and a live Porfiry Petrovich hot on his tail?

⟿

In 1972 another piece of this adventure went beyond the thrill of having a Newark paisano out there who could portray an overbearing Jewish mother and a peevish son so accurately that he seemed a one-man survey research team with so many interviews under his belt that he knew, down to the least standard deviation, what such people were like. I had left California with a sense of inexorable and durable method under my belt and was itching to test it out in a live literary arena. It is a little embarrassing to talk about it now, but since intellectual Marxists are out there, even to this day, writing books about when and how the scales fell from their eyes—when they had their personal Kronstadts[1]—why not at least a few pages about my own version of that adventure?

I was a Freudian. Back then in Berkeley, a bright young assistant professor of English, Frederick Crews, was teaching graduate seminars in applied psychoanalysis and attracting disciples the way a magnet attracts iron filings. It wasn't hard to understand why. Those were heady days of radical thought in Berkeley, and in English, at least, psychoanalysis was the available radicalism. At that time there was no resident Marxist, save maybe a disciple of critic Leo Marx, and Marxism, in those days of home-brew revolutionism, when Friedrich Engels seemed as stolid as a plow horse beside thoroughbreds like Che Guevara, struck most of us as at least musty if not discredited. Whatever else was true, Crews had an odd and offbeat charisma for a radical. He was about the funniest guy going, and classes with him were a treat, no matter what we were talking about. The person we encountered in the classroom might talk about guilt like the Crews of *The Sins of the Fathers*, his book on Nathaniel Hawthorne, but the offhand manner was pure *Pooh Perplex*. For me, at least, if someone that consistently witty and ironic believed so strongly in Freudian theory, then it had a fighting chance of being true. (But let it be said that not even Lenny Bruce could have gotten me to read *Capital*.) We now know that Crews's doubts were festering even as he marched us through our classroom exercises of finding the primal scene in every human struggle and every rustle of garden foliage—and boy did we ever find them. Mom and Dad were never so exposed for the mad fornicators they were as in that seminar! But in those classes, in 1967 and 1968, Crews never let on that we might just be finding what we had set out to look for, and we, in need of some classroom experience that could rival the drama and spectacle of the daily rallies at Sproul Plaza and weekly rumblings out on the streets, clung desperately to the dubious wisdom to be found in Freud's *Standard Edition,* as though it were nothing less than a voice out of the burning bush itself.

I have little recollection of the classes as such: maybe because finally they were more ordinary than I cared then to acknowledge. No, let's be honest. I was bored most of the time. But I have vivid recollections of evenings spent with Crews and members of the San Francisco Psychoanalytic Institute in one psychoanalyst's apartment on San Francisco's Nob Hill, where after drinks and hors d'oeuvres, analysts and lit critters alike sat in a circle and talked theory and literature for about two hours, until dessert came out and we got to freeload amply on Napoleons and Courvoisier, afforded to us by the happy fact that psychoanalysis had emerged in Europe as the treatment of choice for a sexually obsessed middle class and had retained its association with affluence and high culture in the United States. It was certainly a break from the jug wines of student life, and if truth be told, it did not incline one to bouts of skepticism. It was a reassuring way to be young and intellectual in the vortex of a revolution, and as we drove home across the Bay Bridge in my friend Al's MGB, myself stuffed behind the bucket seats like a piece of collapsible luggage, I could only congratulate myself on my luck. Slogging through *Hamlet* week after week with the soigné heirs of the Freudian revolution was a small price to pay for being a privileged student in the back of a sports car roaring its way through the California night with my stomach full of cheesecake and brandy and my head full of the best that had been thought and said—sixty years earlier. Yes, it is true that during one of those soirees a senior analyst had taken me aside to confess that the contents of the Freudian unconscious were, in his words, "few, simple, and boring," but I didn't take it then for a warning, just a bit of late-night personal grousing about the dreariness of having to put up all day with so much kvetching. (A friend reported not long ago of having been fired by her analyst. "I don't want to hear any more about your father," he had said. My sympathies were with the analyst.) It would be a few years yet until I would discover that he was absolutely right: few, simple, and boring, and one thing more—fictitious. That would come later, and Crews himself, having become the Sidney Hook of psychoanalysis, would happily help that reassessment along.

At the time this second storm broke over Roth and *Portnoy* in December 1972—there was an earlier one in 1969 that had driven Roth out of the country—I was casting about for something compelling to do. I had completed my graduate school project and was at loose ends. I didn't want to go any further with the grad school work: it wasn't gripping enough, and I wanted to be gripped. Out of the blue, I had a subject that didn't have to be chosen by lot from a shopping list of options. To take a phrase from WWF wrestling, Podhoretz and Howe had opened a serious can of whoop-ass on Roth, and like the tag-team buddy I fancied myself to be, I sat down and pounded out a riposte that surely didn't take me more than two weeks to write. It was an agitated defense of Roth against charges of being a willful writer "who imposes himself on his characters and denies them any fullness, contour, or surprise"; of lacking all patience for uncertainties, mysteries, and doubts, for "negative capability"; of being vulgar and reductive in his thought; of being a literary "swinger" and a slave to cultural fashion; and of being hampered by a "thin personal culture." These from Howe. After such disemboweling, what forgiveness? Was any hope of dignity left? It was a mugging, pure and simple, and I pegged Howe and Podhoretz for a couple of mugs. All of this is gone over in detail in a subsequent chapter and needs no amplification here, but it sent me flying wildly out of my corner, swinging from the heels. There was a second part to the exercise, much of which is now lost: an attempt to use my newfound tools, my keys to the treasure house of the unconscious, to get down to the bedrock of Alex Portnoy, as though he were my patient. In effect, while defending Roth against detractors, I could also bring Portnoy's strange "case" to light. That those two purposes might in fact conflict with each other did not occur to me at the time.

The entire exercise was exceedingly weird, but at least I had what I wanted: I had been moved at last, first by a book and second by someone else's insistence that my own literary passion—my first since falling hard for James Joyce—was utter trash. If Roth was "Laureate of the

New Class"—Podhoretz's phrase—what was I, then? A face in that depthless crowd? So I rose up, with indignation as my sword and Otto Fenichel's *The Psychoanalytic Theory of Neurosis* as my shield, and wrote about it. And, when I was done, I mailed it off to Roth.

Part of the strategy of that essay was to find a voice, something that was as far as I could get from the prefabricated jargons that were rampant in the profession I had chosen—and have, if anything, grown worse—and from the off-the-shelf middle style of compositional prose that was its immediate alternative. I had written nothing at all since finishing the book on James Joyce two years earlier and felt stymied both by the lack of a compelling subject and a way of writing that could bring ideas to life. By adopting for this diatribe-cum-routine a brash and unbuttoned style, the bratty style of the schoolyard, as it turned out to be, I was able to solve a problem of how to write about Roth without sounding like just another pundit, another sober and wearisome talking head. There would turn out to be problems with this style, including its inappropriateness to other subjects, but for a short while I was able to revel in the freedom that it afforded me; I was able to say things through it that the middle style of expository prose simply ruled out.

About all I remember now is that Roth did not altogether despise it. More than that I can't claim. But the absence of complete contempt was all I really needed to summon up the courage to revise the screed and send it off to *Partisan Review*, where it was accepted immediately. Had Roth called ahead? Now, what I had sent to Roth and what was finally published in *Partisan Review* were substantially different pieces of writing. The first was a screed, a cri de couer, that lit out after Howe on grounds that the character he discovered and scourged in *Portnoy's Complaint* bore distinct resemblances to the person he had anatomized in a self-revealing essay about his own youth, "The Lost Young Intellectual." Howe, I had argued, was in effect tilting at mirrors. Uncertain of how that would fly at *Partisan Review*, I excised that part of the essay, and only recently rediscovered it for restoration in this volume. See chapter 3, "Only a *Weltanschauung:* Howe's Lost Young Intellectual." Without this section, much of the essay's original polemical heat was damped and its velocity was throttled back to the ambling speed of a "study," an "exegesis." The middle style was creeping back.

There was another section, a piece of reckless analysis in which I tried my own interpretive hand at Alex Portnoy's complaint, his struggle between raffish appetites and ethical impulses, and maybe Roth's as well. Recall that *Portnoy's Complaint* is a long analytic confession to one Doctor Spielvogel, who is silent until the end, when he announces his presence with the punchline, "So. Now vee may perhaps to begin. Yes?" My own Spielvogel imitation had to be scaled back: it was fine as a *jeu d'esprit*, but for publication? For the world to see? For literary history? For *Partisan Review*, that Parnassus of my own household gods: Dwight Macdonald, Harold Rosenberg, Mary McCarthy, Saul Bellow, Philip Rahv and William Phillips, Isaac Rosenfeld, Meyer Schapiro? I chickened out and dropped those pages in the wastebasket. In tone it was brash and insouciant, somewhere between diagnosis and shtick, between putting Alexander Portnoy on the couch and putting him on stage, though of course Roth had already beaten me to the punch with both. So, for that matter, had *Partisan Review*, which had published one of the brashest sections of *Portnoy* in 1967: "Whacking Off." But I wasn't Roth and knew that I hadn't the verbal chops or the casehardened nerves to pull it off, and so I put that routine on a short leash, discarding some of the more reckless and jocular speculations.

Here is one I remember. I was running the Freudian chord progression, from oral to anal to phallic, and had this brilliant—to me—anal epiphany. Recall that Mr. Portnoy suffers from a nervous bowel and spends countless hours on the toilet trying to expel as feces some fraction of what he imbibed as food. His bowels, he jokes, are turning into concrete. But Sophie Portnoy, that humming assembly line of symptoms herself, while reminiscing about a man who once paid her court, a businessman in the condiment line, recalls him as "the biggest manufacturer of mustard in New York. . . . And I could have married him instead of your father." Hello! Now, it may be precisely because the contents of the Freudian unconscious are few, simple, and boring that it took me about a nanosecond to see that someone's unconscious— Sophie Portnoy's, Alex's, Roth's?—had dreamed up a rival for the mother's affections whose bowels not only functioned 24/7 but had brought him riches as well. But if it had been too good to pass up the first time around, it was too wild to pass around the second, and out it came. There are those who spend their later years regretting their youthful indiscretions—repentant Marxists in particular are ever beating their breasts about the credulities of their youths. A silent majority, however, regrets their youthful discretions, and I am one of them. Forget the Oedipus Complex. Had Freud given us the Prufrock Complex instead, I'm sure I'd still be quoting him today.

Then again, without regret, would we have any literature? Would there be anything to write about? By the time my denatured essay on Roth appeared in *Partisan Review* in 1974, there were intellectual dramas about psychoanalysis being played out all around. Crews had done an about-face on the subject, now proclaiming it to be a pseudoscience whose authority was rooted in Sigmund Freud's flawed character—the character of an intellectual conquistador—rather than in anything empirically derived and testable. That caused no little bit of consternation among his students, many of whom had founded careers on psychoanalysis, either as academics or, in some cases, as psychotherapists, and felt betrayed. I don't count myself as one of them, and while I maintain to this day a handful of Freudian skeletons in my closet, I don't feel any abiding nostalgia for a system of thought that is so clearly a patchwork of cultural prejudice, guesswork, daring, and blunder, and has so little to do with science. It was on Nob Hill, after all, over drinks, that I was given my mantra of few, simple, and boring, and how hard was it really to go the final yard and detach from a fiction that, like Marxism, makes the world seem so much simpler, meaner, and less fascinating than daily experience tells us it is?

We know too, because Roth wrote about it in *My Life as a Man* in 1974, that he also was undergoing a crisis of faith over his own analysis and analyst—the actual Spielvogel in Roth's life. It comes out in that novel, whose "My True Story" section is close enough to Roth's life to be read as a memoir, that "Spielvogel" had published a case history in a professional journal of his famous patient, the very fact of which struck Roth as a violation of trust and a potential exposure of himself as a patient. In the novel, the Roth stand-in, Peter Tarnopol, is driven to break relations with his analyst, who is accused not only with betrayal of his patient, but with filling his head with ready-to-wear visions of his own life: with, as he puts it, substituting for the character's actual, blessed childhood, "rather Dickensian recollections of my mother as an overwhelming and frightening person." We are expected to read in Tarnopol's break with his therapist Roth's own disaffection from the Freudian world-view itself. Certainly after the minor debacle of *The Breast* in 1972, in which Freud-in-Spielvogel presides over a Kafkaesque farce about a man turned into a giant female breast, Roth clearly was going to have less to say about "the mother."

These simultaneous disaffections, by Crews and by Roth, were very intense for me at the time, in part because I had gotten involved in a situation at my home university that had its own momentum of decay, and in part also because Crews took the opportunity in 1972 to dramatize his disgruntlement in a review of Roth's *The Breast* in *The New York Review of Books* that was so damning, that, when added to screeds by Podhoretz and Howe (and Marie Syrkin and Bruno Bettelheim) only confirmed Roth's special preeminence in the rogue's gallery of literature. Sure Roth had his defenders: so had Julius and Ethel Rosenberg. But that handful of us out on the picket lines with our "Free Philip" buttons and our "Unfair" placards on high might just as well have put them down and gone home for dinner. The verdict was in.[2]

In a few brisk and slashing phrases, Crews roughed up Roth as surely as the others had, not by professing revulsion at his sexual hedonism or at crimes against the Jews but by finding in *The Breast* a failure of literary nerve, a backsliding into sobriety at just that moment in his career when he should have been pushing the envelope of his forte: "the portrayal of compulsives whose humane intelligence cannot save them from their irrationality. The sharpness and energy of his work have to do with a fidelity to petty idiocies of self-betrayal." Roth instead had swallowed the sour bait of orthodox therapeutic wisdom and made his suffering mastomorphic hero into a "noble survivor." "Roth loses control over the half-developed themes that would have saved his story from banality. It is as if Kafka were to bludgeon us into admitting that Gregor Samsa is the most stoical beetle we have met, and a wonderful sport about the whole thing." And what, asks Crews, "would Alex Portnoy have to say about *that?*"

Why had I neglected Crews's review of *The Breast* while working up a brief on Roth's behalf? Because, painful as it would have been for me to say then, I shared Crews's disappointment, though not for his reasons: the hero's, and presumably Roth's, stoical recipe for enduring catastrophe, Freud's own "put up with it." (British psychoanalyst Adam Phillips refers to classical psychoanalysis as the "noble killjoy" and there it was.) The book struck me as flat in ways that were not so easy to pin down: the élan, the propulsion, the sheer performative excess of Roth at the top of his game, were missing. The problem for me was not where Crews had found it, in the hero's, David Alan Kepesh's, sententiousness, his mammary rendition of Polonius, but in the book's dark, wordless core. The book was depressive, as if produced by a collapse of spirits, for which Kepesh's grotesque transformation was only a metaphor and learning to put up was the only available choice. Roth's next book, *My Life as a Man,* would tell us what that was.

⁓

My own connection to the Freudian enterprise was also under strain. I had taken a teaching job at SUNY Buffalo, which at the time was a watering hole for psychoanalytic theorists through its Center for the Psychological Study of the Arts, presided over by Norman Holland. When I arrived, the center was a raucous ongoing symposium: a place where the Sturm und Drang of the psychoanalytic movement at the end of the last century was particularly sturmy. Its monthly dinner meetings were occasions for airing the crises of faith that psychoanalysis was experiencing and for staging previews of the Next Big Thing, whatever it might be. Everybody conceded that the future of psychoanalysis was up for grabs, and like bookies in some Caesar's Palace of ideas, my colleagues were out there handicapping the contenders. In that hothouse atmosphere I was brought nose-to-nose with bold and free-wheeling speculation from all over the map: from the French Freudians (Jacques Derrida and Jacques Lacan) to the British Kleinians and Object Theorists (Melanie Klein, D. W. Winnicott, R. D. Laing), to American therapeutic radicals from Wilhelm Reich to Norman O. Brown. The meetings were attended by feminists brandishing their copies of Juliet Mitchell; a cigar-smoking composition theorist who fulminated about "reader response" and "discourse communities"; an acolyte of Jacques Lacan who giddily regaled us with stories of how the master stiffed him on his training analysis; a neo-Jungian disciple of James Hillman who touted a polytheistic psychology that hearkened back to Greek theology; a law professor and pornography buff who usually showed up

stoned and sprinkled his tedious filibusters with quotes from the Beatles; and a local psychoanalyst who had cooked up his own post-
Freudian system called "identity theory," whereby personality could be
boiled down to its dominant and repetitive themes. I had fallen into an
academic *Walpurgisnacht,* in which I felt like Leopold Bloom wandering
through a hallucinatory night-town of theories. Although it left me be-
dazzled, I did value the free-wheeling spirit of a forum in which the de-
bates were heated and most questions were open for discussion, except
the crucial one: how can we know if any of this is true?

Then, one day, by some hand signal that I happened not to see—like
a batter who has missed the bunt sign—it was over, and the winner was
declared: identity theory. As if nothing momentous had taken place,
suddenly my colleagues were busily coining these one-liners, summing
up human essences in aphorisms so compact that you could stick them
into fortune cookies and still have space left over for lucky numbers.
From the delirious multiplicity of jostling isms, few, simple, and boring
were back in the driver's seat. This collapse of the marketplace of ideas
into a sectarian sweatshop was my cue to slip quietly out the door and
turn my attention to a body of writing that I had been working up since
Portnoy's Complaint and which extended outward into unknown and
fascinating territory: Jewish writers and New York intellectual life.
There was my cornucopia of ideas: Russia, Stalin, Trotsky, homeless intellectuals, homages to Catalonia, modernism, the fall of Paris and the
rise of abstract expressionism, *Partisan Review,* the death rattle (it then
seemed) of Marxism, the Chicago Dostoevskians, the tragic sense of
life, the fiction produced by the decay of a radical movement, the literature of the fortunate fall.

It is a truism that changes in basic orientation, in paradigm, as they
say, are always experienced as liberations, and it was true that the encounter with psychoanalysis felt to many of us at first like a breakthrough into new and exciting vistas and a permission to speak candidly
of intimate matters that had formerly been taboo. To have the unconscious life at one's beck and call made life seem more intricate, more
mysterious, more unstable and explosive. It lent depth to ordinary life,
drama to any human activity more complicated than a yawn, and ra-
tional purpose to eccentric behavior. For the literary critic, moreover, it
provided a backstage pass to the artist's unconscious, allowing the critic

to trump the writer at his/her own game: an understanding of the heart's true desires. "You call that passion? Why, that's textbook regression." Ten years later, after those mysteries had been packaged as doctrines and the taboos had become brand names—when, for example, the male sexual organ got shipped over from France and marketed as a philosophical nullity called The Phallus—I needed liberation from the liberation. For the next leg of the journey, Philip Roth turned out to be a point of departure: his writing, the energies it engaged in me and others, blustery and provocative though they sometimes were, were embarkation points into the turbulent and unpredictable world I was looking for. Did I want strangeness? Well, there it was. The treacherous? Stick around. Sex? Well, Newark had it too, and as for comedy, it had Vienna beat hands down. The tragic sense of life? Prague. So much of what I've read, thought, and explored for the past thirty years started out with Roth. His books have served me as windows on the one hand and a home base on the other: a certain renegade sensibility that answers to my own need for a familiar, reliable, and above all intelligent rebelliousness. Maybe it is the Newark thing, calling me home like a salmon that lasers in on its own tiny stream a thousand miles out at sea. I'd be the last one to deny that there might be something irreducibly parochial in my interests. Maybe too it is the engaged intelligence in everything Roth puts his hand to, or the grievance and restlessness that keeps his writing fresh, even when, as some of his critics continue to complain, it is a theater of personality or of libido. They are hard to distinguish at times. If a man wants to shill for his own cock, why get in his way? Let's leave it this way: I found in Roth something I needed to stay interested for these thirty years: the opposite of few, simple, and boring and the antidote to the terror of growing stale, routine, and predictable with age. Roth hasn't, an example I would hope to follow.

⤙

Virtually nothing that follows was written initially with this collection in mind. Most of the chapters were written first as book reviews. As a result, there is a degree of overlap and repetition in the book that I have decided not to edit out. Why cripple an essay because its best lines have appeared elsewhere? And why bury your best lines by delivering them just once? The reader should be aware, however, that my saying something two or three times is not intended to browbeat. In Yiddish it is called "hocking a chinik," literally, chopping a teakettle. It means only that I've run out of fresh things to say about a particular book and am in desperate need of a phrase. I've updated much of this writing when I could, appended second thoughts to other essays and reviews. Sometimes the original had to say far less than needed to be said, and sometimes I have had a change of heart and mind. Some initial enthusiasms have faded; some initial disappointments have been rethought. And I've had time to read other commentators and reflect on them. In the passing of time, critical commentary on Roth has grown richer and more varied, as some of the best minds of Roth's generation have tried their hand at coming to grips with his books.

1

The Facts and *The Facts*

This book will have little to say about Philip Roth's life. Biography may or may not be a way into fiction; it all depends on how you read and what you want from fiction, and I've decided that the reader of this book will have to do with the bare minimum of biography and slake his or her curiosity about Roth elsewhere. I have neither the skill nor the patience for that sort of work, and this book will be as biographically thin as I can reasonably make it without pretending that the author doesn't exist altogether. (The pomo theorists who deny the author's existence have dealt themselves a comfy hand. Lucky them. They can press ahead undeterred by life and its complications.) I won't even claim it as a matter of principle that this book will be thin on Roth's life, only that to make it thicker would be to write a very different book than the one I have in mind. Hopefully, soon, someone will write that book; Roth deserves and will eventually get his Boswell. Without being too principled about it, I'm more interested in the reader's experience of Roth's books: that is, my own. And I know from long self-acquaintance that this experience is haphazard, inconsistent, and whimsical. I mean, if you are going to be consistent or rule bound about the business of reading, why do it? Where's the adventure?

However, having issued this disclaimer, I do after all have to say something about the author of the novels and stories of which I am try- ing to make sense, if only to ward off total disorientation on the reader's part and sometimes on my own. And, moreover, to acknowledge the obvious, that Roth has strip-mined his own life for the stony ore of his books, and a little knowledge in his case goes a long way. For those who don't already know something about Roth and are picking this book up out of sheer random curiosity—of course, no such reader exists—the question of who this Roth guy is should at least be answered well enough to encourage them to read ahead, and I feel obliged to say something about where readers might go for more. Roth's own "autobiography" of 1988, *The Facts,* is the obvious place to start, and if I highlight the word autobiography with quotation marks, it is only because the book is surprisingly brief for someone who, at the time it was written, was fifty-five years old, and also because Roth himself, by the time the book was finished, called the entire story into question and begged us not to mistake *The Facts* for the facts.

I find it uncanny, but hardly beyond imagining, that for several years now I had set *The Facts* aside for future reading, only to find, upon opening it recently, that it was already graffitied, from first page to last, by my asterisks and exclamation points of approval and my groans of "get off it" and "not again" and "shit." Am I that out of it that I would not remember a book I had read just fourteen years ago, and one that is both by and about an author whose work I hold dear? Of course, I do forget things; fourteen years ago is not last week, and I had read the book apart from any writing assignment. I'm more likely to forget a book that I had not written about than one that was branded into memory by the necessity of dredging up words about it. Or, was the book just forgettable? I hardly blame myself when a book I reviewed as recently as a year ago has slipped so completely out of memory that I have to look up my review to remember even the first thing about it, including the author's name. In such cases I don't think I'm losing it, just clearing my mind to make room for more urgent or pleasurable things. I doubt that any profound self-analysis is called for here; it is not as though I had forgotten my own past, and it is true that after a rereading I find *The Facts* one of Roth's less mesmerizing books, at least until that last thirty-four pages, which take the form of a letter from Nathan Zuckerman to Philip Roth advising him not to publish the manuscript, because, "You try to pass off here as frankness what looks to me like the dance of the seven veils—what's on the page is like a code for something missing."

Zuckerman then proceeds to chip away at everything Roth had tried to construct, from the aureate memories of a cosseted childhood in

Newark to the vivid early days of literary success to the brutal encounters with reader disapproval and the horrors of marriage in 1959 to Margaret Martinson Williams (he calls her Josie Jensen in *The Facts*), a marriage that was combat from first to last, and was not completely resolved until her death in a car crash in 1968, though they were legally separated in 1963. At that point, *The Facts* drops the pose of "undisguised" narrative (as Roth announces it to be at the start) and takes on the dialectical point-counterpoint of a Roth novel itself, with Nathan Zuckerman playing the role of devil's advocate and something more: psychotherapist digging out of the book's bland narrative the grievances and terrors and culpabilities—the sly motives, the slick defenses, the punishing self-delusions—that the main text leaves unspoken. As Zuckerman observes, "With autobiography there's always another text, a countertext if you will, to the one presented. It's probably the most manipulative of all literary forms." A contemporary literary critic, armed with the jargons of the profession, might say that with this appendix, Nathan Zuckerman "deconstructs" Philip Roth's story, or that, since Zuckerman after all is only Roth's hand puppet, that Roth does that himself. Besides not caring for that jargon, which lumps together almost any degree of dissent from a neighborly demurral to a *New Criterion* disemboweling into a single all-purpose verb of demolition, I don't think that gets us any closer to Roth's own intention than the simple observation that he produces his hand puppet and gives him his withering lines in order to rescue his life's story from an error built into its initial conception: that he could write about himself in a voice of calculated blandness and bemused nostalgia without producing a forced march of recollected events, a talking résumé, unilluminated by imagination, uninvigorated by regret, unanimated by guilt. Roth?

～

Roth began writing *The Facts,* he tells us, in the spring of 1987, after a mental crackup induced by drug use in the wake of what should have been simple knee surgery. To deal with postsurgical pain, Roth's doctor prescribed the drug Halcion, which was already known to induce psychosis, a fact of which Roth was unaware. Roth's account of the experience in *The Facts* is sketchy and no more than a bridge to the exercise in recalling his past in order to reconstruct his present. "In

order to recover what I had lost I had to go back to the moment of origin," he writes in *The Facts*. "Here, so as to fall back into my former
life, to retrieve my vitality, to transform myself in myself, I began rendering experience untransformed." A far more harrowing account of the
dread, the panic, the sense of utter mental chaos may be found in the
early pages of the novel *Operation Shylock,* in which Roth details those
months when his mind had slipped its moorings and come utterly
apart. A readership far larger than the one that read *Operation Shylock*
would have seen that story as part of Roth's account of an interview
with Israeli author Aharon Appelfeld in the *New York Times Book
Review* in February 1988.[1] They would have learned of the origins of the
unusually sober *The Facts* in these terms: "My only chance of getting
through to daylight without having my mind come completely apart
was to hook hold of a talismanic image out of my most innocent past
and try to ride out the menace of the long night lashed to the mast of
that recollection."

It is self-evident to anyone who has read more than one or two of
Roth's novels that his own experience has been the basis for much of his
storytelling. He has come into more than just a little bit of criticism for
that from book reviewers and readers, and readers who have little stomach for a writer who puts himself on display, or at least appears to do so,
are not going to take full pleasure in his work, no matter what else he
does. In *The Facts* itself, in the form of a letter to his reader and literary
creation, Nathan Zuckerman, Roth writes: "In the past, as you know,
the facts have always been notebook jottings, my way of springing into
fiction. For me, as for most novelists, every genuine imaginative event
begins down there, with the fact, with the specific, and not with the
philosophical, the ideological, or the abstract." And by facts Roth has
usually meant experiences. "On the pendulum of self-exposure that os-
cillates between aggressively exhibitionistic Mailerism and sequestered
Salingerism, I'd say that I occupy a midway position, trying in the public arena to resist gratuitously prying or preening without making too
holy a fetish of secrecy and seclusion."

The situation is a lot more complicated. Roth is not a public figure,
and if not so tightly secluded from the public as Salinger or Thomas
Pynchon, he keeps his distance from public life. And yet, as he does
that, he makes certain his books will be provocative enough to arouse

the kind of lurid curiosity about his life and habits that he would be bound to defend himself against. As for the heroes of his fiction, they range to and beyond the freewheeling and exhibitionistic Alex Portnoy to the various faces of David Alan Kepesh, who in one book is a gigantic female breast who wants to go on stage with his "act," and in another is a host of a cultural arts TV show in New York, on which he achieves the notoriety that "breast" Kepesh cherishes without the spectacular disfigurement the latter endures. As if to counterbalance those, we have the figure of E. I. Lonoff, who sequesters himself deep in the New England woods, where he lacks only the perfect solitude of Antarctica, in order to indulge the daily pleasure of rewriting imperfect sentences, and the various latter-day incarnations of Nathan Zuckerman, who, in *American Pastoral, I Married a Communist,* and *The Human Stain,* ventures out of his country bungalow, his anchorite's cell, like some secluded and agoraphobic Studs Terkel, just long enough to hear someone else's life story and take his feverish notes, and then scurries back inside to get it all down on the page while the news is still hot.

Still, you don't have to read much of *Portnoy's Complaint* or *My Life as a Man* or *Zuckerman Unbound* or *The Counterlife* or the latest novel as of this writing, *The Dying Animal,* to find, peeping out from behind those Portnoys, Tarnopols, Zuckermans, and Kepeshes, the real Philip Roth, fiendishly dicing up his own experiences—and tarting them up as well—for all he is worth, because, well, it works for him, and what works is what works. We do what we do because we do what we do. For Roth, personality and its disorders is home base, and the astonished recital of human fallibility is his own one-man cottage industry. By the dogged and obstinate and excessive and self-indulgent and self-flagellating and tasteless and pig-headed and persevering and embittered and resentful and Hebraic and stiff-necked and undaunted and unswerving and unreconstructed and unrepentant and unrepentable—and riotously funny—attention to that ground, Roth shows us just how much can be done with it.

At this point, something formal and obligatory will have to do, something suitable for the textbook that I am determined not to write, but which will suffice for the moment to satisfy anyone who is using this book in lieu of a more seminar-suitable text.

⟿

Philip Roth was born in Newark, New Jersey's Beth Israel Hospital on March 9, 1933, to Herman and Bess (Finkel) Roth. Of his mother we know surprisingly little, and tempted though we might be to take the mothers of his novels—the overbearing and ego-busting Sophie Portnoy of *Portnoy's Complaint* and the indulgent Selma Zuckerman of *Zuckerman Unbound*—as rough approximations of her, we would be cautioned to read them as only fictions and schematic counterlives, kvetching yin and doting yang. Roth's father, however, looms large in his son's writing: in both fiction and memoir he is a pater familias of operatic dimensions. Owner at one time of a family shoe store that went bankrupt, he became an insurance salesman for Metropolitan Life and was a driven and devoted employee who went door to door in the Black neighborhoods of Newark, extracting from his policyholders premiums they had scarcely the means to pay. By dint of persistence and devotion to a gentile-run firm that hired few Jews and promoted even fewer, Herman Roth eventually rose to an executive rank and managed an office staff of fifty-two people. *Patrimony,* a portrait of his father's last year of life as he was dying of brain cancer, portrays Herman Roth as a willful man and a practitioner of "tough love," decades before that concept became a mantra of Parent Effectiveness Training.

Herman Roth was not always easy to love in return, and in portraying his father, Roth does not soften all that was spiky and resistant in him. A man of stern judgment and granite will and a harsh judge of other people's limitations, "He would have told you that you can lead a horse to water and you *can* make him drink—you just hock him and hock him and hock him until he comes to his senses and does it." Hock is a Yiddish word meaning "to badger, to bludgeon, to hammer with warnings and edicts and pleas." He was also the great teacher of the plain vision and the plain style: "He taught me the vernacular. He *was* the vernacular, unpoetic and expressive and point-blank, with all the vernacular's glaring limitations and all its durable force."

From 1946 to 1950, Roth attended Weequahic High School in the predominantly Jewish section of Newark, at a time when, for most Americans, a booming economy and rising expectations did much to buffer the tensions of the emerging Cold War. For Jews, however, the recent slaughter of their European cousins and the subsequent founding of the State of Israel in a condition of peril were still livid in memory, and in America anti-Semitism was still both an institution and a sport.

Roth recalls vividly, in his memoir *The Facts,* how gangs out of other neighborhoods known as "Down Neck" and "The Ironbound," places in their own ways as ominous and legendary as the Russian steppes, would swoop down on the placid Jewish community like marauding Cossacks, with baseball bats in their hands and dreams of pogrom in their hearts, especially if Weequahic's football team had had the audacity to defeat its traditional rival, Barringer High. The Weequahic section of Newark was a sheltered enclave unaccustomed to rumbling, where young people cultivated the qualities that were opposed to hardness of heart and fist. It might well have been called "The Ironybound" neighborhood. Among the high school cheers, recalled in *Portnoy's Complaint,* was one that went like this:

> Ikey Mikey Jake and Sam
> We are the boys who eat no HAM!
> We play baseball football soccer
> We keep MATZOHS in our locker!

After high school, Roth attended Bucknell University, where he received his B.A., and the University of Chicago, where he completed his M.A. and taught English. It was at Bucknell that Roth did his apprenticeship in being a scandal, when, as editor of the literary magazine *Et Cetera,* he wrote a satiric sendup of the school's weekly newspaper, the *Bucknellian,* whose editor-in-chief was also a captain of the cheerleading squad. The satire occasioned an admonition from the Dean of Men, a censure from the Board of Publications, and a threatening visit to his room by a chivalrous friend of the aggrieved editor. The outline of what would become a pivot of Roth's career, to offend by some act of satire and parody—an impulse he suppresses only with the greatest of difficulty—was already sketched in before graduation from college. Higher registers of literary solemnity were also under cultivation, and Roth would publish his story "The Day It Snowed" in *The Chicago Review* in 1954, while still an undergraduate.

Following a stint in the army, from which Roth received a medical discharge—an early short story, "Novotny's Pain" (1962), is about a soldier with psychosomatic lower-back trouble—Roth enrolled in a Ph.D. program in English at the University of Chicago, where he began to work away at his career as a writer. His march toward success was unusually swift; his story, "The Contest for Aaron Gold," was published in *Epoch* in 1955 and chosen for *Martha Foley's Best American Short Stores of 1956.*

Roth's marriage in 1959 to Margaret Martinson Williams, a divorcee with a daughter, proved to be a major watershed in his life, a calamity that diverted him from the lockstep progress toward higher attainments he had enjoyed until then, but which also supplied him with the obsessive and intractable material of problem-fiction that his reading in the great classics of modernism had taught him to revere. A woman from a different social class—a fact of which Roth has made much in his endless brooding over the catastrophe—and the daughter of an alcoholic father, Margaret was a formidable adversary, tricking Roth into marriage by faking pregnancy with a urine sample bought from a pregnant woman. He would say of her in *The Facts,* "She would have seemed to [my grandparents] nothing more or less than the legendary old-country shiksa-witch, whose bestial inheritance had doomed her to become a destroyer of every gentle human virtue esteemed by the defenseless Jew." Although she and Roth were legally separated in 1963, Margaret refused Roth a divorce, and the marriage was only dissolved by Margaret's death in a car crash in 1968. The calamity and Roth's own vexation over his vulnerability to a woman more cunning and determined than he left a lasting mark on him, and he would mine and smelt the ore of that marriage for every carat of pity and terror in it, even comb through the slag, in a host of novels, from *Letting Go* and *When She Was Good* to *My Life as a Man,* that *Encyclopedia Judaica* of conjugal catastrophe, and even *Sabbath's Theater.* If there is any subject that Roth's corrosive sense of humor has never fully laughed out of existence it is that marriage, which calls up no less fear and loathing in *Sabbath's Theater* than it did twenty-one years earlier in *My Life as a Man.*

Roth married again only in 1990, to British actress Claire Bloom, with whom he had been already sharing a life for some time, and that relationship broke up in 1995. Since Roth guards his private life carefully—no, he guards it carelessly—we know little about that marriage or its dissolution, unless one is to take the novella *Deception,* published in 1990, about a wife's discovery of her writer-husband's journal of adultery, as a window onto the trouble behind that relationship. Claire Bloom would give her side of the story a lurid airing in her memoir, *Leaving a Doll's*

House, and Roth would respond quickly, slicing her up neatly with a portrait of her as Eve Frame, née Chavah Fromkin, a silent film actress without a career and "a spiritual woman with decolletage," in *I Married a Communist.*[2] That marriage ended in a public flameout, but it did not crack the front page of *People Magazine* and did not leave behind it a long literary trail. Roth would seem to be learning, at last, to let go.

At the same time that Roth has been capitalizing in literature on the eventfulness of his life, he has spoken often of its corresponding event-lessness. "Outside of print," he wrote in his book, *Reading Myself and Others,* "I lead virtually no public life at all. I don't consider this a sacri-fice, because I never much wanted one. . . . Writing in a room by myself is practically my whole life. I enjoy solitude the way some people I know enjoy parties." It is not for no purpose at all that the fledgling writer Nathan Zuckerman looks enviously at the isolated and self-contained E. I. Lonoff in *The Ghost Writer* and says to himself, "That is how I shall live." Let us say, on the basis of no knowledge at all of Roth's life save what he wishes to tell us, that between aggressively exhibitionistic Mailerism and sequestered Salingerism, Roth has made a life closer to Salinger's than to Mailer's. Surely he has used that isolation to write — how else do you produce a literary oeuvre that by now approaches Dick-ensian proportions?

What we can say with some confidence is that Roth's life *as a writer* has been a full one and that the events that bulk large in his career will, in the long run, be central to his life as well. The privacy he guards is the privacy of a writer whose life has been largely bound up with words, his own and the words of others, and has been far more cloistered than those of his reckless and careening characters. His acquaintances and friendships with Bernard Malamud, Chicago novelist Richard Stern, Israeli writer Aharon Appelfeld, and the Czech novelists Ivan Klíma and Milan Kundera; his championship of writers from Eastern Europe during the bleakest hours of the communist dictatorships; his editing of the series "Writers from the Other Europe" for Penguin books; his im-pressive readings of himself and others; his assembly-line production of books at the almost-metronomic rate of one every two years, despite distractions and crushing bouts of bad health, including chronic neck problems, the breakdown of 1987, and open-heart surgery in 1989; the theatrical, now-you-see-it now-you-don't playfulness of his later books;

his daring reinventions of other writers, most notably Franz Kafka and Anne Frank; his "shop talk" with other writers now collected into a volume of that name, all mark Roth as the most tenaciously bookish of our major contemporary writers, the writer for whom the major arena of risk and reward is the written word. "As for living, our servants can that do for us" goes a famous line from the play *Axel* by Villiers de l'Isle-Adam. Rephrase that for Roth and you get, "As for living, our characters can do that for us." That is a half-truth, and while Roth hasn't been so stubborn an anchorite of the sentence as have Henry James or Marcel Proust or his own novelist-ascetic, Lonoff, he did put enough of himself into Lonoff to let us know that he is to be numbered among those who, in the phrase of W. B. Yeats, have made their art their life.

In the forty-four years between 1959 and 2003, Roth has published twenty-six books and much writing that remains uncollected. This is a capacious and abundant career, whose full meaning will take generations of patient scholars to fully interpret and assess. Mine is a patently impatient book, and I look forward to what future Roth archaeologists, with their carbon 14 dating technologies, will come up with.

Second Thoughts

When just three years after *The Facts* Roth comes to tell the story of his father's last year of life, in *Patrimony: A True Story,* the Zuckerman kibitzing and jeerleading is dispensed with and talk about "manipulative" literary forms is nowhere to be found. It is well and good to take corrosive postmodern views of your own life, especially after you have been through years of psychoanalysis and learned that every motive bespeaks a shameful hidden motive and that every shameful hidden motive stands in for a yet more shameful and more hidden one, all the way on down to the bestial core. But in writing about your father, you had better be all business. You're his Kaddish after all. And this is getting it right, is it not? The "self" may be something you put together afresh every day, or every book, but your father was *your father.* He knew exactly who he was; he was as certain as bedrock. A memorial to him is not an occasion for counterlives.

2

The Road of Excess

This extremely intelligent young Jew does not recognize that what he is trying to do, by reversing the Oedipal situation, is to make fun of me, as he does of everyone, thus asserting his superiority over me and psychoanalysis itself.

Bruno Bettelheim, "Portnoy Psychoanalyzed"

The halvah and hot pastrami, diverting touches, obscure the baleful stereotype which emerges from under the banter. The dark Jew seeking to defile the fair Nordic is standard stuff. While Goebbels would leave out the humanizing halvah, there is little to choose between his and Roth's interpretation of what animates Portnoy.

Marie Syrkin, "The Fun of Self-Abuse"

He is an exceedingly joyless writer, even when being very funny. The reviewers of his novels, many of them sympathetic, noticed his need to rub our noses in the muck of squalid daily existence, his mania for annotating at punitive length the bickerings of his characters. Good clean hatred that might burn through, naturalistic determinism with a grandeur of design if not detail, the fury of social rebellion—any of these would be more interesting than the vindictive bleakness of Roth's novels.

Irving Howe, "Philip Roth Reconsidered"

The original essay, dashed off in white heat over a period of a few weeks in 1973, no longer exists. That was before computers; writing then left no digital record, and sometimes things got tossed. I've scoured my files many times, and no trace of the original in its entire form has appeared. There are fragments. One, about Irving Howe and his "Lost Young Intellectual," constitutes the following chapter. Another, on the subject of the baseball book, *The Great American Novel,* is left out. I misread that book badly enough that I would as soon have that misreading out of public sight for now. About *Portnoy's Complaint,* I have vivid memories of some sentences that I blurted out impetuously and then blue-penciled away in embarrassment a few weeks later. The version eventually published in *Partisan Review,* as rambunctious as it may now seem, was the damage control version, lacking some of the freewheeling humor and polemical attack of the first draft. While the original is beyond restoring, it can be approximated from fragments and notes that I have been able to dust off and piece together after twenty-nine years. What appears here is a portion of the *Partisan Review* essay, with as much of the wild analysis restored as I can now recall. Stripped out is the section on *My Life as a Man,* which I've removed to a chapter of its own. You can see me in all of this tossing the analytical ball from oral to anal to phallic, as though pulling off a one-man triple play. The contents of the unconscious didn't strike me as few, simple, and boring just then. My sense that Roth himself was throwing the same ball around the same infield made it seem plausible, even mandatory, to do that, and we both have Dr. Spielvogel to thank for that.

                                                       —~

I knew something about Philip Roth's writing before 1967. Being from Newark I had read *Goodbye, Columbus* at the very least and even, the Essex County Jewish world being a small one, had an aunt who claimed to know the real Patimkin family. Also, I had kept up sufficiently with the reviews to know that Roth had published two novels subsequent to *Columbus* and that they were indifferently received. Certainly they were long and not about Newark, and I did not read them. So it was after the manner of that stout Cortez or whoever it really was on that Peak in Darien that I first looked into Roth's *Portnoy.* That is, I first looked into Roth's "Whacking Off," a *Partisan Review* story that some of my graduate student colleagues were passing about like, some twenty years earlier, their grammar school counterparts had passed around *The Amboy Dukes.* That was unique, for in our time and in that place, Berkeley, 1967, social exchange did not as a rule form around fiction. Well, maybe Herman Hesse; it did seem for a while that everyone was reading *Steppenwolf.* We communed more spontaneously over Crumb Comics, *The*

Berkeley Barb, the latest exposé or manifesto in *Ramparts* magazine, the Free Speech and anti-War Movements, the sports we played and those we watched, or the latest music that was being produced for our generation by drugs and euphoria just across the Bay. You *could* be a Maoist, a Deadhead, a 49ers fan, and a right fielder on your softball team. There might even be consciousness to spare for medieval studies. It wasn't common, but those were magic days when identity seemed open-ended and shopping for a life like you shopped for clothes was what you normally did.

Even then our motives in recommending Roth to one another were clear enough; spontaneous fraternities that form around literary texts are essentially confessional communities. If none of us shared all of Portnoy's anxieties or identified ourselves with each fear and every confidence, we all discovered powerful connections to components of his complaint. Each of us had his oral or anal or phallic secret that was itching to be revealed. I mean, who didn't whack off? And the serial publication of *Portnoy*, as it rolled on through "The Jewish Blues" and "Civilization and its Discontents" (in *New American Review*), assured us that Roth had enough shareable secrets to go around. He gave the adolescent in each of us a place to hang his obsession: the tyranny of the family, the rites and mysteries of the Jewish diet, the splendors of sexual anthropology, the delights and humiliations of whacking off. Add, for me, a suddenly discovered nostalgia and pride of place. This Portnoy had eaten his *chazerai* and suffered cramps and remorse on my block, maybe even on my corner, in front of Galoff's grocery store. He had consecrated with his seed the men's rooms and alleys of my boyhood. As it turned out, I had no monopoly on that revelation. In Berkeley, California, of all places, strangers and fellow students sidled up to me between classes and tendered their confidences: "I lived on Springfield Avenue," or "It's all changed. The Jews have all gone to Maplewood." How did they find me? Clearly I had told someone who told someone who told someone. The Newark diaspora had gone far and fast. Once, I glimpsed a high school jacket bearing the name Weequahic disappear around the corner of Sproul Hall, not to reemerge at the other end and never to reappear again. What was his club? The Spartans? The Trojans? So, that humblest of all places was to be for me exalted, like Dickens's London or Joyce's Dublin, given a history and dramatic resonance by the creative imagination. Some day, I thought, I might lead my undergraduates through Newark on a field trip and show them Watson Bagel or Halem's Candy Store or the barber shop where I couldn't get my hair cut without singing a song in Yiddish, and share with them that same wild surmise felt by Joyceans from all over the world as they stand before Davy Byrne's pub or peer at the site of Leopold Bloom's house at 7 Eccles Street. Bloom too was a masturbator.

Since then, however, two things have complicated my enthusiasm for Roth's writing without in any way diminishing it. The first has been the discovery that my loyalty to *Portnoy* as a version of truth and my conviction that Roth has talent have not been universally shared, certainly not among Jews. The second source of complication is Roth's own work subsequent to *Portnoy*. While his voluminous writing has kept his talent on full, hilarious display, it has sometimes failed somehow to satisfy my own expectations, unformed though they are. The first matter, the opposition of the Jews, is no barrier to admiration. In the conflict between Roth and the numerous voices of Jewish disapproval, a conflict that goes back to 1959 and the publication of *Goodbye, Columbus,* the critics are out of touch. And I don't mean out of touch with the new age, but with the spirit of fiction itself, with the normal uses of the imagination in literature. For their quarrel with Roth is not properly over literature or any aspects thereof but over touchy matters of culture: over who gets to speak for the Jews and what messages are considered safe to deliver. Institutional Jewry in America these days has a decidedly rigid, defensive posture toward the outside world. That posture, I might add, may be the authentic and inescapable product of history and impossible to root out, but the defenders of the faith are not always the surest guides to the freedoms of the imagination or the pleasures of the text. The second matter is that of Roth's talent and the uses to which he has put it, which I take more seriously. It too, though, points us away from literature and toward, in this instance, psychology. Everything about Roth's recent writing suggests that it might profit from a psychological investigation. (Roth, it is clear, was the first to think so.) *Portnoy's Complaint* itself calls to mind that little-known first book by Sigmund Freud: *Studies in Hysteria.*

But these two faces of Roth-in-the-world, the Jew at odds with the fathers and the patient under analysis, are the two sides of his writer's identity, and to stand up for Roth one first has to be clear about what he is up to. Roth the novelist and culture critic is also Roth the son. Observe the abundant filial torments of Alex Portnoy. Observe too Bruno Bettelheim's psychoanalysis of him in *Midstream,* with its peevish diagnosis of Alex's neurotic conflicts. Bettelheim, in an article titled "Portnoy Psychoanalyzed: Therapy Notes Found in the Files of Dr. O. Spielvogel, a New York Psychoanalyst," wastes no time in expressing his disgust with his client. "He cannot stop the diarrhea of talk, since it is his way of denying his essential constipation, his total inability to give of himself or of anything else." Alex Portnoy, after a mere six hours on the couch, is dismissed by his analyst, Spielvogel, aka Bettelheim, as a three-way loser. He is a bad patient, a bad Jew, and a bad boy. "He permits no one, including me, to make any contribution to his life." As therapy, Bettelheim's countertransference may look like a novelty—I mean, where'd he get his clinical training in empathy?—but as literary commentary it is hackneyed, just another sad complaint about what had already been prepackaged as Roth's "self-hatred."

A parallel line of argument has been taken up by Irving Howe in his "Philip Roth Reconsidered" in the December 1972 *Commentary,* an essay heralded by editor Norman Podhoretz's editorial, "Laureate of the New Class." Howe complains there of Roth's personal and ideological assertiveness, of his stance of adolescent superiority to suburban Jewish life, of his nagging habit of "scoring points" instead of striving for imaginative plenitude, of his failure to render a "full and precise" portrait of his Jewish victims, and of his essential joylessness. This failure, Howe observes, is a failure of culture. Roth's stories and novels fall short of something like Tolstoyan amplitude because "they come out of a thin personal culture." Roth, we are told, has uprooted himself from "the mainstream of American culture, in its great sweep of democratic idealism and romanticism." Aside from the tone of world-historical oratorio here, Howe is not wholly off base. Roth's anger is a crucial property of his art and his books can bring laughter without bringing cheer. His failure of magnanimity is considerable and his ample wit sports a chilling edge. And a book like *The Great American Novel,* which draws its humor from an assemblage of freaks, cripples, dwarfs, stage Jews, and pasteboard goyim, will not improve his reputation for compassion. Nor will the book's loose collection of bits and routines earn him any points toward what Howe has called, with Arnoldian sobriety, "compositional rigor and moral seriousness." But for all that, Howe's lecture on Roth's cultural impoverishment betrays something fatally lacking in a critic's armory of tools: a tin ear for language that makes the abundance of culture—and Jewish culture at that—that Roth does bring to bear on his writing unavailable to him. It is surprising that a scholar of Yiddish culture would be deaf to all that Roth has inherited from it, including its self-irony. Beyond that there is a failure of curiosity, of the desire to understand what those of us who felt ourselves in tune with the book were responding to. Not only Roth, but also his readers come in for chastising, for giving in to cheap thrills when they might have been better engaged in reading Tolstoy. It is this note in Howe's complaint that Norman Podhoretz winds through his own sound system, that in the course of Roth's literary career, "more and more people have come along who are exactly in tune with the sense of things he has always expressed in his work and who have accordingly and in increasing numbers come to recognize him as their own." The New Class. So, this is war. This is Kulturkampf. You can smell the cordite right through the page and hear the click of heels on pavement. Fathers on patrol!

Roth's image of himself as perennial Jewish son would seem to be at the core of his identity. It certainly has everything to do with his attachment to Kafka, another Jewish son with a painful and debilitating relationship to fatherhood (see "'I Always Wanted You to Admire My Fasting'; or, Looking at Kafka").[1] "Marrying is barred to me," confesses this Kafka to his father, "because it is your domain." But the sons we discover in Roth's fiction differ from Kafka's in this crucial respect: it is not the father's power that condemns them to impotence and bachelorhood; it is his weakness. The secret of the terror behind Roth's fiction is the realization that the father too is impotent. In fact, Roth himself may be braced and encouraged by the opposition of the rabbis, for the father's enmity is preferable to his adoration. "Others," he confesses in his Kafka essay, "are crushed by paternal criticism—I find myself oppressed by his high opinion of me." There is no escape from the ineffectual father, for the son's oedipal guilt is renewed daily by the father's failures. "Make my father a father," cries Lucy Nelson *(When She Was Good),* and she, a daughter, broadcasts this appeal on behalf of all the Roth sons, before and after.

Roth rewrites the opening sentence of *The Metamorphosis* this way: "As Franz Kafka awoke one morning from uneasy dreams he found himself transformed in his bed into a father, a writer, and a Jew." This Kafka is no gigantic insect with three pairs of legs quivering helplessly before his eyes but a man with three afflictions: Jewishness, talent, and children, the last, the greatest affliction of all. Imagine a Kafka, or a Roth, trying to love that brilliant issue of his loins known as a son. "Keep him away from me," screams a young, imaginary Roth in the Kafka story. Jake Portnoy's bowels answer in frozen rage from the pages of an earlier book. Paternity is a legal fiction in Roth's books where sons and fathers turn out to be brothers under the skin, locked into generations by an unfortunate biological fate. What is Isaac to do when Abraham drops the knife and gets down on the sacrificial altar with him? That is Roth's real dilemma. And that is why manhood in his books never gets further than a dream of center field. The son's chief concern is not to escape his father's wrath but to short-circuit his sentimentality; the thing he doesn't want to do is make his father cry. With fatherhood in doubt, all other relationships are in trouble. Relationships, in Roth's world, are painful experiments whose failures may be preferable to their shame-ridden successes. Men and women are natural enemies who do horrible things when they mistakenly get together, for marrying is surely as barred to Roth's sons as ever it was to Kafka's. It is a good thing for Aunt Rhoda ("Looking at Kafka") that Dr. Kafka's problem is revealed to her before the marriage at that Atlantic City Hotel, for marriage is a fate worse than lifelong loneliness. Love is a front for aggression; sex is an occasion for failure; childhood is tragedy, adulthood farce. The family, according to Roth, doesn't pass on culture; it transmits symptoms. In such a world, to be a child is excruciating; to be a parent is unimaginable.

If Roth's books read like case histories, so does the profile of his entire career. It begins with an orderly and sedate fiction about straight-laced heroes who fail at some relationship or vital task and manifest their disappointment in symptoms, spontaneous outbreaks of anger, unreason, or vertigo. Mrs. Portnoy calls them "conniption fits." The early books, the *Goodbye, Columbus* stories, *Letting Go*, and *When She Was Good*, with their repressed and driven characters, constitute a fiction of failed renunciation. Their heroes are all characters who repress desires that, as we might expect, refuse to go away and keep returning in the form of compulsive and irrational behavior. In *Letting Go*, the mutual renunciation of Gabe Wallach and Libby Herz (based on their mutual reading of *A Portrait of a Lady*) is prelude to six hundred pages of indecision (his), neurasthenia (hers), confusion, and sudden, irrational tantrums (theirs). In *When She Was Good*, the praise accorded to Willard Nelson in the very opening sentence tells us exactly what is wrong with him. "Not to be rich, not to be famous, not to be mighty, not even to be happy, but to be civilized—that was the dream of his life." A man who has given up that much might prosper in a novel of manners, but when Jamesean pretensions surface in a novel by Roth, the shit hits the fan. When Roth hears the word civilization, he reaches for his discontents. And in fact, Lucy Nelson, who has learned from Grandpa Willard the etiquette of small-town character armor, reaps its rewards when faced with the demands of pregnancy and abandonment. Her studied defenses are revealed to be useless and she goes berserk with terror and righteousness.

Portnoy's Complaint advertises itself as Roth's psychic breakthrough, the book in which the Yid grapples with repression and lays claim to his id. A humiliating childhood is dragged into the light; a wild sexual fantasy life makes its debut seemingly undistorted by style or euphemism; the Jewish mother in all her ambiguous effulgence replaces the father at stage center; her son's masturbation is magnificently confessed and celebrated; food is revealed to be an agent of both repression and liberation, and eating turns out to have something to do with love and sex. The book ends with nothing less than the primal scream, all ninety-six a's and four h's of it, after which Dr. Spielvogel delivers the punch line. This book appears to deliver all the right confessions demanded of an analysis: confessions of undue bondage to the past, of secret humiliations and secret rages, of crimes against the family, of failures of the body, and overcompensations of the will.

Post *Portnoy* we have been treated to the breakthrough books and stories: "On the Air" *(New American Review),*[2] a savage and barely controlled saga of one day in the life of Milton Lippmann, talent scout; *Our Gang*, the book of pure contra-Nixonian malice; *The Breast*, an experiment in controlled regression with an old-fashioned stoical message; "'I Always Wanted You to Admire My Fasting'; or, Looking at

Kafka," a lecture turned fantasy of Franz Kafka's possible adventures in Newark; *The Great American Novel*, a humongous four-bagger of a novel about baseball, exile, and the Shoah; and *My Life as a Man*, a CAT scan of marriage in the 1950s, as though it were diseased and malignant tissue. Up until the last book, which appears to return to older modes of writing, Roth's progress throughout this period seemed to take an identifiable shape: the early books, pre-*Portnoy*, were the documents of repression, the later writings, witnesses to the return of the repressed. Where Roth used to give us stoical characters who bore their misfortunes with the sullen nobility of the civilized, until overtaken by sudden outbursts, he more recently has turned to showing us literary surfaces that look like primary-process thought. Where repression was we now have rage; in lieu of symptoms we now get performances.

Upon its appearance, *Portnoy's Complaint* was the most sensational attempt at Freudian fiction in recent American literature, not only because of the boldness of its confessions, but also because of Spielvogel's summary diagnosis, which challenged us with its crisp Germanic expertise. Alex Portnoy, to be sure, knows his theory also. He annotates his complaint with appropriate references to *The Standard Edition* of Freud's works. We know that he has read "The Most Prevalent Form of Degradation in Erotic Life" and that he practices it, and that he is familiar with *Civilization and Its Discontents*, as both text and personal dilemma. His furtive sexuality is supposed to mediate the demands of a clamorous, infantile id and a vigilant, righteous superego, and fails. Thus, according to Spielvogel: "Acts of exhibitionism, voyeurism, fetishism, autoeroticism and oral coitus are plentiful; as a consequence of the patient's 'morality,' however, neither fantasy nor act issues in genuine sexual gratification, but rather in overriding feelings of shame and the dread of retribution, particularly in the form of castration." That is a cogent and inclusive sentence and, in fact, the complaint (here meaning malady, not *geschrei*), stripped of its cultural paraphernalia and defensive wit, does make sense as a strategy for managing deep-psychic warfare. Moreover, believes Spielvogel, "Many of the symptoms can be traced to the bonds obtaining in the mother-child relationship." The doctor has saved us some research here, though his categories, like most diagnostic labels, are textbookish and preemptive; they substitute the mannerisms of analysis for explanation, and if the analytic sections of

My Life as a Man are any indication of what Spielvogel sounds like when he is under a full head of steam, we, and Alex Portnoy, should be more appreciative of his enigmatic silences in the earlier book. Still, he has the right idea: the fictional imitation of confession is confession, and we as readers have some duty to make sense of what we are being so desperately told.

To set the stage for an analysis of our own we have to set the table, for *Portnoy's Complaint* is an exposé, no, a vaudeville, of the Jewish stomach. Food is to Jewish comedy and Jewish neurosis what drink is to Irish, though only Roth so far has taken the full anthropological plunge into the ethnology of the Jewish digestive tract. Roth's Jews are not a people, a culture, nation, or a tradition. They are a *tribe,* which, after its own primitive fashion, observes arbitrary taboos and performs strange sundown rituals that look like obsessional symptoms. Alex Portnoy's particular neurotic style of observing the world has this virtue: a probing and unsentimental eye for styles of irrational behavior, his own included. As he sees it, the kosher laws are as primitive and irrational as any Australian fetish or Papuan cult of cargo, and the dietary antagonism of milk and meat in the Jewish diet is something, not out of Leviticus, but out of Róheim.[3]

Alex Portnoy's morality, not to mention his immorality, begins at the table. Here is The Law according to that Moses of Manhattan, the Assistant Commissioner of Human Opportunity for the City of New York. "Let the goyim sink their teeth into whatever lowly creature crawls and grunts across the face of the dirty earth, we will not contaminate our humanity thus." Thus spake Portnoy of the superego. Now let's hear a word from Portnoy of the id. "At least let me eat your pussy." It is in that spectrum of possibilities between phobic avoidance and insane lapping that the minute moral discriminations of Jewish life are made. For these Jews, the word *moral* derives etymologically from the word *oral.*[4]

When a sin is committed in the Portnoy home it is more likely to involve gluttony than lechery, though in the muddled dreamwork of a complicated and unreliable memory, primal crimes often become confused. "A terrible act has been committed, and it has been committed by either my father or me. The wrongdoer, in other words, is one of the two members of the family who owns a penis. Okay. So far so good.

Now, did he fuck between those luscious legs the gentile cashier from the office, or have I eaten my sister's chocolate pudding?" This confusion never does get resolved. In the infantile moral system of this household, shared by parents and children alike, pudding and pussy may be equally taboo and proscribed with equal ferocity. Food, of course, is the first medium of love and authority for all of us, and where it retains its primal power, as it does for the Portnoys, young sinners may be heard to confess, "I'm eight years old and chocolate pudding happens to get me hot." It is understandable then that the table is the battlefield on which Alex's bid for manhood is fought and lost. The toilet and the bed are also combat zones, but by the time Alex gets there, the war is over. Rearguard actions still rage, however, and Alex's prime weapons are all the tricks in his stubborn oral trade: "having a mouth on him," refusing to eat, eating *chazerai* (or lobster or pussy), or, and herein shines forth his desperate genius, fucking his family's dinner. All strategies naturally fail since the field of battle has been chosen in advance and it favors whoever has the ammunition.

Hunger striking fails as dismally for Portnoy as it does for Kafka's hunger artist. "I always wanted you to admire my fasting," confesses the dying hunger artist to a bored overseer. Alex Portnoy, a tougher sort, would have survived such boredom, but in a household in which food is mistaken for love, hunger artistry is merely being a bad eater and earns not disinterest but a brandished bread knife and a perverse maternal appeal to a son's future manhood: which does he want to be, weak or strong, a man or a mouse?

The politics of food and guilt at the Jewish table have given rise to a unique taboo: *chazerai*. *Chazerai* is not necessarily unkosher food, unblessed or formally proscribed by the laws; neither the hot dog nor the cupcake is mentioned by name in Leviticus. But *chazerai*, while not unkosher de jure is certainly so de facto. It is cheap, processed, mass-produced snack food, gotten outside the home, behind one's mother's back. Its true purpose, as every Jewish mother knows, is to ruin her son's appetite for dinner—her dinner. Thus the eating of snacks after school is a betrayal, and the boy who stops for a burger and fries at fourteen will, at thirty, be stopping after work for a shiksa, thus ruining his appetite. It is a mother's duty to forestall that, to wish upon her son whatever disability will save him: diarrhea, colitis, and "a plastic bag to do your thing in."

For the son, naturally, *chazerai* symbolizes freedom, sexual freedom. For example, here is Alex's own dietary analysis of the difference between himself and Smolka, that same Smolka who gets blown by Bubbles Girardi after Alex, crestfallen, leaves her house having come in his own eye while bringing himself off. "He lives on Hostess cupcakes and his own wits. I get a hot lunch and all the inhibitions thereof." (And speaking of cupcakes, let us not forget Alex Portnoy's dream girl, Thereal McCoy, who "pushes Drake's Daredevil Cupcakes . . . down over my cock" and plunges into his mouth "a nipple the size of a tollhouse cookie.") But for ultimate aphrodisiacal virtue there is the lobster, a terror beyond *chazerai,* an unambiguous threat to sanity and life. Sophie Portnoy's historic bout with lobster, paralysis, and an Irish insurance salesman is textbook hysteria. "See how I'm holding my fingers," she instructs her son, a neophyte in primitive religious phenomena. "I was throwing up so hard, they got stiff just like this, like I was paralyzed."

Sophie Portnoy's symptoms are prophecies for her son. Within an hour of eating a lobster with brother-in-law Morty at Sheepshead Bay, Alex has his cock out on the 107 bus, "aimed at a shiksa." It is to protect him from such madness that a mother must keep up her dietary vigilance. Naturally this education in taboo-by-diet falls to the mother, for she understands better than anyone how food, love, power, and possession are arranged. Is it any wonder then that this same Sophie invites Jake's new cashier from the office for a nice, home-cooked Jewish meal? Hardly, for once Anne McCaffrey has dined with the Portnoys she's hooked, and not on Jake but on his wonderful *haimische* family. "This is your real Jewish, chopped liver, Anne. Have you ever had real Jewish chopped liver before?" So much for that affair, for if lobster is the Spanish fly of the Jews, real chopped liver is their saltpeter, the all-inhibiting cold hors d'oeuvre of the constipated husband. Could Jake be slipping it to that new cashier on the side? Not after that meal. For this is a totem feast and that is *his* liver they're passing around.

So it is not just a happy conjunction of horniness and opportunity that sets Alex to banging that fresh liver behind the billboard *on his way to a bar mitzvah lesson.* It is another symbol of Alex's private Kulturkampf, with the liver falling victim to his relentless, educated cock. What price such victory? To have your mother serve up the conquest two hours later, healthy as milk, dry as matzo, warm and safe as your own Jewish childhood. In other words, defeat. You did your best to spoil dinner, and your best wasn't good enough. (In the "Salad Days" section of *My Life as a Man,* Roth tries to carry this comedy over into the plant kingdom by having Sharon Shatsky entertain Nathan Zuckerman with her floorshow in which she applies to herself a dildo that happens to be a zucchini. Although inventive in its own way, the scene isn't all that funny; the Jews have never been hung up on vegetables. If she had been Irish and it had been a potato, well that would have been a different matter.)

If Alex Portnoy is telling the truth, and he must be unless this is the most opaque lie or deceptive screen memory known to psychoanalysis, his mother's purposes are plain and sinister. She wants nothing less than the annexation of her son, the full possession of and control over his manhood, and she'll have it by stalling his growth at a level of oral dependence. That is why mealtime is the likeliest occasion for Alex to make that leap to the toilet, for as long as he dines at home, his mouth belongs to mama. When his manhood droops, he seeks refuge in the sure successes of boyhood love, determined to win praise at least as a good eater. Similarly, in *My Life as a Man,* it is appropriate that Nathan Zuckerman tries to face down his boyish disgust and demonstrate to Lydia Ketterer and himself that he is a good man and a proper loser by eating her. The ability to eat anything is one of the many false definitions of manhood that Roth's heroes try on for size. Or *is* it false?

That food and love should be so consistently mistaken for each other is no mystery. The connection between them is built into our mammalian heritage, and the job of learning the difference is an ordinary childhood task that we all perform. The terms of that task are named by Roth in two of his titles, *The Breast* and *Letting Go,* and they stand for the primal situations out of which his characters must negotiate a way of life. For these characters, letting go is a theme of desperate urgency, for entrapment, in the form either of captivity or self-repression, is their most abiding condition. Alex Portnoy's final scream is a gesture of letting go that is native to the Roth novel. At the moment of release, the bonds of repression are torn loose, allowing repressed anger to surge peremptorily to the surface. The tantrum is serious business and sooner or later in these books one is bound to be thrown. In *My Life,* Peter Tarnopol's tantrum is a moment of sexual truth. It finds him donning his wife's panties and bra in order to show her, he later explains, that "I wear the panties in this family." In *Portnoy*, it constitutes Alex's final statement, the last desperate demand before Spielvogel interrupts to commence the analysis.

Holding on and letting go are terrors because they first were desires, and it is in the struggle between those wishes that Alex is paralyzed, not in that starchy tango of id and superego so scrupulously defined by the hopelessly orthodox Spielvogel. That conflict, nurtured by a Jewish family that doesn't know when to call parenthood quits, can ramify into the alimentary insanity of Alex Portnoy's life. Every odd libidinal enterprise of his is an attempt to satisfy those two wishes and to be a man and a baby at the same time.

Every character of Roth's seems to be stuck with this obligation, to satisfy deep-seated but contrary needs at once: to grow up and to regress; to let go and to hold on; to be autonomous and to remain dependent. Totalists that they are, they are unable to find and occupy a human middle ground on which self-reliance need not be isolation and love need not be entrapment. Thus Alex Portnoy steers clear of love by laying sexual traps for himself, insuring that his experiments in love will always end in defeat. His episodes of sexual boredom and his bouts with impotence are strategically timed. It is Peter Tarnopol who, seemingly on Alex's behalf, tries to break out of the circle of sexual isolation by getting married and manages, not unpredictably, to marry a woman he fears and despises. To be sure, Maureen Johnson is a fearsome woman, but that is why Peter wants her. He marries her in order to destroy her, and while any woman will do for that, it is a fine point of conscience that she should seem to deserve what she eventually gets. Now *that's* conjugal Realpolitik.

This same dilemma underlies that curious little book, *The Breast,* which Roth wrote some time between *Portnoy* and *My Life* and which reads like a companion piece to both. In fact, if speculation about the book's origins is of any value, it is my guess that it is an addendum to *Portnoy's Complaint* and is perhaps one of those dreams that Alex Portnoy must have produced in analysis but somehow failed to report to us. Its hero, David Alan Kepesh, reads like a primary process version of Alex Portnoy, his repressed infant perhaps, his latent content. Kepesh appears to be the disguised fulfillment of Alex's most repressed wish, which we may now guess is to undo his ill-fated sonhood altogether in favor of a generational merger, to become, not just an infant, but his own mother. If this is a dream and if we know the dreamer, as I think we do, then we can say in our cold and diagnostic way that he has dreamed of becoming his own mother by way of a regression to that period of his own infancy when the senses were too primitive and diffuse for him to know who was who.[5] The advantages of that are obvious. It is a way of holding on and letting go at the same time, allowing you to have your mother and eat her too. (And the breast, for what this may be worth, confounds the kosher laws by being both *milchig* and *fleischig*.) In such a dream of primal merger, the dreamer is at last on his own, self-contained, androgynous, and pleasantly autoerotic, and can indulge himself forever at the sacred fount of life without two sets of dishes. But since this dream by Alex is also a story by Roth, the fulfillment of this wish is bound to exact a price. It turns out that the dream of merger is also the dream of infancy and the fairy tale of sexual self-sufficiency can turn into the nightmare of total helplessness. Thus Alex Portnoy's dream of independence and autonomy becomes David Kepesh's nightmare of isolation and entrapment.

Such a situation is not propitious for fiction. Kepesh's possibilities are too limited. He can only lie there and suffer and, in the end, grow tiresome. Kepesh's condition is in fact terrifying, and yet the tone of *The Breast* seems askew, because Kepesh refuses to be anything but sensible. Accordingly, while *Portnoy's Complaint* is protest fiction and a brief in behalf of letting go, *The Breast* is a conservative moral fable about the virtues of holding on. It hands us the dilemma of civilization and its discontents at the most primitive infantile level and comes out foursquare for repression. Alexander Portnoy, with his temper, is a tiger of wrath; Kepesh, with his Shakespeare and his Rilke, is a horse of instruction. But he may have no choice; all he can do is want, and want, and want, and learn how to behave when he doesn't get. That may be why *The Breast* is so unsettling a book, for to us, Kepesh's mature prescription of a daily anesthetic to reduce his polymorphous appetites reinforced by therapeutic doses of Shakespeare seems like a defeatist strategy for a meager endurance. We want a magical release from breasthood and Kepesh gives us, English majors all, the lesser magic of poetry. We want the primal scream and he delivers lessons about Mr. Reality. We want the heavy cream and he gives us the two percent milk. *The Breast* is the Rothian nightmare at its most radical and its most pedantic. Kepesh, having become his own mother, thumps her Bible; his text on renunciation and endurance may be wisdom but of a familiar kind. He has been reading Irving Howe and he's shaping up. He's thickening his personal culture. Farewell New Class, hello Western Civ. As breasts go he is an overachiever. Nipple and all, he is learning how to be a good boy—and an English professor.

3

Only a *Weltanschauung*
Howe's Lost Young Intellectual

When the first version of the previous essay had its print debut 1974 in *Partisan Review,* it was intended to be a defense of Roth against his principle detractors, Norman Podhoretz and Irving Howe. By the time it found its way into print however, much of its original polemical thrust had been toned down and the essay was well on its way to becoming a "study," an "exegesis." Between the conception and the publication fell the self-consciousness. In going back through notes, however, I found this outtake on the subject of Irving Howe and a once-famous essay of his titled "The Lost Young Intellectual." Roth himself had read it and apparently had it in mind in the original composition of Alexander Portnoy and possibly others of his heroes, and may well have imagined in writing his more rebellious fictions that he was working a territory that had already been opened up by Howe himself. With that in mind as an ironic backdrop to Roth's troubles with his Jewish critics, it seemed well worthwhile to dust off these notes and restore to this book the contentiousness that was taken from that essay.

What had set off my own writing, and would long remain an irritant for Roth as well, were two articles that appeared in the December 1972 issue of *Commentary* magazine: "Philip Roth Reconsidered," by Irving Howe, and "Laureate of the New Class," by Norman Podhoretz.[1] They constituted a devastating one-two punch by two highly politicized literary intellectuals who had decided that Roth constituted a threat to civilized values that they held dear and that he had to be publicly, and

44

vehemently, neutralized. Howe had written earlier in praise of Roth's first book of stories, *Goodbye, Columbus,* when it first appeared, praising Roth for his "ferociously exact" portraits of the moral flabbiness of the suburban Jewish middle class, and observing: "Still, none of this should detract from Mr. Roth's achievement. Nor should it give an inch of encouragement to those in the 'Jewish community' who have begun to mutter against his book as an instance of 'self -hatred.' Even if only a fraction of what Mr. Roth portrays is true, it ought to create the most intense heart-searching among the very people who will soon be hectoring him." Thirteen years later he felt that it was time to retract his earlier praise and join the chorus of those hectoring Roth.

⁓

In 1946, Irving Howe published a remarkably candid self-portrait defense of his estrangement from family and culture, "The Lost Young Intellectual."[2] As a young radical with literary ambitions in the 1940s, Howe chronicled with patience the stages of his own separation from the Jewish middle class, gathering his own poignant observations into a self-portrait that was also, taken broadly, a first halting sketch toward his group portrait of the New York intellectuals. Its basic themes were *marginality, alienation,* and *rebellion,* each interwoven and modulated by *irony, circumspection,* and *doubt.*

Estranged equally from America and Judea, this young intellectual creates his own culture and adopts his own patron saints—Marx, Freud, Thoreau, Kierkegaard, Kafka, Chagall—in an effort to ordain for himself a modern and radical sensibility. For all that, he remains a Jewish son, saturated with the life from which he demands independence and bound to the family from which he claims estrangement. "Literally homeless," he will say of himself, "he has become the ultimate wanderer," *even though* his peregrinations seldom take him west of the Hudson and commonly lead him, with all due ambivalence, toward his parents' apartment.

This intellectual's most problematic relations are those with that family, which is neither a haven in a heartless world nor a transmitter of culture but an arena of conflict, mainly over his apostasy from Jewish life and the practical considerations of economic survival. He is educated, much to his father's delight, but he has no skills, only a *Weltanschauung.*

"What is the good, asks the father, of my son's education, his intelligence, his *edelkeit*—if he can't make a living?" Nor is the mother less demanding, for she has her own claims on the prodigal son, claims of the heart that arise from her own loneliness and heartbreak.

> She constantly hovers over him, developing in him—as if with unconscious skill—the sense of dependence on her which he is later to find so difficult to overcome. The psychoanalyst Helene Deutsch, in her book, *Psychology of Women,* notes that "Jewish women show an overstressed oral-motherly giving toward their children. . . . [T]he mother develops a special interest in the nutritional process of the objects of her love and shows much solicitude about their food." . . . Even when the son is a grown-up man, the mother will still fuss and fume about his food when he comes to visit her, as if to maintain the same modes of affection and dependence.

Where simple doting will not suffice, "Mothers develop neurotic complaints and psychosomatic illnesses as a means of binding the straying son to the family."

Buffeted by contradictions for which neither his upbringing nor his studies, including psychoanalysis, have prepared him, Howe's young intellectual assumes a mask of irony and cultivates Kafkaesque symptoms and Dostoevskian stratagems. So profound may his alienation be that he may trust only words and yearn to become a writer or a fiery orator for whom language is a sword of Jehovah or a cocoon of pleasure.

Howe's young intellectual, then, is a neurotic, stalled by contradictions in every area of his being, including his love life, which is marked by a conflict between longing and shyness and an inability to throw himself totally into a romantic relationship. He is, one might say, a historical instance become a case history, a child of transition poised between the couch and the National Book Award. What he is not is a candidate for is an *aliyah* to Delancey Street, which is no longer available to him. "He must continue as what he is: the rootless son of a rootless people. He can find consolation and dignity, however, in the consciousness of his vision, in the awareness of his complexity, and in the rejection of self-pity. To each age its own burdens."

For all the differences of tone, this sounds remarkably like what Roth intended to depict in the character of Alex Portnoy, and for good reason. Although Alex Portnoy is firmly grounded in personal fantasy and personal crisis, Roth had also assimilated to his vision whatever supporting documents came to hand. By the time he had come to compose *Portnoy,* the age of alienation had long since vanished, but it had left behind some influential texts, from Saul Bellow's *Dangling Man* and *The Victim* to Isaac Rosenfeld's novel *Passage from Home,* a full range of stories and novels by Norman Mailer (*Barbary Shore* and *The Deer Park* in particular), the novels and stories of Bernard Malamud, and much much more. Howe's essay "The Lost Young Intellectual" was only one attempt of many to codify a mood that in the 1950s seemed almost doctrinal for young, Jewish, secular intellectuals. Alexander Portnoy is Howe's young Jewish intellectual two decades later, libidinized, psychoanalyzed, and propelled by bursts of Vietnam-era panic and countercultural libertinism.

Of course, Roth didn't need Irving Howe or Helene Deutsch to teach him about scornful fathers or the "overstressed oral-motherly giving toward their children" of Jewish mothers; he needed only parents. Nevertheless, it was from these predecessors, among others, that he took the authority to draw Sophie Portnoy as a social type, and if she should appear to some a vulgar stereotype, that is largely because Roth, obedient to his authorities, was not the first to stereotype her.

Compounding that irony is Howe's own invocation of the very same essay and portrait as a yardstick by which to measure Roth and find him wanting. It appears that Howe, in assigning Roth the status of a cultural "case," resurrected old formulas in the service of new designs, formulas initially configured for praise and now turned to purposes of condemnation. Consider that marginal young Jew who, as he wrote then, "has largely lost his sense of Jewishness, of belonging to a people with a meaningful tradition, and he has not succeeded in finding a place for himself in the American scene or the American tradition. At the same time, his feelings toward the Jews are troubled, indecisive, and conflicting. His attitude to the Jewish cultural tradition in which he was reared is an ambiguous compound of rejection and nostalgia. What these writers, artists, politicals, and others have in common is a *marginal status* and sense of estrangement in their relation and attitude toward both general American society and their own Jewish background."

That might have been said about Roth years later, and was, though marginality was recast as a "thin personal culture," and estrangement, once a fact of life about which Howe thought it useless to moralize, became Roth's moral handicap and the source of his resentment and exasperation. "When we say . . . that a writer betrays a thin personal culture we mean . . . that he lives at the end of a tradition which can no longer nourish his imagination or that he has, through an act of fiat, chosen to tear himself away from that tradition. . . . It is, of course, a severe predicament for a writer to find himself in this situation; it forces him into self-consciousness, improvisation, and false starts; but if he is genuinely serious, he will try . . . to make a usable theme of his dilemmas."

Reading Howe on Roth we may think ourselves uncannily in a hall of mirrors, watching the critic rage at fractured and grotesque images of himself. His charges against Roth resound with ironic self-references, among which is this astonishing cluster: "Unfocused hostility often derives from unexamined depression, and the latter, which I take to be the ground-note of Roth sensibility, fully emerges only in the two novels he wrote after *Goodbye, Columbus.* But even in the early stories one begins to hear a grind of exasperation, an assault without precise object, an irritable wish to pull down the creatures of his own imagination which can hardly be explained by anything happening within the stories themselves. If sentimentality is defined as emotion in excess of what a given situation warrants, what are we to say about irritability in excess?"

What indeed? Without irritability in excess, there would have been no New York intellectuals, no *Partisan Review,* no *Commentary,* no *Dissent,* Howe's own magazine. And anyone familiar with Howe's own low threshold of indignation would be forgiven for drawing the inference that in admonishing Roth, Howe was also drawing a bead on his own revolutionary youth and at traits of his own, which he had found parodied in Roth's unpalatable books.

Second Thoughts

There was more, much more to this story, though how much of it needs to be recited in a book about Philip Roth is uncertain. Here is a quick overview. For several years before writing "Philip Roth Reconsidered," Howe had been on the warpath against the New Left, and in 1968 had written for *Commentary* a lengthy essay titled "The New York Intellectuals," about a third of which was a bitter screed against what he had seen as a fatal turn in leftism.[3] Howe himself had come out of the Trotskyist movement in the 1930s, had been a disciple of Max Shacht-man, renegade Trotskyist and founder of the Workers Party, and con-sidered himself throughout his career a democratic socialist. In the early days of the anti–Vietnam War movement and SDS, Howe had tried to make common cause with the New Left and failed. Reports of meetings between them, at which Howe sought to instruct his youthful cohorts on the dangers of allowing communists into their movement, suggest that there never was a chance of rapprochement between them, and the dialogue broke down, leaving Howe deeply troubled. There remained, it seems, lingering wounds from those encounters, kept livid by outrage and self-doubt, that would never properly heal.

With "The New York Intellectuals," Howe took the offensive, not only against the New Left, which he regarded as symptomatic of a pro-found ground shift in the terrain of ideas, but against the new sensibil-ity that had come into existence as its cultural *Doppelgänger,* "the psy-chology of unobstructed need." It teaches that "men should satisfy those needs which are theirs, organic to their bodies and psyches, and to do this they now must learn to discard or destroy all those obstructions, mostly the result of cultural neurosis, which keep them from satisfying their needs." Taking a phrase from the sixties itself, he identified it as the doctrine that everyone "should do his own thing." Moreover, he found this cultural trend not in California but at the heart of New York intellectual life, and identified it with writers such as Norman Mailer and Paul Goodman, and found as its high priests Norman O. Brown, Herbert Marcuse, and Marshall McLuhan. "Classics of the latest thing, these three figures can be employed to suggest an organic link between cultural modernism and the new sensibility, though in reality their rela-tion to modernism is no more than biographical." This was 1968, and Roth and *Portnoy's Complaint* were just coming over the horizon. When they appeared, the circuit of reasoning was already live; Roth had only to be plugged in.

Provoked to fury by the apocalyptic fervor of much New Left be-havior, Howe saw in Roth a literary fellow traveler to those chiliastic frenzies, and vented upon Roth his rage at events taking place else-where in the culture. Given an instinct for broad syntheses, it would have been easy enough for Howe to connect SDS's "days of rage" in

1969 with Alexander Portnoy's cries of rage on the couch. Since atmospherics, vast tremblings in the Zeitgeist, were at issue, it did not matter that Roth himself was by no stretch of the imagination either a New Leftist or a counterculture groupie, as Mailer tried to be. He was always, as he remains, a dissenting and distraught son of the secular, bookish, Europeanized, diasporic Jewish culture that created him and that Howe himself spoke for. And yet of course, who would deny, then or now, that the extremity of expression that Roth had permitted himself in *Portnoy's Complaint* had been authorized by a cultural environment in which such extravagance seemed a valiant, even heroic, expression of resistance to the modulations of civilization. Willy-nilly, Roth was a footnote, a remarkably handy case study of ressentiment and unobstructed need, those new fetishes, as Howe saw them, of the ecstatic, postmodern Jewish tribe.

I doubt that any New Leftist read or took counsel from Roth, or that he took any from them. He was decidedly not out there trying to levitate the Pentagon with Norman Mailer, Robert Lowell, and Paul Goodman in October 1967. As for the counterculture, in its broader lifestyle aspects, there is little reason to think that Roth encountered it in any form more immediate than newspapers and television, where its basic issues, its tragic dramas, and its staged spectacles were all melted down and packaged as network infotainment. But that little was enough for him to absorb the vibrations of the time-spirit, the de-authorization of the superego, the debunking of middle class life and constraints, and the celebration of "letting go" or letting fly with one's rage. Howe didn't need much. For him, Roth was another rivet to hold tight his grandiose polemical boilerplate. It felt to Roth, however, as though the whole boiler, steam, pipes, valves, and all had come crashing down on top of his head.

4

Analysis Terminable
Life as a Man

Ketterer came to hate me, Monica to fall in love with me, and
Lydia to accept me at last as her means of salvation. She saw the
way out of her life's misery, and I, in the service of Perversity or
Chivalry or Morality or Misogyny or Saintliness or Folly or Pent-
up Rage or Psychic Illness or Sheer Lunacy or Innocence or Ignorance or Experience or Heroism or Judaism or Masochism or Self-
Hatred or Defiance or Soap Opera or Romantic Opera or the Art
of Fiction perhaps, or none of the above, or maybe all of the above
and more—I found the way into mine.
Nathan Zuckerman in My Life as a Man

I am the Dagwood Bumstead of fear and trembling.
Peter Tarnopol in My Life as a Man

The therapeutic novel in America has been, as often as not, the divorce
novel, the miseries of the marriage bed being to modern fiction what the
anticipated delights were once to Elizabethan comedy. To the contemporary writer, the dramaturgy of courtship and union is not half so appealing as that of divorce, and between the chapel and the courtroom
falls the battle, the accusation, the demand, the denial, the strategy, the
maneuver, the duplicity, the scrutiny, the disclosure, the alibi, the self-
deception that believes the lie (thank you, Rogers and Hart), and the
analysis. Roth's *My Life as a Man* bears something of the same relation to
his writing that *Herzog* and *The Last Analysis* bear to Saul Bellow's and

After the Fall to Arthur Miller's. It is a testament of freedom, a memorial to trauma, a report card on psychoanalysis, and an exorcism of the ex.

Peter Tarnopol of *My Life as a Man* is a thirty-four-year-old writer—author of the celebrated *A Jewish Father*—widower, neurotic, narcissist, teacher, and outpatient who has squandered his talent and manhood in a marriage that has left him frantic, suspicious, over his head in debt and guilt, and barely able to salvage material for a book from this tangled ground zero. That book is a novel in three parts: two stories or "useful fictions," "Salad Days" and "Courting Disaster (or, Serious in the Fifties)," and an autobiographical novella, "My True Story," a confession of a young writer's marital desperation cleverly rendered as a "True Confession." Due partly to the ironbound divorce laws of New York State and partly to the tenacity and cunning of Maureen Johnson Tarnopol, formerly Mezik, formerly Walker, Tarnopol's marriage could be dissolved only by Maureen's death. It had been a trumped-up affair from the start, founded on a false pregnancy, a faked urine sample, and a phony abortion, for which a Jewish boyfriend had paid through the nose. Three years into this marriage, in the heat of the daily brawl, this one over Tarnopol's brief affair with an undergraduate student, Maureen feigns a suicide attempt and threatens to expose her professor-husband to the university, and he reacts by firing off the last salvo in his emotional arsenal, a tantrum. He tears off his clothes and dons Maureen's underclothes. Confronted by her husband feminized and in tears, Maureen relents and confesses her original sin and, as such things go in stalled marriages, turns her confession into an instrument of further coercion: "If you forgive me for the urine, I'll forgive you for your mistress," a quid pro quo that only a mugger could love. Now, 1967, four years after Tarnopol's flight from Maureen and a year after Maureen's death in a car crash, he is finally writing the novel, episode by bloody episode, in the monastic isolation of the Quahsay writer's retreat in Vermont.

Like *The Breast*, *My Life as a Man* is largely a dissertation on entrapment, a disclosure of how a man can find himself irredeemably beyond the pleasure principle just when he had so much pleasure to expect. As Roth conducts it, the inquiry is less philosophical than accusatory. The two forms of inquiry differ as "how?" differs from "who?" or a Bellow novel differs from a Roth novel, for where Moses Herzog and Artur

Sammler presuppose evolutionary conditions behind their predicaments and pose such questions as "What is this life?" and "What is the
heart of man?" the likes of Portnoy, Kepesh, and Tarnopol presuppose
transgression, guilt, and blame, and tend to ask, "Why is *she* doing *that*
to *me*?" and "Where did I screw up?" Tarnopol is quick to accuse the
culture. He was deceived into making that vain and calamitous gesture
of a marriage, he believes, by the moral climate of the fifties, in which
decade, "Decency and Maturity, a young man's 'seriousness,' were at
issue precisely because it was thought to be the other way around: in
that the great world was so obviously a man's, it was only within marriage that an ordinary woman could hope to find equality and dignity.
Indeed, we were led to believe by the defenders of womankind of our
era that we were exploiting and degrading the women we *didn't* marry,
rather than the ones we did."

Augmenting that moral climate for a young English graduate student was the great tradition of literary high seriousness, a tradition epit-
omized for Tarnopol by an epigram from Thomas Mann that he had
appended to *A Jewish Father* (and Roth himself had used in *Letting Go*):
"All actuality is deadly earnest, and it is morality itself that, one with
life, forbids us to be true to the guileless unrealism of our youth." Such
a courtship of cultural superegos has always been the English major's
stock-in-trade, and Tarnopol suffers an English major's catastrophe—
to have been ruined by the tight-lipped austerities of the great Protestant tradition and by those smothering lessons about duty, renunciation,
and endurance that adorn a literary education. "To live profoundly,"
saith the superego, especially one nurtured on Dostoevsky, Conrad,
Hawthorne, Leavis, Trilling, and Irving Howe, "is to suffer." The great
dialogue of Western Man says precious little about the morality of
pleasure, about, not to put too fine a point on it, whacking off.

The ubiquitous Spielvogel, who is Tarnopol's analyst too, sees it differently. What Tarnopol had taken for cultural coercion, he sees as the
victim's collusion, as the "acting out" of his ambivalence, narcissism, and
libidinized aggression, which he had initially directed toward a "phallic
mother" but eventually displaced onto his wife. What Spielvogel sees is
not a man victimized by an era that placed a premium on self-sacrifice
and moral accountability but a tactical arrangement between two people
out to enjoy some serious misery. So taken is Spielvogel with his own

diagnosis and the purchase it gives him into the dynamics of creativity that he publishes a paper on it while Tarnopol is still under his care.

Behind Spielvogel's jargon about libidinized aggression and phallic mothers is the suggestion that the marriage had its purposes for Tarnopol and that Maureen's duplicity not only posed a threat to him but opened up opportunities as well. On Maureen's part, the signs of wanting something more than "true love" are there from the start: she courts punishment with all the conviction of a journeyman welterweight out to prove he can still take a punch. Even before the marriage, when she attacks Peter with her purse and he threatens in his harmless way, "CLIP ME WITH THAT, MAUREEN, AND I'LL KILL YOU," she responds, "Do it! Kill me! Some man's going to—why not a 'civilized' one like you!"

Although readers are in no position to disentangle the Byzantine maneuvers of a marriage gone sour, they may observe that Maureen's death plea is wholehearted and that Peter, in marrying her, had homed in on her self-destructiveness. Guilt, submission, intimidation, and sudden moral collapse had all played their part in leading Tarnopol to the altar, and yet one suspects that such marriages tend to befall a special class of man: those who bear a grudge against women. Maureen had an instinct for finding such men: Mezik, the saloonkeeper who made her go down on his buddy while he watched, and Walker, the homosexual who broke his promise to give up boys. Tarnopol has more in common with such company than he imagines. All three found in Maureen the right type of woman, one for whom their misogyny could seem a just and reasonable hatred. Indeed, the circumstances surrounding Maureen's death are ambiguous enough to suggest that it is Walker at last who kills her, for he was driving the car in which she died.

The news of Maureen's death has hardly arrived when Peter finds himself contemplating his newest problem, girlfriend Susan McCall, who, until then, had merely been a sweet burden: a helpless, mildly neurotic, leggy heiress who is incapable of an orgasm but cooks a marvelous *blanquette de veau* and spikes her fruit salads with Kirsch. In short, she is not morally challenging enough for an aspiring young hunger artist who must take off for Quahsay and sexual quarantine, to a life of hard work, regular hours, calisthenics, a hot breakfast, and a simple boy's lunch, to relive, in short, the easy ascetic triumphs of those salad days when to finish your homework and clean your plate were the only evidence needed that you were a good boy.

My Life as a Man offers less instant gratification than *Portnoy*, perhaps because it is so labored a performance and a more intricately woven book than the spontaneous *Portnoy* and the ad libbed *Our Gang* and *The Great American Novel*. Its mixed styles and shifting perspectives, the thick inlays and elaborate overdubs, reflect many years of labor and doubt. But for all its intricacy and art, the book strikes deeper than *Portnoy*, whose formulas for the sources of Alex Portnoy's complaint come down to a couchful of theories and notions from Freud, Otto Fenichel, Isaac Rosenfeld, and Spielvogel, brilliantly applied though they may be. *My Life as a Man* is a book of uncertainties. It suggests that the truth, if one exists, lies beyond the scope of psychoanalysis in its customary forms. *The Mother* scarcely makes an appearance; *the phallic mother* is only a figment of Spielvogel's imagination. The point of Tarnopol's quarrel with Spielvogel over the latter's interpretation of his truant sexuality is that there are no privileged explanations, only points of view. Spielvogel is granted one, Tarnopol's brother Morris another, sister Joan yet another, Maureen still another. Even Frannie Glass of J. D. Salinger's *Frannie and Zooey* is permitted a neurasthenic word on the subject. By means of his "useful fictions," Tarnopol plies himself with several others, making *My Life as a Man* a *Rashomon* of critical interpretation. The book may even be understood as Roth's answer to Spielvogel, his explanation of why psychoanalysis finally fails as a basic and comprehensive guide to motives and why fiction, with its freedom, its variousness, and its possibility, is far more faithful to life than case history. No single interpretation, the book warns us, will explain the mess Tarnopol is in, and nothing less than a symposium on the subject can begin to approach it.

In *My Life as a Man*, Tarnopol's, and the reader's, doubts about Spielvogel's judgment and about the integrity of the entire analytic process are brought to a head by Spielvogel's paper on Tarnopol, "Creativity: The Narcissism of the Artist," in which Tarnapol is thinly disguised as "a successful Italian-American poet in his forties." Tarnopol's dismay at the essay stems largely from the fact that while the history is familiar, if distorted, the interpretation strikes him as entirely fanciful. "I could not read a sentence in which it did not seem to me that the observation was off, the point missed, the nuance blurred—in short, the evidence rather munificently distorted so as to support a narrow and unilluminating thesis at the expense of the ambiguous and perplexing actuality."

Spielvogel's analysis *is* couched in a distressing jargon. In adverting to Tarnopol's "enormous ambivalence" about leaving his wife; his "castration anxiety vis-à-vis a phallic mother figure"; his "acting out with other women," and "reducing all women to masturbatory sexual objects" it so reduces Tarnopol's tangled motives to catch phrases that Tarnopol is filled with wonder that the man to whom he has poured out his soul could so have turned his heartaches into platitudes. There is simply no relationship between that language and his life, and Tarnopol, his confidence shattered, is poised to forsake analysis for Quahsay and isolation to apply to himself the one therapy he can trust for nuance, if not results: writing.

Indeed, the distinction *My Life as a Man* enjoys as a modern psychological novel lies in the analysand's battle with analysis, initially refusing the ritualized explanations offered by Spielvogel. "Does your wife remind you of your mother?" Spielvogel asks Tarnopol in one of their first sessions, causing Tarnopol to balk and enumerate all the differences between the despised wife and the sainted mother. The scenes of angry rejoinder between Tarnopol and Spielvogel, though not always the freshest writing in *My Life as a Man,* cast a critical light on psychoanalysis: on the reductiveness of its diagnostic terminology and its power to browbeat the skeptical patient simply by charging him with resistance. Initially, upon getting wind of Spielvogel's bias, Tarnopol challenges Spielvogel's textbook interpretations, but as time passes he begins to question his own recollections of a blessed childhood, calling up in their stead "rather Dickensian recollections of my mother as an overwhelming and frightening person."

A charge commonly levied against psychoanalysis, that it bullies the patient into accepting interpretations that violate his or her memory, is tellingly illustrated here as Tarnopol learns in analysis to dislike his mother, even as he suspects that the diagnosis Spielvogel has given him "revealed more about some bête noire of his than of my own." And yet, despite that realization, the desperate need to be unbound from the past rather than any conscious assent to the doctor's findings keeps Tarnopol in analysis for three years and drives him through bouts of sullenness with his mother whom, until entering analysis, he believed he adored.

This episode reflects back on *Portnoy's Complaint,* a book whose very slant on Alex Portnoy's childhood takes its cues from psychoanalysis. The myth on which the book rests—when in pain, *cherchez la mère*—is now revealed to be a delusion foisted on Alex Portnoy by his analyst, the selfsame Spielvogel. *My Life as a Man* is, it seems, the first of several novels written contra-*Portnoy,* a son's plea that it was Freudian doctrine or the Zeitgeist or the great books that led him astray, not his mom.

My Life as a Man is, all in all, Roth's best book. Its prose is pungent and aquiver with the asperities of a sour marriage, the jargon of the clinic, the argot of the street, and random voices from out in left field. Roth reproduces the language around him better than any American writer today, and when he is listening well his prose is gratefully free of his characteristic mannerisms: those of precocious insight and those of high purpose. And it is the sensitivity to language that explains the final assessment of psychoanalysis in this book, for it is language at last that drives a wedge between Tarnopol and Spielvogel and sends the latter back to Quahsay and his typewriter for a session of autotherapy that may produce, if not good feelings, at least good books. Spielvogel, in contributing his "useful fiction" to the symposium on Tarnopol, violates not just a code of professional ethics but one of style. The analysis goes swimmingly until the analyst bursts into the artist's medium and reveals his own inadequacy with words. By breaking into prose, the one domain over which his patient is master, he demystifies himself and de-authorizes his craft. The mask of omnicompetence is off and the writer/patient, finding himself a character in a routine case history that goes from formula to banal formula with dull predictability, must terminate the analysis. He'd given Spielvogel his best lines and Spielvogel had botched them. In *My Life as a Man,* Roth takes his lines back and takes charge of his own story, laboring to show how, with sensitivity, imagination, and a flair for *le mot juste,* it might properly be told.

Second Thoughts

With a few minor phrase changes, I have left this pretty much as I wrote it in the mid-1970s. Clearly I was using Roth here as a stalking horse for my own disaffections, but since he suited the role so well, no great violence was done to the book. Reviewing the book now, some twenty-seven years later, I'd probably be less message-ridden and more attuned to the composition of a book that is so clearly *written*. *My Life as a Man* was Roth's first foray into the business of self-improvisation and the telling of one story from multiple points of view. Having Peter Tarnopol invent Nathan Zuckerman in "useful fictions" that played extra variations on the theme of personal catastrophe was not just a way of flexing his writer's muscles; it was a way of gaining purchase over some pretty tender and confounding stuff. It was his way of having art take up where therapy had left off, and to do what therapy had failed to do: produce usable fictions.

What Roth's years of analysis had taught him was the inescabability of meaning, how inevitable it was. Freud had used the term "overdetermination" to stand for it, by which he meant that everything you do takes place in a sticky web of people and circumstances and history and language and every sort of mental activity, from the most primitive demands of the medulla to the last conversations one has overheard. A tremor in any of it sends shock waves through all of it. If Spielvogel—the real one—had betrayed Roth and theory finally disappointed him, the habit of mind gave him a subject and a method. He learned to cross-examine his misery and make it speak. He graduated from his earlier writing by learning to see all of experience with a compound eye. And he learned as well that a whole life could be brought to bear on a single moment. This book's extraordinary density comes out of that awareness.

That training happened to coincide perfectly with his reading. Roth was the perfect English major: he took books seriously, and in one of the "Useful Fictions," "Courting Disaster (or, Serious in the Fifties)," Nathan Zuckerman, having been medically discharged from the Army for migraine headaches, decides to see a psychoanalyst in Chicago who has, he is told, a Freudian orientation. Zuckerman's self-presentation is bafflingly literary to the analyst.

> I did not know that it was a Freudian orientation so much as a literary habit of mind which the neurologist was not accustomed to: that is to say, I could not resist reflecting upon my migraines in the same supra-medical way that I might consider the illnesses of Milly Theale or Hans Castorp or the Reverend Arthur Dimmesdale, or ruminate upon the transformation of Gregor Samsa into a cockroach, or search out the "meaning" in Gogol's short story of Collegiate Assessor Kovalev's

temporary loss of his nose. Whereas an ordinary man might complain, "I get these damn headaches" (and have been content to leave it at that), I tended, like a student of high literature or a savage who paints his body blue, to see the migraines as standing for something, as a disclosure or "epiphany," isolated or accidental or inexplicable only to one who was blind to the design of a life or a book. What did my migraines signify?

Figuring out what it all signifies is the work of the book. *My Life* is so clearly a "working through" book, a kind of novel that is far less likely to be written today in our climate of quickie therapies and pharmaceutical mood regulators and personality patches. It was authorized by a climate of thought in which "confronting" and "working through" were the keys to recuperation. But that can be dreary as literature, and Peter Tarnopol's disgorgings tend to be both sodden and long. I can hardly imagine what it must be like for the poor therapist. What makes the book work for me, however, is not the spiritual ditch digging that takes us into the storm drains of Peter Tarnopol's depression, but the voices from outside Zuckerman/Tarnopol's head that ventilate the book with Roth's comedy, which not even disaster can repress. For starters there are Tarnopol's brother Morris and sister Joan, the former a practical tough guy, a reality instructor who pipes in editorially with a kind of Bellowesque bluster on the subject of Tarnopol's taste in women (first Maureen, then Susan McCall): "The gray eyes and the 'fine' bones have got you fooled, kiddo. Another fucked-up shiksa. First the lumpenproletariat, now the aristocracy. What are you, the Malinowkski of Manhattan? Enough erotic anthropology. Get rid of her Pep. You're sticking your plug in the same socket." Sister Joan, who has married into wealth and ascended into the empyrean of culture and taste in California, offers a place to stay, but not a pat on the head. "We won't ever bother you with our goatish ways, if you should just want to sit around the pool and polish your halo. If it pleases you, we will do everything we can to prevent you from having even a fairly good time. But reliable sources in the east tell me that you are still very gifted at that yourself."

Tarnopol sends Joan copies of his two stories or useful fictions, "Salad Days" and "Courting Disaster (or, Serious in the Fifties)," and she turns them over to the twenty-four-year-old associate editor of the literary magazine *Bridges,* one Lane Coutell (wrack your brains for that one—clues to follow). Coutell writes, acutely for a twenty-four-year-old, "To the degree that this is so serious [i.e., that "Serious" is an allegory of Tarnopol and his muse], to the degree that the character of Zuckerman embodies and presents the misguided and morbid 'moral' imagination that produced *A Jewish Father*, it is fascinating; to the degree that Tarnopol is back on the angst kick, with all that implies about 'moving' the reader, I think the story is retrograde, dull, and boring, and suggests that the conventional (rabbinical) side of this writer still has a stranglehold on what is reckless and intriguing in his talent." This may be mannered and guarded, but it is not stupid. And here is the clue. Coutell's wife is one Frances Coutell, described by Joan as "a delicate, washed-out beauty of twenty-three, bristling with spiritual needs; also a romantic masochist who, as you will surmise, has developed a crush on you, not least because she doesn't like you that much." And Frances writes: "My two cents worth, only because the story J. admires most seems to me smug and vicious and infuriating, all the more so for being so *clever* and *winning*. It is pure sadistic trash and I pray (actually) that *Bridges* doesn't print it." Well, that's of course Franny Glass of J. D. Salinger's *Franny and Zooey*, and Lane Coutell is the date who meets her for the big Yale game. Roth is marvelous at these sendups, and I only wish there were more of them. Franny closes her letter to Joan: "Life is awful. Yours, Franny."

The best of the rest is an imaginary college essay on the useful fictions by one Karen Oakes, the senior at the University of Wisconsin, with whom Tarnopol has a brief fling. Imaginary because she doesn't actually write it: Tarnopol dreams it up. "In order to dilute the self-pity that (as I understand it) had poisoned his imagination in numerous previous attempts to fictionalize his unhappy marriage, Professor Tarnopol establishes at the outset here a tone of covert (and, to some small degree, self-congratulatory) self-mockery; this calculated attitude of comic detachment he maintains right on down to the last paragraph, where abruptly the shield of lightheartedness is all at once pierced by the author's pronouncement that in his estimation the true story really isn't funny at all. All of which would appear to suggest that if Professor Tarnopol has managed in 'Salad Days' to make an artful narrative of his misery, he has done so largely by refusing directly to confront it." Tarnopol gives her an A+.

Sure, this is all preemptive self-criticism, Roth's way of getting to the shortcomings in his writing before the critics do and softening the blows by striking them himself. And it also sets the stage for the "My True Story" section of the book, in which Tarnopol presumably makes amends for his fictional evasions and comes clean with the nasty truth, not only about Maureen but also about himself: that whatever befell him, he richly earned. But for me, at any rate, it is Roth airing out what is reckless and intriguing in his talent—vide Lane Coutell—the gift for mimicry, and letting the delight of liberating one's talent wrestle the book away from the drudgery of working through, of mourning.

Toward the end there are other voices: Maureen's friend in "group" Flossie Koerner and Maureen herself, through her diary, which Peter takes from her apartment while she is in the hospital after a suicide attempt. While they have the effect of taking us down yet other corridors in the book's hall of mirrors, I don't find them terribly fascinating. Maureen, writing in the soubrette's voice she saved for her diary, turned out to have little to say besides the clichés of romantic disappointment. "Where have I been? Why haven't I realized this? Peter doesn't care for me. He never did!" That sort of thing. She does have a few smart things to say about her own future role in her husband's writing: "If it weren't for me he'd still be hiding behind his Flaubert and wouldn't know what real life was like if he fell over it. What did he ever think he was going to write about, knowing and believing nothing but what he read in books?" True enough, though about what it is she gave him, what "reality" she brought into the home, not a word. Roth missed a chance here at a final exorcism in the form of a confession of sadism toward her husband. But then, having already spoken sufficiently ill of the dead, he wasn't up to having her speak ill of herself. Mourning has its decorum; even Roth knew when to leave bad enough alone. "Wear a dark suit," advises Tarnopol's father, "put in an appearance, and that'll be that."

5

The Convalescence, or
The Man That Got Away

By contrast, *The Professor of Desire* is a mopping-up operation, a recapit-
ulation of second-hand themes at reduced levels of panic. It is a transition piece between the mayhem-ridden "breakthrough" books and the
modulated *The Ghost Writer,* a convalescence novel, tracking the flight of
an emotion from illness to health and featuring a hero who is discharged
from analysis because he no longer needs it. Although Kafka and entrapment crop up as motifs in *The Professor of Desire,* the book finally
puts away Kafkaesque determinism and testifies to the medicinal prop-
erties of simple love, and while its hero, David Kepesh, is haunted by
transformations to come, *The Professor of Desire* on its own terms gives
reason to believe that there are second acts in Jewish-American lives.

David Alan Kepesh, in a pre-breast incarnation, experiences his
bleak marital strife with Helen Baird, a Southern California coed man-
qué who had spent seven years as an international seductress and Asian
femme fatale before returning home to marry, and torment, a young
Jewish English professor. The marriage, the affliction, the conviction
that fate possesses an imagination not unlike Franz Kafka's, are tedi-
ously familiar to the reader of Roth. They are the threads of domestic
disarray that draw *The Professor of Desire* into the company of *Letting
Go, When She Was Good,* and *My Life as a Man* as a novel of that sordid
Roth obsession: marriage. What is new is the countertheme, which
finds Kepesh being rescued from his agony and his impotence by Claire
Ovington, a warm, patient, doting woman of twenty-four, whose very

physicality provides him, as if by sheer weight, with the emotional ballast he lacks in himself. Peter Tarnopol may justly complain to Spielvogel that his wife does *not* remind him of his mother, but even the staunchest antagonist to Freudian doctrine is bound to observe in Claire a decidedly maternal presence in David Alan Kepesh's life. *The Professor of Desire* makes scant sense unless we assent to the proposition that Kepesh is plucked from depression and released from psychoanalysis by expert mothering.

The Professor of Desire, then, is a novel of rebirth, that Bellovian theme. Roth's version of it, however, could not be more different, for where Bellow's characters are reborn to themselves and stake out their new lives as isolates and even, as in the play *The Last Analysis,* as enemies of the family, this Roth character is reborn to love and be brought back into the family. Through his love of Claire, Kepesh is also reunited with his father, who discovers in Claire a lifeline to his son. What Kafka, what Bellow, could have conjured up such a scene as the one in this book that finds the Jewish father embracing in both arms the prodigal son and prodigal son's shiksa girlfriend with tears of appreciation gleaming in his eyes? Whatever happened to alienation? To Kafka? This is borscht, served with Wonder Bread, perhaps, but borscht all the same. *The Professor of Desire* signals Roth's turn from outrage to *poshlust* and from Kafka to Catskill, where all trials are resolved in sobs of forgiveness. But if *The Professor of Desire* is Yiddish theater, it is Yiddish theater suburbanized, eroticized, and brought up-to-date by sweet dreams of healing miscegenation.

It is noteworthy that the books of convalescence that depict the Roth hero as "getting better" should also feature a turn toward the illnesses of history. History replaces individual pathology in these books and the basic strategy of postwar fiction is reversed. *The Professor of Desire* and, more centrally, *The Ghost Writer,* are history-laden books: the Jewish past weighs heavily upon them. In *The Professor of Desire,* the past is implied through the metaphor of Kafka; in *The Ghost Writer* it breaks through in Nathan Zuckerman's dream that a young woman whom he meets at the house of E. I. Lonoff is in actuality Anne Frank. Kafka, it seems, does dual service for Roth, standing as a metaphor for marital entrapment and sexual failure in some writing and elsewhere as a metaphor for life under totalitarianism.

But in *The Professor of Desire,* the shift of gears from the personal to the historical is incomplete: the novel seems to have been conceived in one frame of mind and completed in another. *The Professor of Desire* is not a novel but a grab bag of moments and reflections, some of them dull, others rising to Irving Berlins of rhapsody. Themes rise but never converge, and we never know for certain what Herbie Bratasky, Kepesh's boyhood idol who is a tummler at Abe Kepesh's "Hungarian Royale" resort in the Catskills and did "Petomaine" routines for David Kepesh's private delectation, has to do with Helen Baird or Claire Ovington or the mystique of Kafka or with what appears to be the book's grand theme: Kepesh's initiation into love.

The Professor of Desire is Roth's tenderest book, the one in which he takes the greatest risks of love. It dispenses almost entirely with irony, crisis, compulsion, moral intricacy, and the comic strategies of self-defeat, and attempts to make a simple statement of the power of nurturance to heal what is broken in a life. But Roth as a writer is not a practiced hand at sweetness and for the most part doesn't know how to dramatize it as anything but effusion. The book stumbles over its own gratitude. Tenderness only becomes charged with imagination when it is the father, rather than Claire, upon whom it is lavished. Abe Kepesh, widower and retired owner of Kepesh's Hungarian Royale resort, is the ubiquitous voluble Roth father, whose fears and obsessions, all packaged in a charming immigrant naiveté, come pouring forth in an unrelenting stream of blessings and non sequiturs, pushcart nostrums and dizzy flights of diaspora fancy. He has a molten heart that secretes affection, and even if you do not prick him he bleeds love. He and Claire, creatures of untutored love, are spontaneously drawn together, recognizing in each other the simplicity of heart with which each is endowed.

Simplicity of heart! What in the world is that doing in a Roth novel, where doubt, unreason, duplicity, and panic are the stocks-in-trade of all characters, all *except* the father, who is always, everywhere, untainted? In a fallen world, he is the pre-lapsarian patriarch, a bewildered Adam who has shlepped innocently into the wrong garden and knows of no more of evil than the failure of his own business. Through the years, in many books, from *Portnoy's Complaint* through *The Breast* (where Abe Kepesh is ostensibly the same) through the marvelous story, "'I Always Wanted You to Admire My Fasting'; or, Looking at Kafka" to *The Professor of Desire,* this portrait of patriarchy-with-a-human face has been the counterweight to the Kafkaesque nightmares of entrapment and impotence that these Roth sons invariably suffer. For though the father is himself trapped and hemmed in, he meets his fate with dignity and provides the distraught son with an emotional safety valve. The love between them would seem to go deep. In later books, *The Ghost Writer* and *Zuckerman Unbound,* their bond of blood and wacky conversation will unravel, but up through *The Professor of Desire,* it will prove to be the most powerful and sentimental bond of all, making all others, including those of sexual love, seem fragile and makeshift by comparison.

Hegel's parable of the honest soul giving way in the modern world to the disintegrated consciousness finds its image in Roth in the simple father raising the neurotic son, who then struggles to get back to a lost and elusive simplicity. But even as Kepesh remarks on his great fortune in having found Claire and contentment, he awakes from bad dreams filled with portents of disasters to come and lets us know that contentment is only provisional, if only because, we may surmise having read this book, it provides him with too little material.

Perhaps this book is a boundary marker for Roth's talents, an indication of what his imagination can*not* encompass, for there does not seem to be enough aggression or despair or irony or perversity or misogyny or folly or pent-up rage or psychic illness or sheer lunacy or Judaism or masochism in Kepesh's predicament to bring into play Roth's full talent, a talent so completely keyed to incipient panic that it appears to be the imaginative equivalent of Georg Simmel's definition of a highly developed culture: a crisis constantly held back. One finally sees *The Professor of Desire* as a book between books, an unfinished project, a rough beast, its hour come round at last, slouching toward Zuckerman and a trilogy.

Second Thoughts

I've left this pretty much as first written in 1977. *The Professor of Desire* did not grow any more compelling to me with age, its or my own. By 1977, Roth had been spending considerable time in Prague, had already been expelled by the Czech authorities, and had already begun editing his Writers from the Other Europe series for Penguin. Kepesh's dream encounter with Kafka's whore in this book seems more usefully taken up in the context of those visits and that editing project, for which, see chapter 9, "The Prague Orgy and The Other Europe."

6

This Is How I Will Live
The Ghost Writer

Like a patient etherized upon a table
>>> T. S. Eliot, "The Love Song of J. Alfred Prufrock"

Sing me a song. Oh, imitate the great Durante.
>>> Amy Bellette, from *The Ghost Writer*

What if? What if the Prince of Denmark should be visited one night by a ghost that claims to be the spirit of his dead father and informs him that his peaceful passing away was actually a poisoning and that the prince must take revenge on the guilty parties, the prince's mother and his uncle? What if a petty clerk in Prague should awaken one morning to find that he has become an enormous insect, or what if Franz Kafka himself should survive his bout with tuberculosis in 1924, live long enough to have to flee the Nazis, and immigrate to Newark just in time to become Philip Roth's Hebrew School teacher? Such is the premise of what is surely Roth's finest piece of short fiction, "'I Always Wanted You to Admire My Fasting'; or, Looking at Kafka."[1] In that story, Roth brings Professor Kafka home for dinner; Mr. and Mrs. Roth fix him up with Aunt Rhoda, the spinster, and Kafka eventually takes her away one weekend to Atlantic City where, being Franz Kafka, he falls short of being a man. Because Roth refuses to cure him of all his afflictions, Kafka loses not only another woman but also a chance to put down roots in New Jersey. He remains as wifeless in Newark as he had been in Prague, and never does become Philip Roth's uncle.

And what if Anne Frank should have survived the Holocaust and immigrated to America to become a coed at a small college near Stockbridge, Massachusetts. And what if, some years later, she should meet up with Nathan Zuckerman, a young writer from Newark, who is about Roth's age and is currently in hot water throughout Essex County because of a story he has written, featuring his own family, that is taken to be anti-Semitic? Stop there. The difficulties are immediately obvious. Anne Frank can't be reinvented like Franz Kafka. Kafka was so wholly of the imagination that it remains his medium even after his death, but Anne Frank belongs to history, and to a history so tragic and irredeemable that the imagination has to feel chastened before it. But what if our Zuckerman, whose fantasy life sometimes overpowers him, were only to imagine that a young woman he meets might be Anne Frank, and that for his own personal motives it is reason enough to fall in love with her? Then you have Philip Roth's *The Ghost Writer,* a book about how Anne Frank might be invented by a young man who has need of inventing her.

This encounter takes place at the isolated country home of the writer E. I. Lonoff, a gray, Jewish eminence who, despite seven books and a National Book Award, which he refused, has scarcely any popular following and desires even less than he has. Lonoff is a recluse who has renounced all passions except for his art and is a master of style who has devoted his life to *le mot juste,* or turning sentences around and around until he has gotten them right. His stories may go to twenty-seven drafts. As for the stories themselves, they are Jewish minimalist, comic parables "in which the tantalized hero does not move to act *at all*—the tiniest impulse toward amplitude or self-surrender, let alone intrigue or adventure, peremptorily extinguished by the ruling triumvirate of Sanity, Responsibility, and Self-Respect, assisted handily by their devoted underlings: the timetable, the rainstorm, the headache, the busy signal, the traffic jam, and, most loyal of all, the last-minute doubt."

Upon first stepping into Lonoff's rural retreat Zuckerman is struck by its prevailing civility and composure and decides, as well an embattled young man fresh out of Newark and the culture wars might, "This is how I will live." What he believes he sees is a life pared down for work and stripped of inessentials, including inessential passions. And so it is, though such a life has its penalties. Lonoff has either repressed the fire in him or has none to repress. He is a man with "autumn in his heart and spectacles on his nose"—Isaac Babel's definition of the Jewish writer. As another character in *The Ghost Writer* observes, he is as "unimpressive as he is unimpressed."

Zuckerman is in awe of so much dedication, and Lonoff, in turn, has taken a shine to the young writer whose voice, Lonoff tells him, "is the most compelling voice I've encountered in years, certainly for somebody starting out." (Irving Howe, in reviewing *Goodbye, Columbus* in 1959, had found in Roth "a unique voice, a secure rhythm, a distinctive subject.")

Not everyone is ready to concur in that, least of all Zuckerman's own father, who is outraged by his son's most recent story in which the messy details of an old family squabble are laid bare and all of Jewry, thereby, has been informed against. "It is about kikes," he tells Nathan. "Kikes and their love of money. That is all our good Christian friends will see, I guarantee you." Although the outline of the story we are actually given sounds a good deal more like Saul Bellow's "The Old System" than anything Roth has ever written, the predicament is vintage Roth. "Doc" Zuckerman, the pharmacist, even takes the offending story to Essex County's most distinguished Jewish jurist, Judge Leopold Wapter, who sends Nathan a ten-point questionnaire about his Jewish loyalties and beliefs that might well have been made up from Roth's own brimming files on betrayal. "Why in a story with a Jewish background must there be (a) adultery; (b) incessant fighting within a family over money; (c) warped human behavior in general?" "Can you honestly say that there is anything in your short story that would not warm the heart of a Julius Streicher or a Joseph Goebbels?" And more, as if that were not enough.

It does Zuckerman no good to invoke the example of Isaac Babel's Odessa stories, or to protest that Uncle Sidney, the villain of his story, is a descendent of Benya Krik, the legendary Jewish gangster of Babel's Odessa. Little wonder that he seeks refuge from this onslaught of relatives and elders of Zion in the company of the Jewish master of Flaubertian indifference, whose sole morality is renunciation in living and a firm mastery of every shade of expression. If that makes Lonoff sound a little like a Jewish Henry James, that is intentional. In depicting him, Roth has been less interested in the sharp contrasts between Jewish and

American cultural traits than in the blendings and overlappings of Old and New World species of asceticism. Lonoff is one whose Jewish-American hyphen stands for a confluence, not a contradiction.

How better for Zuckerman to turn the tables on Judge Wapter and the legions of relatives poised to strike him down than to apprentice himself to the "most famous literary ascetic in America," and then, for extra leverage, become a sort of son-in-law by marrying Lonoff's young assistant, Amy Bellette, who offers not only her own devotion to the master's art but something more: a history of suffering? Amy is a D. P. who, with Lonoff's aid, had come to America just after the war some ten years prior, to become, Lonoff insists, the best student of writing he ever had. In a phrase that could only clutch at Zuckerman's literary heart, Lonoff tells him, "She has a remarkable prose style." She also has a remarkable appearance, dominated by large pale eyes and a marked disproportion between body and head, hinting of early injury, misfortune, deprivation. Hinting of the camps.

Zuckerman is smitten. Why shouldn't this woman with the remarkable style, false name, and mysterious European past be Anne Frank herself, miraculously alive and in America and, out of her survivor's stubbornness and pride, refusing to reveal herself? Zuckerman can scarcely wait to give his father and all the other enemies of the imagination at home a taste of their own medicine. "This is my Aunt Tessie, this is Frieda and Dave, this is Birdie, this is Murray. . . . This is my wife, everyone. She is all I have ever wanted. . . . Remember the dark hair clipped back with a barrette? Well, this is she. . . . Anne, says my father—the Anne? Oh, how I have misunderstood my son. How mistaken we have been!"

It can be hard at times to distinguish a mea culpa from a hard right to the *kishkes*, but Roth seems willing to settle for something less than severe reprisals. The idea of marrying Anne Frank is certainly one of the more ideologically assertive admissions of error on record. But Roth does not seem as close to this Zuckerman as he has been to other heroes, and if he isn't exactly above his handiwork paring his fingernails, neither is he scoring points with abandon. It isn't the intractability of Zuckerman's situation that interests Roth here but the strangeness and unpredictability of a world that continually surprises Zuckerman with its own ingenuity.

Amy Bellette may not be Anne Frank, but she is, in her way, a beguiling mixture of dependent child and accomplished young woman, an émigré Peaches Browning with a remarkable prose style who privately addresses Lonoff as Dad-da and has apparently spent years trying to seduce the famous literary ascetic. But Lonoff, who has given everything to art, lives a life so austere that even he complains of its emotional poverty. And yet, in his unguarded moments, that is, when his wife is not about, he entertains his Amy by doing impressions of the great Durante. As Zuckerman sits up late into the night in Lonoff's study, his perusal of Lonoff's books is interrupted by voices from Amy's bedroom above. What is he to do but stand atop Lonoff's desk, atop a volume of James's stories at that, and apply his ear to the ceiling? What he overhears are Amy's efforts to lure Dad-da into her bed. But he is steadfast, and even when she sheds her nightgown to stand naked before him, he remains firm and sensible. He is a married man and will not hear of an affair. ("I've had the bed," he confides elsewhere to Zuckerman.) Only once does he yield to her wishes, when she cries out, "Oh, tell me a story. Sing me a song. Oh, imitate the great Durante, I really need it tonight." And for just a moment Lonoff gives in. "O, I know don well I can do widout Broadway—but . . . can Broadway do widout meeeee?" *Oh, imitate the great Durante!* The guy has got some spunk in him after all.

∽

What is the point of such shenanigans, or of the bitter domestic blowup that follows, in which Lonoff's wife, for whom he has never done the great Durante, or much else for that matter, marches out in despair, calling out to Amy as she goes, "The classroom daydream has come true! You get the creative writer—and I get to go!" In a sense there is no point at all, if by point we mean something like weighty moral purpose. This is the least tendentious of Roth's books, far more the bemused slice of life than the anguished self-exculpation. Here it is the other guy's marriage that is on the rocks. Lonoff has chosen the perfection of the work over the perfection of the life, and Roth looks on the consequences with detachment. Maybe it is Lonoff's own imperturbability, his peculiar absence of conflict or normal passion, that robs the moment of its desperation, but situations that were disastrous in earlier books are merely ironic in this one.

Even the element of self-examination here is unlike the turbulent self-inquisition we have come to expect of Roth, since it is not destructive motives that are being mercilessly scrutinized but the imagination itself. Accordingly, the regressive portions of the personality that elsewhere have been central take a back seat to such considerations as history and literature. The Roth who wrote this book is the Roth who edits the Writers from the Other Europe series for Penguin Books and spends much of his time in London or Prague in the company of Czech writers like Milan Kundera, to whom he dedicates this book, and Ludvík Vaculík. It is the Roth, in other words, who has set his sights on becoming a European novelist. While Newark is still very much with him, it is now Newark under the shadow of Amsterdam in 1944, thus infinitely diminished in scale. Newark is now only the embarkation point for a flight into the greater world, while Prague and Amsterdam are the cities of night and fog out there beyond the sheltered confines of Weequahic High. Doc Zuckerman and Judge Wapter's fears may be misapplied, but they are not unfounded.

This book finds Roth poised ambiguously between his old obsession with sexual failure and domestic crisis and a more recent involvement with history on the tragic plane, but unable to take the full plunge into matters on which he has so tenuous a grasp. Here, and in *The Professor of Desire,* he introduces some catastrophe of historic proportions—the Holocaust or the Soviet rape of Czechoslovakia—and then scales the story down to the level of a domestic blowup. Even while his imagination wrestles with horrors of world-historical magnitude, his writing stays close to what he knows firsthand.

No idea lends itself to fiction except through a strategy of presentation, and Roth, who has not been a student of Henry James for nothing, knows that better than anyone. The strategy of placing an Anne Frank look-alike in Stockbridge in 1956 and introducing her to Roth's own alter ego gives Roth freedom to invent characters, entertain fantasies, and shuttle at will between continents, which are now only places in the mind, while any direct assault on history would have closed off these possibilities. And yet, for my taste, *The Ghost Writer* could have been bolder with its modest premises and taken a few more risks. This is Roth's most restrained book since *When She Was Good,* and his circumspection is certainly in keeping with the hazardous nature of his material. You want to walk softly with this stuff. Still, I'd like to know more about the Lonoff who does Durante imitations in the bedroom and less about the one who says of himself, "I turn sentences around. That's my life. I write a sentence and then I turn it around. Then I look at it and I turn it around again." It occurs to the reader, though not to the starstruck Zuckerman, that Lonoff's studied composure is a symptom of an impenetrable egotism, and that to be unimpressive as he is unimpressed is to be so full of himself that nothing can puncture his shield of self-conceit. Unless we can imagine that there is something fairly wild lurking beneath all that composure, Lonoff must seem an unappealing figure, and maybe his wife, as she walks out the door, is telling us all we need to know about him. "Nothing can be touched, nothing can be changed, everybody must be quiet, the children must shut up, their friends must stay away until four—There is his religion of art, my young successor: rejecting life! *Not* living is what he makes his beautiful fiction *out* of!" Is that because Lonoff is in mourning for the Jews of Europe, or because he has mastered the art of civilized sublimation, turning all his sex into prose, or because he simply lacks his fair share of life force? His canons of reticence give us not a clue, and Roth, for once, has settled for telling us far less than we want to know.

Second Thoughts

Was I being hard on this book? After all, there is much to admire in it. The slow ripening of the sentence, that unerring instinct for how words are stitched together, reaches its full maturity in *The Ghost Writer* and remains a constant throughout Roth's subsequent writing. John Leonard touched on something important in reviewing *The Ghost Writer* in *The New York Review of Books*.[2] Never mind all the questions about the book, he observed, "What matters more is the music." That's right, though I'm not sure I'd agree that Leonard and I hear the same music, not if what he hears is an "odd sonata, as if Mahler had tried his hand at a bit of Mozart and just couldn't resist bringing in one of his inevitable marching bands." What? But *The Ghost Writer* is one of those books worth pausing over and listening to just a little bit. Here is a scene in which Lonoff stands at the door as Hope leaves to drive Amy into town. "From [the back of the house] the wooded hills began their impressive rise, undulating forest swells that just kept climbing into the next state. My guess was that it would take even the fiercest Hun the better part of a winter to cross the glacial waterfalls and wind-blasted woods of those mountain wilds before he was able to reach the open edge of Lonoff's hayfields, rush the rear storm door of the house, crash into the study, and, spiked bludgeon wheeling high in the air above the little Olivetti, cry out in a roaring voice to the writer tapping out his twenty-seventh draft, 'You must change your life!' And even he might lose heart and turn back to the bosom of his barbarian family should he approach those black Massachusetts hills on a night like this, with the cocktail hour at hand and yet another snowstorm arriving from Ultima Thule." We're beyond landscape here. Roth has packaged irony, wit, midwinter bleakness, and imaginative drama into a tight little lyric that sounds to me a lot more like Cole Porter composing "Atilla, the Musical" than Mahler or marching bands. From now on, Roth is the master of this music of ideas no matter what he is writing.

Anatole Broyard took the occasion of remarking on Roth's voice, which Roth himself defines for Zuckerman in the book as something apart from style.[3] "I don't mean style. I mean voice: something that begins at around the back of the knees and reaches well above the head." Broyard said, "In his last few books, including the forthcoming *Zuckerman Unbound,* his voice is unmistakably his own, immediately recognizable. It is rueful, optimistic, anxious, exalted, defensive and aggressive. It is a voice that excels at embellishing or rationalizing but breaks when it tries to dissemble. It is a city voice, full of the rush of human traffic and the calling of horns." Indeed, it is an unmistakable pleasure to go back to Roth's novels and re-encounter this voice, so sure of itself, so varied, so melodic, in *The Ghost Writer* in particular. One of the pleasures of assembling this book from old essays and reviews has been that of rediscovering that voice. In one of those crotchety essays that are now and then secreted by *Commentary* magazine, Joseph Epstein wrote in 1985 that while he found Roth readable, he did not find him rereadable.[4] "Trial by rereading is a tough test for a novelist, and I am not sure exactly what it proves, except of course that it is obviously better to write books that can be reread with pleasure than not. . . . Roth, on a second reading, begins to seem smaller." I simply scratch my head at that and wonder whether we have the same writer in mind. But then that is

Commentary and its killjoy notion that the primary role of criticism is to grant or withhold permission to enjoy, and morality is all on the side of withholding.

It is not hard to see what Roth was getting at in *The Ghost Writer* and Lonoff. He was creating an image of all that he was not: reclusive, prohibitive, wholly removed from the cultural firing line, and letting us know finally that it is not for him; indeed, having Lonoff bestow a blessing on his not being so nice in his writing. Even through the book's glassine surface, the ghost sonata that stirs passion up toward the surface and then submerges it again beneath glissandos of prose seems to promise some new direction for his writing, an assimilation of the old turbulence and an artist's desire to move on. I had hoped it wasn't so, and it wasn't. It isn't just that Lonoff provided Roth with a technical problem he couldn't solve; he was a human problem that Roth had to keep at arms' length. To give him subjectivity, to do for Lonoff what Roth would do years later for another prohibitive character and a father, Swede Levov in *American Pastoral,* would have been beside the point. He is put there to offer the vision of an alternative life to Nathan Zuckerman and then to withdraw it, by being disappointing. He may be the old master who has perfected Isaac Babel's thrift of language and can say that "no iron spike can pierce a human heart as icily as a period in the right place,"[5] but he has nothing of Babel's abundance of life, and he can no more be imagined writing a story like Babel's "My First Goose," in which a Jewish correspondent proves his worth to a band of Cossack horseman by plunging his sword into a peasant's goose, than writing *Portnoy's Complaint.*

For all I found there to admire, I finally had to agree that *The Ghost Writer,* as a stand-alone novel, was too thin for my blood, and for Roth's as well. But then I don't read it now as a stand-alone novel, but as the first movement of a Zuckerman quartet, which rises in crescendos of irony and turbulence through *Zuckerman Unbound* and *The Anatomy Lesson* and ends with the crashing encore of "The Prague Orgy." That is where you find Broyard's city voice, "full of the rush of human traffic and the calling of horns."

7

The Jersey Bounce
Zuckerman Unbound

Yes, he thought, life has its own flippant ideas about how to handle serious fellows like Zuckerman. All you have to do is wait and it teaches you all there is to know about the art of mockery.
> Nathan Zuckerman, from *Zuckerman Unbound*

Kafka once wrote, "I believe we should read only those books that bite and sting us. If a book we are reading does not rouse us with a blow to the head, then why read it?"
> Nathan Zuckerman, from *Zuckerman Unbound*

They call it the Jersey Bounce
A rhythm that really counts
The temperature always mounts
Whenever they play the funny rhythm they play
> "Jersey Bounce"

If Roth's books are not precisely autobiographies, neither are they wholly fictions as, say, Tolstoy's or Dickens's novels are fictions. And unlike James Joyce's godlike artist, Roth is not high above his creations, paring his fingernails. Rather, his stories are fables of identity, improvisations on the theme of the self designed to heighten and refine essential elements, highlight basic terms of being, and dramatize recurring conflicts. "He used to wonder how all the billions who didn't write could take the daily blizzard," muses Zuckerman in *The Anatomy Lesson*, "all that beset them, such a saturation of the brain, and so little of it known or named. If he wasn't cultivating hypothetical Zuckermans he really had no more means than a fire hydrant to decipher his existence." These fables are experiences, mined, smelted, and cast by the imagination, so that each novel, for all its extravagant invention, develops a fairly narrow range of ideas, which can be captured in singular phrases and gripping images. We might call *The Ghost Writer* a fable of the artist as a martyr to language, *Zuckerman Unbound,* a fable of the artist as a martyr to his fame, *The Anatomy Lesson,* one of the artist as a martyr to himself. (And, might not *My Life as a Man* be the artist as a martyr to marriage; *The Breast,* the man as a martyr to his own desires; *Portnoy's Complaint,* the son as a martyr to the family; and *The Great American Novel,* the team as a martyr to history?) None of these books is a perfectly neat rendering of an idea, and yet the ease with which such captions come to mind does suggest two things about the turn of Roth's imagination: one, that despite its improvisational brilliance, it can be theme bound; and two, that it is prodded into invention by a sense of persecution.

The censure Roth has endured has played into it, and it stands to reason that he would periodically bow to the chorus and tailor his books to humor it, or worse, to plead the case that he was, all along, not so frightening a fellow as his books let on but just another modern alienated author plying his lonely trade. It was also inevitable, given his image of himself as a man torn between his ethical impulses and his appetites, that he would silence the unsocialized self now and then to permit his more measured and prudent inclinations, his inner Jane Austen, to have their say, even if the voice in which they spoke was shaking with silent laughter. Thus it was, I suspect, that *The Ghost Writer* was conceived, a book in which Roth affected a studied modulation of voice that muted the trademarks of his personal style: the brashness, the mordant wit, the careening associations, the shtick for shtick's sake. His reward for such a sacrifice was a quieting of the gallery and a modicum of critical deference that had normally been withheld. That Roth having courted it is determined to live without it, is demonstrated in *The Anatomy Lesson,* in which he fires off round after round of antipersonnel ordnance against the elders of Zion, and then impales Zuckerman on a Jewish gravestone, breaking his jaw and demonstrating conclusively to the kibitzers at *Commentary* that they had their man pegged right all along.

Zuckerman Unbound lacks the ethical ambition of *The Ghost Writer*, for which I find myself grateful. It does not flirt with tragic history—the Holocaust or Anne Frank. It is not so ostentatiously European, its cultural references being American quiz shows rather than Russian-Jewish storywriters. Its tragic moments, such as they are, take place entirely within the family, as Nathan Zuckerman's father dies cursing his son, calling him a "bastard" with his dying breath. And it has no Lonoff to make a desert of the emotions in the name of Flaubertian ideals. Rather, it has Alvin Pepler, escapee from Newark, ex-Marine, ex-quiz show contestant, egotist, bully, extortionist, and idiot savant who has the trivia of a generation, including the pop hits of 1950, at his fingertips. Like Zuckerman, he has a raconteur's instincts; like Zuckerman he is unhinged; like him he collects grievances in much the same spirit as he collects odd facts—he adds them up and keeps a running total. A contestant who had gained celebrity on the show *Smart Money*, only to be dumped by the producers who felt they could get higher ratings with Hewlett Lincoln, Pepler carries this fix, this betrayal (the producer fed Lincoln the right answers) around with him as his desperate claim to being somebody.[1]

But Pepler is not so completely other, any more than Lonoff was other. Zuckerman sees Pepler as his "pop self" as perhaps Lonoff was his high culture self, his Jersey self as opposed to the Weimar self. In these fables of identity, the supporting characters tend to be facets of Zuckerman, essentialized and given voice as if to see how his proclivities, pushed to extremes, might produce monsters. Recalling Roth's myth of himself as a man torn between the measured and the reckless, the civilized and the untamed, we might think of Lonoff and Pepler as bookends, examples of what can happen when either side takes full command. Pepler is someone torn between comedy and mayhem. Lonoff is a monk of the sentence, Pepler "another contending personality for ringside at Elaine's." What, then, is Zuckerman himself, for all his antics and his *Carnovsky*, but an appeal for sanity—if not quite a demonstration of it—and the best of both worlds? The difference between *The Ghost Writer* and *Zuckerman Unbound*, then, corresponds to Roth's choice of monsters and is the reason why the book with the more spirited monster is the livelier of the two.

Zuckerman Unbound bears resemblances to Saul Bellow's *Seize the Day*. It possesses a similar maniacal verve and sardonic humor, and has in Zuckerman a character who, like Tommy Wilhelm, is dispossessed of a wife — Zuckerman has recently left her — a father, and a family, and in Pepler a cunning little madman and a word-intoxicated gonif, like Tamkin. It even comes equipped with a father's curse, the elder Zuckerman's dying word to his son: "bastard." But this resemblance is mostly tonal: an occasional flurry of repartee, a breakneck pace, and a shared vision of the scalded nerves and blasted hopes of urban life. Pepler lacks the dimension that renders Tamkin so authentic a figure of the urban fantasmagoria, that of the popular shaman and philosopher-charlatan, the professional healer-stealer. He is finally just another plaintiff in Roth's serialized court of appeals. Trying to "do" Bellow as he had elsewhere "done" Kafka, Roth nonetheless had his own preoccupations to work out: the penalties of success, not failure, success beyond expectation, and to examine that in its most critical domain Roth needed more than just a phantom heckler. He needed an injured family, and it is in the family feud that develops over Zuckerman's writing that his success takes on its proper meaning.

The source of Zuckerman's notoriety is his novel, *Carnovsky*, a recent *succès de scandale* (this is 1969) that has catapulted him into fame and fortune and made him a national celebrity and the most snickered about writer in America. *Carnovsky*, a novel about a young man's masturbations and his battles to become a man against the determined opposition of his mother, has brought him unwanted attention, opened a breach between his family and himself, and made him a spectacle on the streets of New York. Strangers accost him: "Hey, careful, Carnovsky, they arrest people for that!" The Fifth Avenue bus comes alive when he gets on. A woman steps into his path: "You need love, and you need it all the time. I feel sorry for you." The man from Con Ed: "Hey, you do all that stuff in that book? With all those chicks? You are something else, man." But of all Zuckerman's admirer-assailants, it is Pepler who captures his, and Roth's, imagination. A *landsman* and a maniac, the Ancient Mariner of the marginal, he stoppeth Zuckerman in a deli, commandeering his sandwich and demanding an audience for his tale of woe.

Pepler had been a quiz show prodigy in the 1950s, starring for three weeks on the rigged TV sensation, *Smart Money,* before the producers pulled the plug on him because, as he believes, a Jewish champion was bad for their ratings. His unhinged life ever since has been devoted to baring his stigmata and demanding justice, and he wants Nathan to help him write the book, claiming in fact to have a Broadway producer, Marty Paté, interested in the story. (Paté only goes after big projects, having an option on the Six-Day War for a musical, with Yul Brynner as Moshe Dayan.) It will take Zuckerman just a short time to determine that Pepler is a complicated case of delusion and eidetic memory: a madman who is separated by mere degrees from being an imaginative genius. But his genius has slipped its moorings and gone drifting in the Great Lakes of resentment. His last desperate acts are to accuse Zuckerman of having stolen *Carnovsky,* which is *his* life's story, and to leave in Zuckerman's mailbox a handkerchief, which Zuckerman had loaned him, in which he has masturbated. Zuckerman does not know what to do with him, and as it turns out Pepler doesn't have a clue to what he should do with himself, as he turns quickly into a stalker and an extortionist, demanding money to prevent any harm from coming to Zuckerman's mother. Are we to take it that this is what might have happened to Alex Portnoy if his analysis had failed? Or worse, succeeded? This erosion of boundaries between art and life and between one book and the other, as Roth's books and characters become embedded as fictions within other fictions, presents the reader with a hall of mirrors. His books begin to collide like subatomic particles, throwing off exotic fragments. *Zuckerman Unbound* points us back in one direction toward *Portnoy's Complaint* (it takes place in 1969, the year *Portnoy's Complaint* is published), in another toward *The Ghost Writer,* and looks ahead toward *The Anatomy Lesson,* in which Zuckerman Peplerizes himself and becomes a lunatic assailant and a dangerous grievant, dangerous in the main to himself.

If *The Ghost Writer* is a book about the penalties of art, then *Zuckerman Unbound* is about those of fame. Zuckerman enjoys a one-night stand with the actress Caesara O'Shea (who is also being wooed by Fidel Castro), who is reading Kierkegaard's *The Crisis in the Life of an Actress,* in which she has marked this passage: "And she, who as a woman is sensitive regarding her name—as only a woman is sensitive—she knows that her name is on everyone's lips, even when they wipe their mouths with their handkerchiefs." Such fame resembles Zuckerman's own, his name on everyone's lips even as they wipe their mouths with their handkerchiefs, with, indeed, *his* handkerchief, as Pepler does after finishing Zuckerman's sandwich. (It is the same handkerchief Pepler later returns impregnated with his semen, a token of fame that not even Kierkegaard's actress was likely to receive. Or was she?) With *Carnovsky,* Zuckerman has been thrust into such public attention, which he experiences as gossip and invasion, since people take his books for confessions or declarations that demand angry or intimate responses.

But though Roth tries to show how painful this public assault can be he makes it look equally diverting. He receives threats and protests but he also gets proposals and propositions. He becomes a target for the fantasies of others that, however trying they may be, always fall short of being lethal. Even Pepler, for all his antics, is only a spectral emanation of fractured Newark sensibility who doesn't captivate Zuckerman so much as circumnavigate him, firing in salvos from way offshore.

The public side of fame, then, is a divertissement from what is central to the book: Zuckerman's crime against his parents by the writing of *Carnovsky.* At the very height of the uproar over *Carnovsky,* Zuckerman's father suffers a fatal stroke. Once a vigorous man, he now lies helplessly in bed while members of the family troop past to pay their respects. As he lies on his deathbed, barely conscious and unable to speak, Nathan eschews the opportunity to say a simple, loving farewell. He is an artist, after all, wedded to the elaborate, the indirect, the metaphorical, and he recites to his father instead the big bang theory of the universe, telling him about "the universe expanding outward . . . the galaxies all rushing away, out into space, from the impact of that first big bang. And it will go on like this, the universe blowing outward and outward, for fifty billion years." Now, that may be a metaphor for love (orgasms don't come any bigger or last longer than the big bang), but it is also a fatuous routine that Nathan's father, mustering his remaining strength, damns with his last word, the barely audible but painstakingly pronounced, "Bastard!"

Zuckerman Unbound's conclusion finds Nathan in Black Newark, reconnoitering his old neighborhood, now blasted by riot and neglect. Zuckerman has gone there to contemplate whatever there was to contemplate, mainly, Zuckerman being Zuckerman, himself. A Black man with a shaven head steps out of a house and stares at him.

"Who you supposed to be?"

"'No one,' replied Zuckerman, and that was the end of that. You are no longer any man's son, you are no longer some good woman's husband, you are no longer your brother's brother, and you don't come from anywhere anymore, either."

This is one of Roth's bleaker conclusions, but does Zuckerman deserve it? Does a man get this for just writing a shocking book? To be bombarded by the Peplers of the world or gang-tackled by the Judge Wapters (and the Irving Howes, Norman Podhoretzes, Bruno Bettelheims, Marie Syrkins, and Joseph Epsteins) of the world comes with the territory: You take your lumps. But to be lost in the stars like some ricochet from the big bang? Surely it is to be wondered that Zuckerman, for all the blows he suffers for *Carnovsky*, gets small pleasure from his money or his fame and experiences the latter only as a curse. After the burial of the father, Zuckerman's brother turns on him with this withering indictment: "You *are* a bastard. A heartless conscienceless bastard. What does loyalty mean to you? What does responsibility mean to you? What does self-denial mean, *restraint*—anything at all? To you everything is disposable! Everything is *ex*posable! Jewish morality, Jewish endurance, Jewish wisdom, Jewish families—everything is grist for your fun-machine. Even your shiksas go down the drain when they don't tickle your fancy anymore. Love, marriage, children, what the hell do you care? To you it's all fun and games. *But that isn't the way it is to the rest of us.*"

A reader would be pardoned for taking this for a mea culpa, Roth's admission that he had provoked a scandal with *Portnoy's Complaint* and done some damage in the family (though Roth's own father is a fan of his son's writing). He would seem to have taken his Jewish critics to heart, conceding that his revolt in the name of the cerebellum was ill conceived. And it does seem as though *Zuckerman Unbound*, following the lead of *The Professor of Desire* and *The Ghost Writer*, is another contra-*Portnoy* book, more nakedly than the others, and a rueful concession that he'd been a bad boy after all. If so, then let the finger wagging truly begin, for what artist in his right mind these days asks the world to honor him for his good manners? What advantage accrues to the imagination when the artist publicly repents his days as a brat? Zuckerman's outburst in *The Anatomy Lesson,* then, becomes clear as Roth's reminder that decorum, tact, order, and the virtue racket have their place, but not in his novels.

Second Thoughts

Sometimes we need reminding that novels are not always about what they are ostensibly about and that the habit of drawing lessons from them cordons us off from literature in a very narrow cell of meaning. Sure, *Zuckerman Unbound* is about being a son doing injury to his father in order to be true to himself, and certainly it is also about a kind of public notoriety that makes it impossible for a writer to venture out casually in public without being recognized and assailed. But who couldn't have written books about that? Bellow might have done it, Updike, Styron. That material is hardly a distinction. Like so much of Roth's writing, *Zuckerman Unbound* is also about the voice in which it is told, voice as something that starts behind Roth's knees and winds up over his head. You have to be deaf to literature entirely not to notice it right away in picking up a Roth novel, and in *Zuckerman Unbound* that voice is so much of what the book means, or what it does and we need to find ways to talk about it, though talking about voice is not unlike talking about music, which someone said is like dancing about architecture.

It is, for one thing, an urban voice, which means that it is both competitive and brittle, it prides itself on being in the know but admits to vulnerability. It is nervous, querulous, hungry, and needy, sometimes verging on crisis, but it is also resilient: intelligent, dramatic, and surefooted in its grasp of the American vernacular. It makes literature of speech. If you listen to the notes, you can hear the attack and the decay, the burst and the fall. On every page, the voice says to us, "I can handle anything." And what does Roth say? Zuckerman observes of Caesara O'Shea, as they survey the room at Elaine's: "He admired the whole savory mixture, sauce and stew: the self-satirizing blarney, the deep-rooted vanity, the levelheaded hatred, the playfulness, the gameness, the recklessness, the cleverness." Is this not also true of Zuckerman's own conversation and Roth's own writing? It is a very high order of writing, but writing keyed invariably to the cadences and inflections of speech. It is no wonder that Roth has tried his hand from time to time at play writing, since his lines need to be spoken and heard. Unfortunately, much of his best writing is in the great narrative blanket around the dialogue that is lost in drama or film. In writing about Roth, I often want to grab the reader by the sleeve and say, "Listen to this. It's the Jersey bounce."[2] The best I can do is to quote him at length, as I do, since, after all, writing about prose is too much like dancing about architecture.

8

The Jawbone of an Ass

The Anatomy Lesson

And Samson said, "With the jawbone of an ass, heaps upon heaps,
With the jawbone of an ass have I smitten a thousand men."

Judges 15:16

I've gotten such payoffs from being repulsive.

Nathan Zuckerman, from *The Anatomy Lesson*

In a painful-to-read scene in *The Anatomy Lesson*, Nathan Zuckerman, stung by a review of his work by Milton Appel, a critic of national eminence, and by Appel's subsequent appeal to him to write something favorable to Israel for the *New York Times* op-ed page, dials Appel on the phone and showers him with insults.[1] "In that bloodthirsty essay you have the fucking gall to call *my* moral stance 'superior'! You call my sin 'distortion,' then distort my book to show how distorted it is! You pervert my intentions, then call me perverse! You lay hold of my comedy with your ten-ton gravity and turn it into a travesty! My coarse, vindictive fantasies, your honorable, idealistic humanist concerns! I'm a sellout to the pop-porno culture, you're the Defender of the Faith! Western Civilization! The Great Tradition! The Serious Viewpoint!"

Appel's review in *Inquiry* magazine had caught Zuckerman off guard, all the more so because fourteen years earlier Appel had hailed the young writer's dissections of middle-class Jewish life in his collection of stories, *Higher Education*, as "fresh, authoritative, exact." But now, in the wake of his cause célèbre, the novel *Carnovsky,* all his books seem, as

Zuckerman paraphrases Appel, "tendentious junk, the byproduct of a pervasive and unfocused hostility . . . mean, joyless, patronizing little novels, contemptuously dismissive of the complex depths."

Compounding Zuckerman's injury is the fact that some of his books, including the despised *Carnovsky,* owe their slant on Jewish life to an essay by Appel who, as a self-conscious, *alienated* intellectual in the forties, had expressed the perplexities of second-generation Jewish boys too thoroughly Americanized to rest easily in their parents' Jewish world but too Jewish, too inward, too painfully intellectual to embrace confidently a rude, jostling America. The essay had served Zuckerman as a beacon of intellectual alienation, expressing a generational dilemma in the ennobling language of literary study. "He wrote about Camus and Koestler and Verga and Gorky, about Melville and Whitman and Dreiser, about the soul revealed in the Eisenhower press conference and the mind of Alger Hiss—about practically everything except the language in which his father had hollered for old junk from his wagon. But this was hardly because the Jew was in hiding. The disputatious stance, the aggressively marginal sensibility, the disavowal of community ties, the taste for scrutinizing a social event as though it were a dream or a work of art—to Zuckerman this was the very mark of the intellectual Jews in their thirties and forties on whom he was modeling his own style of thought."

Zuckerman might have suffered this rejection by this once-admired father in fretful silence had not Appel, with a curious mordant flourish, prevailed upon a mutual friend, Ivan Felt, to ask Zuckerman to write that op-ed piece in defense of Israel, which had just rallied to defeat the combined Egyptian and Syrian armies in the Yom Kippur War in October 1973. Israel was roundly condemned by the United Nations Security Council, the European press, and even the United States Congress, and its defenders were looking for allies. But the phrasing did not lack Appel's customary belligerence. "Why don't you ask your friend Nate Zuckerman to write something in behalf of Israel for the Times Op Ed page? He could surely get in there. If I come out in support of Israel there, that's not exactly news; it's expected. But if Zuckerman came out with a forthright statement, that would be news of a kind, since he has prestige with segments of the public that don't care for the rest of us. Maybe he has spoken up on this, but if so I haven't seen it. Or does he still feel that, as his Carnovsky says, the Jews can stick their historical suffering up their ass?"

As any friend would, Felt xeroxes the letter and passes it along to Zuckerman who, given his volatile temper, his delicate nerves, his chronic upper lumbar pain (a sharp, persistent pain in the neck), and his fragile self-esteem, erupts in Krakataus of rage, throws a tantrum, and makes his call. Appel's answer is measured, austere, and crushing. "Mr. Zuckerman, you're entitled to think anything you want of me, and I'll have to try to live with that, as you've managed obviously to live with what I said about your books. What is strange to *me* is that you don't seem to have anything to say about the suggestion itself, regardless of your anger against the person who made it. But what may lie in store for the Jews is a much larger matter than what I think of your books, early or late, or what you think of my thinking."

Properly rebuked, Zuckerman silently sets down the phone. His reply comes only later, after Zuckerman's imagination has taken stock of the situation and devised a symbolic and wholly private response. Flying to Chicago with the idea of calling an end to his career as a writer and entering medical school, and high as cirrus on Percodan, which he takes for his neck, and marijuana, which he takes for pleasure, he introduces himself to a fellow traveler as Milton Appel, publisher of *Lickety Split* magazine and former owner of Milton's Millennia, New York's hottest sex club. Ripped, enraged, and twenty-five thousand feet up somewhere over Lake Michigan he lets his imagination roam freely over the rare possibilities of being Milton Appel, the sleaziest man in all New York, the Jewish Larry Flynt. "My magazine is a mirror and we reflect it *all*. I want my readers to know that they shouldn't feel self-hatred if they want to get laid. If they jerk off it doesn't make them beneath contempt. And they don't need Sartre to make it legit. I'm not gay, but we're starting to run a lot of stuff on it. We help out married men who are looking for quick sex. Today most of the blow jobs are being given by guys who are married. You married?"

Neither Roth nor his delirious Zuckerman proposes this wild fantasy of Milton Appel, sleaze king, as a proper answer. It is simply a private release, a device for easing the pain while admitting defeat. Zuckerman is suffering from a powerful, chronic pain in his upper lumbar region, "a hot line of pain that ran from behind his right ear into his neck, then branched downward beneath the scapula like a menorah held bottom side up." He is unable to work—typing is agony, composing manually no better—and often unable to sit up at all, and all efforts at diagnosis and therapy have proven fruitless. He lies on a play-mat wearing prismatic glasses that allow him to see at angles without moving his head, and dictates, when he can, sentences to a secretary who takes down his words when she isn't otherwise busy taking down her pants. She is one of four women who come into his life. Diana, Jenny, Jaga, Gloria. "They were all the vibrant life he had: secretary-confidante-cook-housekeeper-companion—aside from the doses of Nixon's suffering, they were the entertainment." This is 1973, and the Watergate hearings are on television.

Efforts to diagnose and deal with the pain have proven unsuccessful. He has tried three orthopedists, two neurologists, a physiotherapist, a rheumatologist, a radiologist, an osteopath, a vitamin doctor, an acupuncturist, and an analyst. "The acupuncturist had stuck twelve needles into him on fifteen occasions, a hundred and eighty needles in all, not one of which had done a thing." The analyst wondered aloud if he wasn't holding onto his illness in order to retain his "harem of Florence Nightingales." He has tried a collar and something called Dr. Kotler's Pillow, sent to him by the doctor himself, an elderly physician who grew up in Newark and had his office in the Hotel Riviera, before it was purchased by Father Divine. The purgation of repressed rage by verbally assaulting Milton Appel by phone has done no better. "Standing atop the paper-strewn bed, his hand clutched into fists and raised to the ceiling of the dark tiny room, he cried out, he screamed, to find that from phoning Appel and venting his rage, he was only worse."

Zuckerman's best results have been pharmacological, various combinations of alcohol, marijuana, and Percodan, and to manage the ordeal of traveling to Chicago, he loads up on all of them. A Web site devoted to pharmaceuticals says the following about Percodan: "Adverse Reactions: The most frequently observed adverse reactions include light-headedness, dizziness, sedation, nausea, and vomiting. These effects seem to be more prominent in ambulatory than in nonambulatory patients, and some of these adverse reactions may be alleviated if the patient lies down. Other adverse reactions include euphoria, dysphoria, constipation and pruritus." Zuckerman, who started using it for his

neck, stays with it for the euphoria. It was one of Elvis's drugs for producing a high, and a Web page out in Cyberia with the endearing name
of elvispercodan.html lets us in on the following: "Percodan is . . . an ef-
fective painkiller and induces a state of euphoria. It is quite similar to
dilaudid, except much less potent. Elvis used it recreationally to basi-
cally just feel better." So, Zuckerman unlocks the entertainer in himself
much as The King prepared for a night on stage. By the time the plane
lands in Chicago, Zuckerman is still flying. Hammered by the fast-
running tides of pain, bitterness, and euphoria, he has fallen into a
monologue that is too exuberant, too surprising, too urgent to be sup-
pressed. Purgation by pity and terror can't hold a candle to purgation by
pharmaceuticals. Off he rages, continuing with Ricky, the young female
chauffeur of his limousine, what he had begun with his unfortunate fellow passenger on the plane. "And the ACLU, do they help? They think
I give freedom a bad name. Freedom's *supposed* to have a bad name.
What I do is what freedom's about. Freedom isn't making room for
Hefner—its making room for *me*. For *Lickety Split* and Milton's Millennia and Supercarnal Productions." And on and on and on, as far as the
desublimation cocktail will take him: "diatribe, alibi, anecdote, confession, expostulation, promotion, pedagogy, philosophy, assault, apologia,
denunciation, a foaming confluence of passion and language, and all for
an audience of one. Into his parched-out desert, that oasis of words!"

That it will turn out badly we know before it happens. We will find
Zuckerman in an emergency room, with his mouth wired shut after a
fall against a cemetery gravestone. All this, one guesses, from meeting
E. I. Lonoff ten years and two books earlier and saying to himself,
"This is how I will live." Now he has to recover from his misguided decision, and then recover again from the recovery, learning to say again,
as speech returns to him, "This is how I will live."

⟿

What do we make of this appalling refrain of rancor and grief, this return to the agonies of being oneself, punctuated by the usual bursts of
fury at the unfairness of it all? In reviewing *Zuckerman Unbound* for *The
Nation*, Richard Gilman recalled being asked by a bewildered Flannery
O'Connor why a writer like Norman Mailer was displaying himself,
rather than letting his work speak for itself. Gilman's answer had obvious

application to Roth: "I remember saying, wholly unsure of my argument, that like other gifted Jewish writers Mailer, as a historical outsider, saw writing, at least in part, as an embattled 'way in,' and that for many such writers language was a social weapon and a means of justification. Their dwelling so much on their own situations, rather than on the possibilities of language as invention, didn't mean that their work was necessarily inferior but only that it was more tied to contingency, that it was more utilitarian, so to speak, and more deliberately seductive; such writing sought love and power more nakedly."[2]

Such an explanation is appealing because it depersonalizes the issue, turning it into one of culture and history. It even de-ethnicizes it, since to be an outsider one needn't be a Jew. These posturings and plays for attention, then, are simply the gyrations of the arriviste who has dispensed with the protocols of social initiation and just put his rough shoulder to the door. Roth's books, like those of his fellow Newarker Leroi Jones/Baraka, can be as rude as the streets, though their rudeness is calculated, designed to grate on the reader's nerves, stir up disapproval and gather in the rewards of scandal. Still, this explanation tells us less than we want to know about why certain books ask greater indulgence of their readers than others. Why, we might ask, after *The Professor of Desire* and *The Ghost Writer,* books that promised a time out from verbal shock, is *The Anatomy Lesson* so punishing a book? Why this belated overflow of powerful feelings recollected in hysteria? Four plausible answers come immediately to mind: The Offense, The Agenda, The Dialectic, The Demonstration.

The Offense. After twelve years, the offense still rankled.

The Agenda. The Anatomy Lesson was simply the next item on Roth's my-life-as-an-outlaw agenda. *The Ghost Writer* was set in 1956, *Zuckerman Unbound* in 1969, *The Anatomy Lesson* in 1973, and after the publication of *Portnoy/Carnovsky,* the Howe attack was the next shattering event. By then, Roth had no marriage to chafe against and only indignant reviews to suffer. Having made Zuckerman roughly a reflection of his own life Roth was not about to pass up the opportunity to make *l'affaire* Howe his next item.

The Dialectic. Having played the Sensitive Jewish Boy in the three prior novels, Roth felt it time to dust off the Jewboy in the Zuckerman finale and bare his fangs. (For which liberty Zuckerman's fangs get knocked out.) Once he had given himself over to a schematic conception of himself as a man torn between the civilized and the primitive, he began testing the roles, now donning one, now the other, as an actor might play Othello one night and Iago the next. Roth's writing is an extension of his mimicry, and his role-playing comes into keener focus if we see his entire oeuvre as a repertory theater in which he has cast himself in a series of parts based on the vicissitudes of being himself. Now he is Portnoy, now Tarnopol, Kepesh, Lonoff, Pepler, now one of the dozen flavors of Nathan Zuckerman.

The Demonstration. Roth wanted to establish once and for all that Nathan Zuckerman is not Philip Roth but a moral fable that takes its departure from Rothian premises. How else do we account for the carefully timed encounters with Roth in the news weeklies and the Condé Nast publications, *House and Garden, Vogue,* except as demonstrations that Roth is alive and well and cool and in command in Connecticut, not out of his gourd or walking the wards with Nathan Zuckerman in Chicago?[3] It is noteworthy that a book based so closely on Roth's life should in the end prove a demonstration of the difference, but Roth wants it clear that his novels place autobiography wholly at the disposal of imagination. If Milton Appel's attack is taken straight from life, Nathan Zuckerman's crackup is sheer invention. The behind-the-scenes profiles, especially those in the upscale monthlies with their beaumonde chitchat about Philip and Claire making "tofu runs" to far off groceries, are public relations of a low order, and even the hardhats at *Commentary* would be pardoned for smirking at these insider exclusives instructing the credulous that Roth is not out making crank calls or heading for the woodwork with an apple in his back but right at home where he belongs, doing his homework and keeping a high profile.

Whether what we're seeing is a man divided irreparably against himself and courting the bourgeois life in order to write scandalous diatribes against it is uncertain: we have only Roth's word for it. What is certain is that Roth wishes to be seen that way and has taken great pains to make sure we've got the proper image. *The Anatomy Lesson,* then, is a way of restoring the visible balance, even as Roth trims in the other direction by summoning reporters to his Berkshire nest for white wine and cold veal. Such considerations take us far afield from Roth's books, except as they lend *The Anatomy Lesson* a plausible raison d'être:

to redress an imbalance. Prior books had flirted with convalescence, arousing in Roth a need for a bracing howl at the moon, or at the Jewish fathers—excepting, of course, his actual father. (A Kafka by proxy, he allows himself to be oppressed only by proxy fathers.) During the Percodan-fueled diatribe in which he parades as Milton Appel, pornographer, Nathan Zuckerman chatters away about the indecencies of being nice, and though he is playacting, the play permits him to romp recklessly through his antinomian imagination. "Nice. I don't care what my kid grows up to be, I don't care if he grows up wearing pantyhose as long as he doesn't turn out *nice*. You know what terrifies me more than jail? That he'll rebel against a father like me, and that's what I'll get. Decent society's fucking revenge: a kid who's very very very nice—another frightened soul, tamed by inhibition, suppressing madness, and wanting only to live with the rulers in harmonious peace."

It was Irving Howe who called for a "good clean hatred that might burn through" and "the fury of social rebellion." *The Anatomy Lesson* is nothing if not a hatred that burns through. If illness and recovery—and then recovery from the recovery—are usable metaphors for Roth's career, and if Roth himself led us to think of *The Professor of Desire* and *The Ghost Writer* as symbols of convalescence, then what is *The Anatomy Lesson*? A relapse novel? A return of the repressed? A dropping of the mask? A tutorial in the "secondary gains" of illness, as Zuckerman's analyst proposes? *The Anatomy Lesson* is a rude and dissonant book, a nightmare of a novel, really, and the most pugnacious of Roth's books since *Our Gang*. Zuckerman's call to Appel, with its choruses of invective, is particularly painful to read, not least because the reader feels the humiliation from which Zuckerman himself, doped to the nostrils against pain, is insulated. (Performance is, I think, the proper word here, since Roth himself rather than the events in the book draws our attention.) The sheer force of being in it demands consideration. Roth does not always write with taste or with grace—why should he?—but he writes with power, power generated by turning himself inside out and summoning the hidden, the recessive and the shameful, quite as though he were acting on Isaac Rosenfeld's precept that "the sooner we strike shame the sooner we draw blood."[4]

Such a willingness to strike shame is driven by a moral imperative, to strike deep, to descend into the trenches of the imagination, the deep subduction zones, to probe for insight and health in the blackest corners, and to bring them back up like pearls. It is symptomatic of the moment in which the book is set that marijuana and Percodan are Zuckerman's royal roads to the unconscious. But behind Zuckerman's turning on to tune in and drop *in* stands the iron suzerainty of Roth's conscience, demanding that Zuckerman stop beating around the Lonovian bush and face the tough issues: his profession, his eventless life, his pain, himself. "Had he kept a pain diary," Zuckerman notes, "the only entry would have been one word: myself." *The Anatomy Lesson,* then, does not offer itself to any ready-made audience. Lacking the sexual comedy and inventive gusto of *Portnoy's Complaint* while being every bit as self-punishing, to whom could it appeal? Answer: to Roth himself. It is his own approval that Roth is always courting, but not the approval of the instincts, which neither condemn nor bless but only want. It is the approval of a strict code of conduct that commands him to tell the truth, to stand alone, to remain defiant, to take the shots, to tell the jokes, to plumb the depths, to reach the next level, *to be fearless.* And to be funny. Fearless and funny.

Second Thoughts

The Anatomy Lesson is funny, recklessly, bawdily, funny. The book blazes with Roth's black and blue humor. We can open it anywhere, but here is one of Zuckerman's smoking perorations, on the subject of giving up writing and going into medicine:

> Enough of my writing, enough of their scolding. Rebellion, obedience—discipline, explosion—injunction, resistance—accusation, denial—defiance, shame—no, the whole God damn thing has been a colossal mistake. This is not the position in life that I had hoped to fill. I want to be an obstetrician. Who quarrels with an obstetrician? Even the obstetrician who delivered Bugsy Siegel goes to bed at night with a clear conscience. He catches what comes out and everybody loves him. When the baby appears they don't start shouting, "You call that a baby? That's not a baby!" No, whatever he hands them, they take it home. They're grateful for his just having been there. Imagine those butter-covered babies . . . with their little Chinese eyes, imagine what seeing that does to the spirit, *that* every morning, as opposed to grinding out another two dubious pages. Conception? Gestation?

Gruesome laborious labor? The mother's business. You just wash your
hands and hold out the net.

This is only one of the more lighthearted of Nathan Zuckerman's routines, which rise in huge hot air balloons right up through the Kafka-
sphere and beyond.

Then again, is nothing but personal moral combat at stake here?
Nothing but pleading a case to the world, to your detractors, to yourself? Nothing but "working through"? Still? Is attitude all we have to
talk about, impoverished and message-besotted readers that we are?
Sure, attitude is up front and inescapable in this book; Roth hauls it
around like a trucker hauls around his eighteen-wheeler. But what an
eighteen-wheeler it is! In looking at what I have written before, I find
that I've made too much of Roth's moralized theatrics and left out a
fairly obvious alternative way of making sense of *The Anatomy Lesson.*
The Music.

Suppose this aerobic progression of moods, attitudes, weathers, seasons were planned out in advance, as a composer plans out a symphony:
allegro, andante or adagio, scherzo, allegretto? As Vivaldi planned out
The Four Seasons. Well, then, here we have the scherzo, or better, the furioso, the blast of winter. We don't need recourse to psychology or personal history or to suppose that only blowtop volatility is at work here,
that Roth has been going through another round of violent mood
swings and ought to get back on his lithium. Although of course what
would Roth be without that volatility, those scalded nerves, that meas-
ureless indignation? Why not suppose instead that he had planned out
the full *Zuckerman Bound* sequence in advance, by mood, attitude, linguistic feel, and cadence? This was to be the book of detonations, the
one where the cannons go off. And so they do. Why not allow style to
dictate the terms, instead of the mercurial heart? When Beethoven runs
us through a furious passage, with the tympani pounding away and the
horn section sending a boisterous and joyful noise unto the Lord, do we
stop to grumble, "What's eating this dude? Why can't he chill out?
How about a little toccata and fugue, a little Bach?" Especially when
books are sequenced like these are and eventually bound together as
Zuckerman Bound, we may begin to suspect a program, a stylistic work-
out in which time, signature, and rhythmical imperatives come first.[5]

Whether that changes anything for others I can't say. For me it means that I don't have to take Roth's emotional or moral temperature every fifteen minutes. Or my own. Is this acceptable now? Is it safe for me to be enjoying this? If, like Samson, he takes up the jawbone of an ass and slays a thousand, do we need to work it through? I can relax my scruples and take pleasure in Roth's blackest comedies and in his formidable command of that most sonorous and pliable of instruments, the rowdy, bruising, muscular American vernacular, without needing permission to rejoice in the pandemonium of his Schadenfreude, not to say my own.

9

"The Prague Orgy" and
the Other Europe

Kafka! Thou shouldst be living at this hour: the White House has
need of a new Press Secretary.
> Philip Roth, "Our Castle" in *Reading Myself and Others*

Kafka's prescient irony may not be the most remarkable attribute of
his work, but it's always stunning to think about it. He is anything
but a fantasist creating a dream or a nightmare world as opposed to
a realistic one. His fiction keeps insisting that what seems to be unimaginable hallucination and hopeless paradox is precisely what
constitutes one's reality. In works like "The Metamorphosis," *The
Trial*, and *The Castle*, he chronicles the education of someone who
comes to accept—rather too late, in the case of the accused Joseph
K.—that what looks to be outlandish and ludicrous and unbeliev-
able, beneath your dignity and concern, is nothing less than what is
happening to you: that thing beneath your dignity turns out to be
your destiny
> Philip Roth, conversation with Ivan Klíma in *Shop Talk*

I imagine Styron washing glasses in a Penn Station barroom, Susan
Sontag wrapping buns at a Broadway Bakery, Gore Vidal bicycling
salamis to school lunchrooms in Queens—I look at the filthy floor
and see myself sweeping it.
> Nathan Zuckerman, from "The Prague Orgy"

In the early 1970s, in flight from America, where his fame had become a
curse and the "herd of independent minds" (Harold Rosenberg's
phrase) was on full stampede, Roth began spending his springs in

Prague, in the company of Czech writers. Besides wanting to be away from America, Roth was on the trail of Franz Kafka, who had written about the crushing and the relentless as the normal state of affairs. Who else but Roth would have imagined Prague under communist rule for his spring getaway? Why not a cell in San Quentin? It might, indeed, have been easier to get into, since Roth's visits were closely monitored by Czech authorities and were brought to a halt in 1976, when Roth was denied a visa. The situation of Czech writers was especially desperate in the wake of the Prague Spring of 1968, Alexander Dubček's experiment in "socialism with a human face" that was abruptly cancelled by Soviet tanks and two hundred thousand Warsaw Pact troops.[1] Writes Roth of these visits, "Ivan Klíma was my principle reality instructor. He drove me around to the street-corner kiosks where writers sold cigarettes, to the public buildings where they mopped the floors, to the construction sites where they were laying bricks, and out of the city to the municipal waterworks where they slogged about in overalls and boots, a wrench in one pocket and a book in the other. When I got to talk at length with these writers, it was often over dinner at Ivan's house."[2]

Those visits brought about a remarkable new direction in Roth's writing: a Europeanization of outlook and a deepening of his fascination with the intractable, the perverse, and the unattainable, Kafka's version of our own life, liberty, and the pursuit of happiness. Of all the accusations in Irving Howe's screed, the most injurious was that Roth suffered from a "thin personal culture," by which Howe meant, or claimed to mean, "that he comes at the end of a tradition which can no longer nourish his imagination or that he has, through an act of fiat, chosen to tear himself away from that tradition. . . . It is, of course, a severe predicament for a writer to find himself in this situation; it forces him into self-consciousness, improvisation, and false starts; but if he is genuinely serious, he will try, like a farmer determined to get what he can from poor soil, to make a usable theme of his dilemmas." It had to rankle, it was meant to, though like much else in Howe's manifesto, it had arisen out of the troubled self-reflections of a man who, like the farmer in his parable, had bootstrapped himself up from alienation into culture, both Yiddish and European, by the ferocity of his intellect and will. Compared with Howe, Roth was indeed shy of comparable range, and as a spiritual stepchild of the same New York intellectual culture that produced Howe, he was sensitive to what he lacked. He was neither European nor Russian born, nor were his parents. He inherited nothing of the high culture of Mitteleuropa, though he would absorb some of it second hand, through his psychoanalysis. The folk life, the vitality, the creative ferment, and the heartache of the Ashkenazi diaspora he would know mainly from what could be picked up on the street: in the nervous patter and exuberant comedy of Chancellor Avenue. He grew up knowing neither Beethoven nor Sholem Aleichem, Bach nor Socialism, Trotsky nor Herzl nor Rashi, neither Zionism nor Yiddishism, Talmud nor Torah. For music he had Jimmy Dorsey and Frank Sinatra, for drama he had *The Green Hornet* and *The Shadow*. His Spanish Civil War, his Battle of Stalingrad, was the World Series. On the score of personal culture understood that way, Roth was vulnerable, and to acquire it he was going to have to do it the hard way: on his own, by the sweat of his brow, and by total immersion. He made Franz Kafka his point of entry into that larger world, and literature, having gotten him into hot water, was going to have to get him out of it. So he fled New York for Prague, left the world of contending vanities and tin-horn ideologues and headed for one of the epicenters of world tragedy. He'd had, you might say, his fill of minor league crap and took off in pursuit of major league crap.

The predicament of writers in Czechoslovakia and elsewhere in the Soviet imperium became of vital importance to him, and as he became familiar with their plight and a partisan of their writing, he turned to editing, for Penguin Books, a series to introduce many of these writers, and some earlier ones, to English-speaking audiences for the first time. Out of the series, Writers from the Other Europe, would come books that had a profound impact on American consciousness, by Milan Kundera, Ludvík Vaculík, Tadeusz Borowski, Tadeusz Konwicki, Bruno Schulz, George Konrad, Witold Gombrowicz, and Géza Csáth.[3] It is unclear how personally engaged Roth was in the entire series: he seems to have been closer to some books and writers than others, and only Milan Kundera's *Laughable Loves* bears his introduction. And as if to underscore the ironies that attended everything Roth did in those days, the introduction to George Konrad's *The Caseworker* (1974) was contributed by Irving Howe, which either tells us a lot about Roth and Howe behind the scenes or nothing at all. At best it tells us that both were, finally, professionals who made their rapprochement, not over Israel, but over communism. Whatever the extent of Roth's practical involvement with the series, Penguin emblazoned his name on its series covers throughout its run in the late 1970s and 1980s, before the surprising events of 1989 rendered it moot, by rendering moot the very idea of an "other" Europe. While it lasted, Writers from the Other Europe performed an indispensable service, not only in providing an outlet and an international audience for writers who could be read at home only in samizdat, but also by alerting the West to a creative explosion taking place behind the Iron Curtain, an explosion that the Czech government sought to suppress by punishing writers with jobs as street cleaners and window washers.[4] Alexander Dubček himself in 1974 was an inspector in a trolley factory in Slovakia. Although these efforts at suppression lacked the full Stalinist ferocity of a bullet behind the ear, they were brutal in their own way and hastened the fall of communist governments after the Russians withdrew.

Taken together, these books added up to a tragic literature that reflected not only the daily oppression and humiliation of writers under the boot of bureaucracies that were at once banal and omnipotent, but looked backward as well to the Second World War, under whose shadow the people of Central Europe still lived. Tadeusz Borowski, for example, a Polish writer who had been a political prisoner at Auschwitz during the war and part of the "Kanada" corps that relieved the condemned of their belongings, wrote a series of swift and steel-hard vignettes about the operations of the camps. Borowski, one of the young stars of Polish literature and a rising figure in the Polish Communist Party, took his own life in 1951 and is commonly thought of as one of the delayed victims of the death camps: one who survived only to find his survival unbearable. Another of the discoveries brought to light by that series was Bruno Schulz, a Polish-Jewish writer and art instructor living in the town of Drogobych, where, during the war, it was said that he was protected by an SS officer. "One day in 1942," according to Jerzy Ficowski's introduction to *Street of Crocodiles*, "he ventured with a special pass to the 'Aryan' Quarter, was recognized by another SS man, a rival of his protector, and was shot dead in the street." Little known in the West before the publication of this book in a highly visible series, Schulz is now widely regarded as one of the Jewish, and Polish, masters of surrealism, whose writing out-Kafka'd Kafka in its depiction of the impotent, the magical, and the perverse.

The seventies were a high time for revelations about the Soviet empire. Books seemed to pour out of the Soviet Union and its satellite countries, as the underground movements of Prague, Budapest, Leningrad, and Warsaw significantly reshaped literary thought in the United States and Western Europe. Aleksander Solzhenitsyn's *The Gulag Archipelago*, first published in Paris in 1973, appeared in English translation the following year, while Nadezhda Mandelstam's magisterial memoirs of life under Stalin, *Hope Against Hope* and *Hope Abandoned*, were published in English in 1970 and 1974 respectively, and these books so towered over the landscape that some commentators were prompted to conclude that great literature could be produced only under conditions of oppression, while liberal democracy, by contrast, was fated to specialize in light, popular entertainment. One heard references, virtually homages, to the "muse of censorship." Forget the creative writing centers, the poetry workshops and the humanities research institutes, intoned George Steiner at the time. "[We must look] to the studios, cafés, seminars, *samizdat* magazines and publishing houses, chamber-music groups, itinerant theatres, of Krakow and of Budapest, of Prague and of Dresden. Here . . . is a reservoir of talent, of unquestioning adherence to the risks and functions of art and original thought on which generations to come will feed."[5]

Roth was not among those to celebrate the gift of totalitarianism to the imagination, though he did return from his Prague sojourns with this much-quoted aphorism: "There, nothing goes and everything matters; here, everything goes and nothing matters." But as for literature, he never doubted that "we" needed it as much as "they" did. "I think it's also true," he would say in his interview with Ivan Klíma, "that in a culture like mine, where nothing is censored but where the mass media inundate us with inane falsifications of human affairs, serious literature is no less of a life preserver, even if the society is all but oblivious to it."

Roth's writing would be marked by this experience, profoundly and permanently. What he discovered in his Prague visits was a world as paradoxical, irrational, and infuriating as any invention of Kafka's, and a literature that took the horrifying and the ridiculous as the normal state of affairs. He felt, moreover, a continuity between his own imagination of entrapment and a world in which it need not be imagined. But to discover himself as a European, Roth had to invent his connection to that middle-European world, since for a boy from Newark to imagine himself a stepchild of Prague required a recycling of the self into a richer and more formidable creature than Weequahic High School commonly produced. Not just Weequahic: any American high school that was not ringed by tanks and run by sadists.

Franz Kafka was the catalyst for this recycling. If Klíma was Roth's actual Virgil through the inferno of Eastern Europe, then Kafka was the dark, kibitzing angel on his shoulder, telling him where to look. The Kafka influence first emerged in two short publications of the early 1970s: his novella *The Breast* in 1972, his erotic reprise of Kafka's *Metamorphosis,* in which the hero is turned not into an insect but a gigantic female breast, and, the following year, Roth's most appealing and to my mind most successful work of short fiction, "'I Always Wanted You to Admire My Fasting'; or, Looking at Kafka." In that story, which begins as a lecture about Kafka to Roth's class at the University of Pennsylvania and then veers off into reverie, Kafka escapes both tuberculosis and the Nazis to turn up in 1942 in Newark as the young Philip Roth's Hebrew School teacher. Brought home one evening for a hot meal and some homespun wisdom, Kafka is maneuvered by Roth's parents into a courtship with Roth's Aunt Rhoda, a clerk at a dry goods store with frustrated aspirations toward the stage. After a proper courtship, including a resuscitation of Aunt Rhoda's acting career—she has a starring role in Chekhov's *The Three Sisters* at the Newark Y—Kafka and Rhoda go off for a weekend in Atlantic City where, Kafka being Kafka, something misfires and Kafka disappears from Rhoda's, and the fictive Roth's, life. Was it sex, as Roth and his brother overhear from their parents, or, preoccupied with spiritual starvation, did Kafka read to her aloud from "The Hunger Artist" over dinner, surrounded by glowing honeymooners and serenaded by the Atlantic surf roaring in the background? Years later, while in college, Roth receives from his mother this obituary notice: "Dr. Franz Kafka, a Hebrew teacher at the Talmud Torah of the Schley Street Synagogue from 1939 to 1948, died on June 3 in the Deborah Heart and Lung Center in Browns Mills, New Jersey. Dr. Kafka had been a patient there since 1950. He was seventy years old. Dr. Kafka was born in Prague, Czechoslovakia, and was a refugee from the Nazis. He leaves no survivors."

Consider the story's implicit proposition: "If only he could have married, Franz Kafka could have been my uncle," though marriage, as Kafka wrote to Felice Bauer, was barred to him. Here was one way to forge the Newark-Prague connection, to have Newark imagine Prague through Prague's taking refuge in Newark. Here Roth could imagine Kafka as a shy refugee while Kafka could experience Roth as a bratty student and the son of meddlesome parents. What not even this New World Kafka could do was imagine a happy sybaritic weekend in Atlantic City and the joys of domesticity that might follow from it. Joys of domesticity? Kafka? Roth?

With Newark, marriage, therapy, and the bruises of the literary vocation seemingly exhausted by the end of the 1970s, Roth made of Prague a source of usable myth, a substitute for Spielvogel's couch or the marriage bed or the scathing book review or the orthopedic playmat. The old myths, of infancy, of libido, of a mother's love and tyranny, of Newark as paradise lost, of New York City as the snake pit of contending egos, had given way to myths of humanity in torment, in which Franz Kafka stood as an exalted, and *echt* Jewish, symbol. Prague does double duty, as a new model unconscious that was far from simple and anything but boring and a more capacious, more mysterious, and more convoluted version of Jewishness than the one Roth experienced as a boy in Newark. Was this an *aliyah* by other means, a raising of *The Trial*, "The Metamorphosis," and "The Hunger Artist" to the status of Midrash, if not Torah itself? Prague, for all its straitness and repressiveness, appeared to offer new possibilities for the self: involuted and ironic, all the more so for being the city that Hitler chose to be his museum of the Jewish culture he was exterminating. Here was a link to Jewishness more mysterious and unfathomable than anything Roth could have learned at the dinner table or the Talmud Torah after school.

The Professor of Desire would be Roth's next effort at imagining Kafka, and in it Roth drew upon his visits to Prague and encounters with writers and professors, including one Professor Soska, a former research chemist who, for his acts of resistance to the regime, has had to find work as a typist in a meat packing plant. Kafka, Soska informs

David Kepesh, Roth's alter-ego, or really alter-id, in this book, has be-come a shorthand for the political situation and the daily absurdities of bureaucratic coercion. "Yes, this is true; many of us survive almost solely on Kafka. Including people in the street who have never read a word of his. They look at one another when something happens, and they say, 'It's Kafka.' Meaning, 'That's the way it goes here now.' Meaning, 'What else did you expect?'" When asked about the nature of his fasci-nation with Kafka, Kepesh, Roth's professor of desire who had for a spell lost his desire, answers in terms of his recent sexual difficulties that, thanks to the patience and good sense of his new woman friend, Claire Ovington, are now at an end. "I can only compare the body's utter sin-glemindedness, its cold indifference and absolute contempt for the well-being of the spirit, to some unyielding, authoritarian regime. . . . I sometimes wonder if *The Castle* isn't in fact linked in Kafka's own erotic blockage—a book engaged at every level with not reaching a climax." He is embarrassed to be saying this, but Soska brushes the embarrass-ment aside. "To each obstructed citizen his own Kafka."

Later that night, as Kepesh dreams uneasily beside his sleeping Claire, he dreams that a Czech guide has taken him to meet the woman who calls herself Kafka's whore, and he interviews her through a trans-lator. The old woman remembers little about Kafka himself, except as a clean, well-behaved Jewish boy—"Clean underwear. Clean collars. They would never dream to come here with so much as a soiled handker-chief." Sure, he had erection troubles, but she took care of them with her mouth. For five more dollars she offers the American professor a chance to touch her cunt—for literary history. His translator encour-ages him: "First of all, given your field of interest, the money is tax-deductible. Second, for only a fiver, you are striking a decisive blow against the Bolsheviks. She is one of the last in Prague still in business for herself. Third, you are helping preserve a national literary monu-ment. You are doing a service for our suffering writers. And last, but not least, think of the money you have given to Klinger [Kepesh's analyst]. What's five more to the cause?" Of course this professor of desire places his hands between the woman's legs. Here is the last word in intellectual tourism—no, cultural immersion—and for a mere five bucks. Professor Kepesh will get a scholarly monograph out of it—"Touching History," no doubt—as surely as Roth gets a book.

All of this was a warm-up for "The Prague Orgy," the splendid no-vella that Roth appended to the Zuckerman novels when Roth pub-lished them together in a single volume as *Zuckerman Bound* in 1985. Roth would tell an interviewer that the Prague story in some version was there from the start, but that he was not entirely sure where to put it or what to do with it. "It wasn't clear to me until midway through the third book *[The Anatomy Lesson]* that this material—which in fact had inspired the whole enterprise—belonged at the very end. In order for Prague to have the impact upon the reader that it originally had on me, I had to write a 697-page introduction."[6] While David Kepesh's dream of Kafka's whore in *The Professor of Desire* delivers the swift coup of a perfectly timed punch line, "The Prague Orgy" is a single sustained punch line from beginning to end. It has all the density and brio, the humor and weight of something that has been percolating a long time. Here all of Roth's wit and extravagance, his anger and his social con-science, his sexiness and his contempt for authority, are simmered down to a quintessence.

Zuckerman goes to Prague on a mission, to retrieve the stories of a Yiddish writer of the prewar period named Sisovsky. According to his son, who visits Zuckerman in New York, Sisovsky is the unknown ge-nius of Czech Yiddish literature, whose stories are in the possession of the younger Sisovsky's wife, who hates him and refuses to let them go. Zuckerman is forewarned about Sisovsky's wife, Olga, who is "very well known for her writing, for her drinking, and for showing everybody her cunt." And he is cautioned as well: "The only thing is not to lay her too soon." This is not just protest fiction—even Roth's protest fiction is not just protest fiction. This is Roth writing under the influence of Franz Kafka, Milan Kundera, his Czech instructor in dialectical eroticism, and Bruno Schulz, the Polish Jewish writer to whose death at the hands of a Nazi officer the story makes chilling allusions. (Sisovsky the elder, his son tells Zuckerman, was shot by a Nazi officer in a feud with an-other Nazi officer, who explains to the commandant: "He shot my Jew, so I shot his Jew.")

In Prague, Zuckerman finds himself at a party in a film director's palace, and the reader would be forgiven for imagining that he is in Kafka's castle. Here assembled are Prague's banned and debauched, amply supplied with whisky and fifteen-year-olds, boys and girls, to suit all inclinations. "Come to the orgy, Zuckerman—you will see the final stage of the revolution." So here is socialism with a human face at last. Or, at least, human genitalia. Zuckerman's tour guide and reality instructor is the banned writer Bolotka, who would appear to be Ivan Klíma in all but name, who points out the fired journalists, novelists, abstract painters, the writers, and Olga, a novelist whose best-selling novel is titled, *touha,* "longing," the emotion in which she specializes. All are marking time on their treadmills of humiliation. This is surely Kafka's castle, but it is a castle of stories, an echo chamber in which all the tales of desire and devastation are told again and again: everybody knows everybody else's story, including the secret police who bug every hotel room, restaurant, telephone. "Here is where literary culture is held hostage," Zuckerman thinks, "the art of narration flourishes by mouth. In Prague, stories aren't simply stories; it's what they have instead of life. Here they have become their stories, in lieu of being permitted to be anything else. Storytelling is the form their resistance has taken against the coercion of the powers-that-be."

Whether this is right or not, it certainly makes sense of the totalitarian rulers for whom it is not enough to get their legitimacy from the barrel of a gun; they also have to control the stories, lest they topple regimes. Where everything matters, nothing goes. It is not always clear what to make of the histrionic sexuality of the story: Olga does indeed show her cunt to everyone, including a strangely reluctant Nathan Zuckerman, whom she wants to marry and leave for America with. This is a Zuckerman we hardly know: a sober fellow, a chaste visitor from another world. Here he is on his best behavior. He wants to get possession of Sisovsky's father's manuscripts and then clear out as efficiently as he can.

Nothing is efficient in this Prague. There are microphones everywhere and a clear guide to reality nowhere. Bolotka tells a story about his student days, when his friend and fellow writer Blecha was assigned to spy on him. Blecha got drunk and confessed and showed Bolotka the reports. They were so terribly written that the authorities could make no sense of them, and so Bolotka volunteered to write his own surveillance reports and give them to the friend to hand in, in exchange for half the money. "They will wonder how your rotten writing has improved overnight but you just tell them you were sick. This way you won't have anything damaging on your record, and I can be rid of your company." Only the reports were now so good that Blecha was promoted and put onto bigger troublemakers. And so Bolotka had to become Blecha's writing instructor, to teach him how to write spy reports in plain Czech, well enough indeed that he became a nationally prominent composer of poetry, plays, and novels, in all of which he displays the same gifts of observation and articulation and realism he first brought to spying. Bolotka of course remains in disgrace because he is an alienated writer, and alienation is not approved from above.

Yes, Zuckerman gets the manuscripts, without having to fuck Olga for them, and they are promptly taken from him by the police, who inform him that he must leave the country immediately, Zionist spy that he is. Driven to the airport by the Czech minister of culture himself, he is quizzed about the fate, in America, of Betty MacDonald, author of *The Egg and I*, whom the minister regards as a neglected American master.

"And what has happened to Miss Betty Macdonald," the minister demands to know.

"I have no idea," Zuckerman replies.

"Why does something like this happen in America to a writer like Miss MacDonald," he persists, insinuating that some fate worse than the Gulag—utter neglect—has befallen her in barbarian America. As Zuckerman has been reminded, "The police are like literary critics—of what they see, they get most wrong anyway. They *are* the literary critics. Our literary criticism is police criticism." "Mightier than the *sword*?" he reflects to himself. "This place [Prague] is proof that a book isn't as mighty as the mind of its most benighted reader."

"I don't think even Miss MacDonald expected her book to endure forever."

"You have not answered me. You avoid the question. Why does this happen in America?"

"I don't know."

Of course Zuckerman does not know. He is a character from one novel, an antihero of alienation, who has found himself thrust into a novel of *touha* without a clue to the plot, and to be expelled from communist Czechoslovakia is to be expelled from a book in which there is a starring role for Betty MacDonald but not even a walk-on for him,

Zionist agent that he is. "Ah yes," says the man at passport control to Zuckerman as he passes through, "Zuckerman the Zionist agent. An honor to have entertained you here, sir. Now back to the little world around the corner."

In the paradoxes of life under communism, that boot camp of absurdity, Roth's imagination, schooling itself on Freud and Kafka, on Schulz and Kundera, found its ideal subject. He could improvise extravagantly, without ever leaving the plausible behind. And with the completion of the *Zuckerman Bound* quartet, Roth made a demonstration of literary virtuosity and historical awareness that was stunning. He had become formidable. Fierce in his convictions, exact in his observations, and as crafty in his imagining and he was imaginative in his craft, Roth had harnessed his irony to a fully formed personal mission—to open new frontiers for the American imagination—and emerged from the shadow of his earlier, more capricious books to be America's most cunning and capacious novelist.

This question lingers: *Could* Zuckerman have been a Zionist agent? Read ahead to *Operation Shylock*.

10

The Five Books of Nathan
The Counterlife

I can only exhibit myself in disguise. All my audacity derives from masks.

Nathan Zuckerman, from *The Counterlife*

The Interpretation of Dreams may have passed from the scene of American intellectual life as a vade mecum of human behavior, but not before making a permanent contribution to our common understanding of how fiction is to be read. Among the ideas to survive the demise of the system are ambivalence, overdetermination, an unconscious mental life, and the belief that all expressions of human desire save the most basic and biological disclose a collision, rather than a harmony, of desires. Certainly, without such concepts at hand, we are disarmed before anything as complex and indirect as contemporary literature, and without doubt we are disarmed before a writer as mercurial as Philip Roth, who has made of mixed emotions not only an art but a principle of art, producing out of his quarrels with himself a literature both richly conceived and intricately fabricated. No longer case histories, as they once seemed to be, his books have lately evolved into theaters of uncertainty in which characters perform dramatic charades of ambivalence that in the past might have been interpreted as "acting out." *The Counterlife* is the most recent and most impressive of Roth's late theatrical novels, all the more impressive for possessing at once a peformative brio and a historical gravity. An elegant novel, it performs an elaborate counterpoint between the inertia of history and the agility of the imagination and is evidence that it is possible for a novel to contradict itself repeatedly and appear to be all the more convincing for its contradictions.

The Counterlife is a story cycle featuring Nathan Zuckerman, his brother Henry, Henry's wife Carol, and the usual troupe of delectable shiksas, all different and all named Maria. A tale told in five movements, *The Counterlife* more closely resembles *Gulliver's Travels* than a conventional novel, though the five acts rather than four voyages may be Roth's way of suggesting Shakespeare as its patron saint. Or is it the five books of Moses that we are expected to recognize? If the Zuckerman novels up until now are the Zuckerman variations, this one by itself is the Zuckerman fugue: a Grosse Fugue to round out Roth's late quartets.

The movements are "Basel," "Judea," "Aloft," "Gloucestershire," and "Christendom," which form a circuit, insofar as the end of "Christendom" represents no particular resolution of the problems posed in "Basel." Each movement restates in different terms the book's central problem: what is a Jew and how is he (and it is always *he*) to live? Setting the variations into motion is "Basel," the account of Nathan Zuckerman's brother Henry, a New Jersey dentist whose exhausted marriage has driven him into a couple of affairs, the first being with Maria from Basel. (Recall that the first Zionist Congress, called by Theodore Herzl, took place in Basel in 1897.) Although Henry and Maria are in love, their mutual marriages eventually win out, and in time Maria returns to husband, Basel, and oblivion. Ten years later, Henry develops an attachment to his dental assistant, Wendy, who treats him to regular after-hours fellatio, until Henry begins taking a beta-blocker for his heart condition, a side effect of which is the inhibition of potency. In despair over his inability to gratify Wendy's "oral hangup," he opts for bypass surgery and dies on the operating table. The chapter ends after the funeral, with Nathan pondering his notes on his brother's affairs and his own guilt for failing to dissuade Henry from the operation.

The import of the book's title becomes apparent at the start of "Judea," where Henry, fabricating a counterlife for himself, turns up alive and in flight from dentistry and domesticity for Israel and a militant Zionist kibbutz on the West Bank. Here, the dream of Herzl's Zionism is being put into action. This counter-Henry, now calling himself Hanoch, packs a revolver and sits at the feet of one Mordecai Lippman, an apocalyptic Zionist and pioneer of the settlement movement in Judea and Samaria. It is to this settlement, Agor, that Nathan goes to visit Henry, only to find himself under siege from Henry's colleagues for his "Diaspora abnormality"—four gentile wives—and for his failure to make his own *aliyah*. Despite this, or maybe because of it, Nathan comes to appreciate, without falling under, the spell of Lippman, whose apocalyptic scenarios are charged with the elements of a primitive and powerful art: prophecy. Among his prophecies is one of a coming pogrom in America carried out by Blacks, whom the gentiles are secretly grooming to wipe out the Jews. The gentiles, goes the story, will then fall upon the Blacks and wipe *them* out. The story is screwball enough to condemn Lippman as a paranoid and yet faithful enough to the racial tensions of American life to blur the line between paranoia and prophecy. And it is vivid enough to make it mesmerizing to the credulous. Lippman is a gifted storyteller, like Roth himself, with a flair for making implausible dramatizations sound like imminent catastrophes, and Zuckerman, who has an appreciation for what the imagination does, has to be warned by an Israeli journalist friend not to mistake vividness for intellectual depth or moral incisiveness. It is a lesson about art itself, not just apocalyptic messianism.

Previously, at the Wailing Wall, Nathan had been accosted by a young American pilgrim, Jimmy Ben-Joseph Lustig of West Orange, New Jersey, who is a reader of Nathan's books and author of his own prophetic tractate, The Five Books of Jimmy. A baseball fan to boot, he laments, "That's the thing that's missing here. How can there be Jews without baseball? . . . Not until there is baseball in Israel will the Messiah come! Nathan, I want to play center field for the Jerusalem Giants!" Vivid, galvanic, his eyes aglitter with prophecy, he finds himself in major league trouble in "Aloft," where he turns out to be a highjacker who sneaks a gun and a grenade aboard an El Al airliner in the name of abolishing the Jewish past. But Jimmy is jumped by Israeli security guards, stripped, searched, and beaten. Nathan, for sitting next to him, is forcibly undressed, given an anal search, and treated to a long, blithering, inspired lecture on Jews, gentiles, Satan, Billy Budd, T. S. Eliot, and Eliot's Bleistein with a cigar by a security guard who coaches Nathan along the way: "If only we had T. S. Eliot on board today. I'd teach him about cigars. And you'd help, wouldn't you? Wouldn't you, a literary figure like yourself, help me educate the great poet about Jewish cigars?" Nathan, naked, handcuffed, and frightened out of his wits can only be agreeable: "If necessary."

This is vintage Roth, playing terror as vaudeville, playing Jerusalem as Prague, playing Judea as "A Day at the Races," and devising fiendish new steps for the choreography of comedy and the abyss that has been his stock-in-trade from the start. I'll stop short of summarizing "Gloucestershire" and "Christendom," which, in any event, are rich and surprising and beyond paraphrase. Suffice it to say that in "Gloucestershire" it is Nathan who suffers the heart trouble, takes that beta-blocker, and dies on the operating table for the sake of *his* Maria, a young Englishwoman. But death doesn't prevent Nathan from interviewing Maria from beyond the grave, nor Maria from answering him in the cool phraseology of the English Midlands that makes her a dead ringer for something out of *Pride and Prejudice.* Finally, in "Christendom," Nathan is brought back to life in England, as Henry had been in Israel, to settle down in London with his proper, ladylike Maria. However, a brush with English anti-Semitism sends him into a nasty tantrum that drives Maria not only out of his life, but out of his book as well. "I'm leaving the book," she announces when he refuses to be reasonable, and poof, out she goes.

This summary hardly does justice to a book so calibrated and nuanced and so attuned to the conundrums of Jewish identity that the reader has to attend it page by page to stay even with its maneuvers. And seldom have those maneuvers been more agile. Beyond the deaths and resurrections, the sure-handed changes of pace, the swift and confident changes of costume and locale, and the brittle Tom Stoppard repartee, Roth is up to something major in *The Counterlife* that makes it seem a more auspicious novel than the three that preceded it: *The Ghost Writer, Zuckerman Unbound,* and *The Anatomy Lesson.* What is it?

The answer I think is two-fold, encompassing Roth's method on the one hand and his conception of himself on the other. Roth has put himself in unfamiliar territory, dissolving Zuckerman while building a stage for his performances. Nathan Zuckerman not only lacks a firm and defined sense of self, which might describe any Roth character who has slipped his traces, but lacking here even a consistent story to give his life the unity of action. What was psychological in earlier books is structural here; neurosis has become technique, and technique is discovery. This softness of profile has been Roth's compact with Zuckerman from the start, in *My Life as a Man,* and in one extreme moment, indeed, he empties Zuckerman of virtually everything that had once constituted his identity. In a coda of despair at the end of *Zuckerman Unbound,* Zuckerman, having lost both father and mother, having alienated his brother and left his girlfriend, returns to the point of his origins to contemplate the ruins of Newark, and standing before his old house in what is now a Black neighborhood, he is confronted with a young Black man, his head shaved, with a German shepherd in tow. "'Who you supposed to be?'" the man asks. "No one," replied Zuckerman, and that was the end of that. "You are no longer any man's son, you are no longer some good woman's husband, you are no longer your brother's brother, and you don't come from anywhere anymore, either."

This is as despairing as any of Roth's bleak conclusions, yet it also holds out the promise, if only in the reader, for regeneration. For to be no one is to be potentially anyone, and Zuckerman could be invented afresh, as in fact he is in each of the Zuckerman novels. In *The Counterlife,* Roth reinvents him fully five times, giving him a different character profile and destiny in each chapter. If that bears some resemblance to repertory theater, it is intentional, since Roth seems committed in his recent books to a peformative view of the novel as inventive, playful, and improvisational, because, it seems, *life is that way.* The American myth of the self-made man is postmodernized: improvisational man takes his place in the novel as a metaphor for the self-improvising character of our time. "Look, I'm all for authenticity," announces Nathan Zuckerman during a squabble with Henry, "but it can't begin to hold a candle to the human gift for play-acting. That may be the only authentic thing that we *ever* do."

We know, because Roth has uttered such sentiments before, that we are being treated to a Wildean lesson about the authenticity of masks, and if we've been reading Roth right along we can even guess why: to deny, for the nth time, that his characters can be identified with their author, an error for which Roth has taken more than his fair share of abuse. One aim of the Nathan-Henry-Maria repertory theater in *The Counterlife* is to drive home the point once and for all about the separation of art and artist and to close the book on the question of whether Nathan Zuckerman or Peter Tarnopol or David Kepesh or Alex Portnoy is or is not Philip Roth.

But, then, read this way the book is not only discomfitingly defensive, it is also embarrassingly trendy: a work of fictive deconstruction in which Roth catches up at last with the Coovers, the Barths, the Hawkeses, the Gasses, the Austers, the Federmans, and the whole international coterie of Frenchified writers who take their outlook from Jacques Derrida, their authority from Yale, and their styles from the more opaque chapters of James Joyce's *Ulysses*. Read as a theater of fashionable indeterminism, *The Counterlife* seems a shell game, one, moreover, without a pea. Under which Zuckerman do you find the Roth? Under which Zuckerman do you find the Zuckerman? But Roth is not a shell artist, and intuition tells us that he is after bigger game than an exegesis in *diacritics* and that beneath the carousel of charades and improvisations there is a very substantial Roth, whose presence may be felt everywhere if located precisely nowhere.

It is an unfamiliar Roth, however, *Roth the Jew*. Of course, Roth's Jewishness has never been precisely under wraps, but it has been in the past a Jewishness of sensibility and self-consciousness—a bromide of panic and responsibility, to borrow a phrase from Richard Gilman. It was a psychological condition and a form of disablement for which Kafka supplied the metaphor, impotence or inhibition or clumsiness or amorous shiksas or a thin skin the symptoms, and psychoanalysis the remedy. The Jewishness of *The Counterlife* is, by contrast, a historical Jewishness and a source of meaning, if not precisely of strength. In *The Counterlife*, Roth begins to examine the collective identity and situation of the Jews, first through Henry/Hanoch and his *aliyah* and then, tentatively, carefully, inconclusively, through Nathan as well.

In "Judea," Roth plants in Henry's mouth a rejection of the very brand of selfhood—"the American-style psychiatric soul-searching in which my own heroes could wallow for pages on end"—that Roth's books, up until now, have been largely about. Nathan has been pestering Henry to tell him more about himself, until Henry, provoked, responds: "The hell with *me*, forget *me*. *Me* is somebody *I* have forgotten. *Me* no longer exists out here. There isn't time for *me*, there isn't need of *me*—here Judea counts, not *me*!" Henry, as Hanoch, has submitted himself to the collective and turned against all that Nathan stands for: psychiatry, soul-searching, irony, self-dramatization, exhibitionistic indulgence, childish self-dramatization, the narcissistic past, the purely personal—his diaspora abnormality. Nathan is not prepared to forswear that abnormality just yet; it remains the root and ground of his being, but he is not unmoved by sentiments of group solidarity, and for the first time in Roth's books, one senses that immersion in a culture is no longer entirely out of the question. It is not embraced, but neither is it rejected completely out of hand. All that is rejected is apocalyptic messianism, which is simply one of the forms that Jewish collective identity may take.

Where Roth remains steadfast is that the formation and understanding of the *self* is still very much his project, only now operating under new ground rules: the rules of *performance*, in which one exhibits oneself only in disguise, and the rules of *history*, in which the self appears as a resultant of forces: powers, cultures, traditions, movements, emigrations, wars, bloodlines, blood. Those ground rules are in conflict, however, since the theatrical view of the self denies authenticity while the historical demands it. The writer may play fast and loose with the *I*, turning the self into a company of actors, but he dare not tamper with the *we*. Jewish history is not something that can be arbitrarily reinvented. And it is this collision of basic agendas, the theatrical agenda and the historical, that gives *The Counterlife* its tension and makes it the unsettling and absorbing book that it is.

⁓

It is not for nothing that *The Counterlife* unfolds into five distinct stories, featuring five Zuckermans in radically different situations. If repertory theater hadn't given us the model for understanding this, psychiatry might have, and there was a time in reading Roth when we'd have routinely reached for our Freud, if not our Havelock Ellis, to make sense of it all. In the books from *Portnoy's Complaint* through *The Breast*, *My Life as a Man*, and *The Professor of Desire*, and including the comic capers, *The Great American Novel* and *Our Gang*, all that was problematic, mysterious, and beyond reason in human behavior was subject to understanding, when at all, in terms provided by the mental health professions, and Roth was quick to cite the analyst, Spielvogel in some books, Klinger in others, in case we failed to grasp the point.

All that is now overthrown, and drama is the new, and more capacious, metaphor and justification for the irrational self. Besides permitting more without the charge of pathology, it also just plain permits more, as illness has ripened into dialectics. At the end of "Christendom," Roth, speaking in propria persona, addresses the Maria who has taken a voluntary leave from his book and explains to her as best he can what he has been up to in the performance of Zuckerman. "I realize that what I am describing, people divided in themselves, is said to characterize mental illness and is the absolute opposite of our idea of emotional integration. The whole Western idea of mental health runs in precisely the opposite direction: what is desirable is congruity between your self-consciousness and your natural being. But there are those whose sanity flows from the conscious *separation* of those two things. If there even *is* a natural being, an irreducible self, it is rather small, I think, and may even be the root of all impersonation—the natural being may be the skill itself, the innate capacity to impersonate. I'm talking about recognizing that one is acutely a performer, rather than swallowing whole the guise of naturalness and pretending that it isn't a performance but you."

This is a step beyond a description of the Zuckerman tales as Roth's repertory theater; it is a statement of life itself as inherently theatrical, and the Zuckerman variations then being faithfully mimetic, true-to-life. That is all very postmodern of Roth, and I don't completely buy it except as a statement of method. It isn't as if the artist, anymore than the rest of us, recasts the ground of his being every time he sits down at the word processor to cut and paste another self. The contemporary cybernetic self is notoriously mobile, but mobility has limits that define sanity in the individual and character in the novel. For a literary character to come to life, he or she needs the consistency, the plausibility, and the limitedness of life itself. Zuckerman's roles all have that: the Zuckerman Follies is a determined and law-abiding theater. To cite a simple example: Zuckerman may marry a gentile—he may marry five of them—but he can never become one. Thinking in terms of music may make the point clearer. The variations have neither spirit nor charm without the theme.

In the sixties, when Roth took up psychoanalysis out of the pain and perplexity of his life, it was also to expand his language of being: to find out what was in the unconscious and to enrich his characters, as well as himself, with a deeper and darker vocabulary of motives. But psychoanalysis was publicly overthrown when Peter Tarnopol in *My Life as a Man* walked out on his Dr. Spielvogel without looking back and used the book not only to chastise Spielvogel for sloppy ethics in publishing an article about him but also to register the claim that there were depths beyond the Freudian unconscious—few, simple, and boring—that a man had to explore on his own. In fits and starts, Roth's career since *My Life as a Man* has been an exercise in getting beyond the platitudes of the Freudian system and finding resonances and amplitudes that nourish and enliven the character rather than, as psychoanalysis finally does, infantilize and deplete it. And that points eventually away from analysis toward synthesis, toward putting the self back together through history and culture.

As he was working on the Zuckerman trilogy, Roth was also editing *Writers from the Other Europe.* What Roth discovered in his forays into Eastern Europe was a literature as paradoxical, as erotic, and as darkly comic as his own and a continuity between his own most florid imaginings and the main lines of modernist thought. But to discover himself as a European, Roth was obliged to invent his connection to that middle-European world, since for a boy from Newark to imagine himself a stepchild of Prague required a recycling of the self into a more formidable creature than Weequahic High School commonly produced.

Prague, however, is only a halfway house on the road to Judea, and *The Counterlife* comes into focus as the next station on the journey of self-integration, the port of call where the rootless cosmopolitan fits himself out with historical roots, not by surrendering himself to militant Zionism, but by listening, questioning, and absorbing the problematic in contemporary Jewish life. *The Counterlife* is steeped in perplexity *and* in Jewish history; it grafts the theatrical onto the historical, quite as if Roth has extrapolated his own ambiguities onto the Jewish nation and discovered in the world without as actual what was in his world within as possible. In a shrewd review of *The Counterlife* in *Commentary,* Robert Alter notes that the book's uncertainties reflect the condition of contemporary Jewish existence. "It may sound puzzling that all this intense engagement with what deserves to be called, without apology, reality, should occur in a novel constructed by playing one fictional premise against another. However, the self-conscious fictionality of *The Counterlife* proves to be the perfect vehicle for confronting the questions of what it means to be a Jew, given the ambiguous burdens of Jewish history at this particular moment of the twenty-first century. Roth doesn't supply answers, but he recognizes that the dimensions of the question can be seen only by following out a collision of ideas."[1]

Exactly. The Jewish experience is a maze, a series of open questions that can be posed without being answered, and there is no guide to the perplexed handy for quick reference. We may even say that what Roth has done in *The Counterlife* is to attach himself to Jewish history as a particular instance of the problematic: finding in the turbulent I a reflection of the troubled we. Nathan's brother Henry, casting off the merely personal for the collective, is trading in one unidimensional Jewish life—suburban dentist and after hours hedonist—for another—latter-day pioneer and gun-toting Zionist. One set of blinders is exchanged for another, while Nathan, who is too mercurial, can no more become a settler in Agor than he can be a squire in Christendom. Nor can Roth, who will take his own route to Judea, by way of England and Prague.

What saves Zuckerman's meanderings from being just tourism—just, one is tempted to say, rootless cosmopolitanism—is the constant testing of the new world against the self and the self against the world. It is a laboratory approach to life and is not without its problems. In "Christendom," Nathan, now married to his Maria and trying to settle in England, comes under fire from Maria's sister Sarah for playing the "moral guinea pig." It is a charge, which Nathan doesn't really deny; he simply parries it.

> "I think you like to play the moral guinea pig. . . ."
> "How does a moral guinea pig play?"
> "He experiments with himself. Puts himself, if he's a Jew, into church at Christmastime, to see how it feels and what it's like."
> "Oh, everybody does that . . . not just Jews."
> "It's easier if one's a success like you."
> "What is easier? . . ."
> "Everything, without question. But I meant the moral guinea pig bit. You've achieved the freedom to knock around a lot, to go from one estate to the other and see what it's all about. Tell me about success. Do you enjoy it, all that strutting?"

"Not enough—I'm not a sufficiently shameless exhibitionist. . . . I can only exhibit myself in disguise. All my audacity derives from masks."

Roth often puts the truth in the mouths of peripheral characters, and Sarah has hit upon a portion of it, though she doesn't know what to make of it, seeing Nathan's rootlessness as merely an irresponsible deployment of freedom—the freedom of fame and money—rather than as a search for meaning in a life whose meaning has always to be constructed. Zuckerman himself seems to mistake his restless and exploratory impulse for nothing more than a propensity for role-playing, as he testifies in his last letter to Maria after she has absconded from the book. "All I can tell you with certainty is that I, for one, have no self, and that I am unwilling and unable to perpetrate upon myself the joke of self. It certainly does strike me as a joke about *my* self. What I have instead is a variety of impersonations I can do, and not only of myself— a troupe of players that I have internalized, a permanent company of actors that I can call upon when a self is required, an ever-evolving stock of pieces and parts that forms my repertoire. But I certainly have no self independent of my imposturing, artistic efforts to have one. Nor would I want one. I am a theater and nothing more than a theater."

If this is Roth peeking out from behind the mask of Zuckerman— and there is no test for this except intuition—it is foxhole talk, situational ethics, and while it may have some marginal utility in keeping the New York critics at bay or entertaining the professors with those feints and tropes that academic criticism thrives on, it also keeps readers from consciously grasping what subliminally they must surely sense: that Roth's Jewishness (as opposed to his Judaism) is growing deeper roots and becoming more certain of itself. Despite all the fancy footwork, the book possesses a logic, a weight, and a center of gravity that no troupe of players will conceal. That center of gravity may be roughly defined as a movement eastward: elsewhere to Prague or to Anne Frank's Amsterdam, here to Jerusalem, London, Gloucestershire. Along the way, certain goods are acquired: a different slant—many different slants—on his Jewish identity, which he now is rather vehement to defend, and a richer personal culture. The writer from Newark whom Irving Howe once charged with possessing a "thin personal culture" is no longer vulnerable to such accusations, if in fact he ever was. Roth has not settled with Jewishness just yet, and it is likely that he never will, but his compass needle points eastward, back toward the old country and an even older country before the diaspora began, and the personal culture he has picked up along the way is thicker than ever.

Second Thoughts

This review-essay of *The Counterlife* first appeared as "Zuckerman's Travels" in *American Literary History* in 1989 and was republished in my collection of essays, *The Conversion of the Jews.* This chapter and the one on *Operation Shylock* might be read together, since the latter is clearly a sequel to the Israeli sections of *The Counterlife. The Counterlife,* at least parts of it, was the beginning of Roth's efforts to find some common ground with Israel, but without yielding any of his own ground as a secular, diaspora Jew with a distinctly liberal politics who finds fundamentalism terrifying. Later on, in *American Pastoral, I Married a Communist,* and *The Human Stain,* Roth goes head to head with other fundamentalist zealotries: Weatherman-style revolutionary romanticism, Depression-era communism, and French feminism. We come away from all these books with an unmistakable profile of Roth quite different from, say, Roth the compulsive, Roth the blowtop, Roth the sex hound, Roth the moral guinea pig, Roth the son, Roth the husband, Roth the stranger, or Roth the Jew. It is Roth the liberal, and if this book were being written now from scratch from a different point of view, with a greater emphasis on political and ideological matters, I could call it, without embarrassing either Roth or myself, *Studies in Liberalism.* It is liberalism, with its broad sympathies and tolerant views, and, yes, its brief on behalf of sex, that comes under assault in Roth's books, from all points on the political compass, and it is a sentiment that throughout his career he never waivers from. Erections come and go; regimes, whole empires, break apart; marriages happen and come apart; curtains rise and curtains fall; the devotion to tolerance endures.

11

Impuritanism and Postmodernism

Deception

Deception isn't quite a novel; it is rather a scrapbook that has been pasted up and padded out with broad margins and lots of white space into a book roughly the length of a novella. It belongs to a novelist named Philip, who lives in England, has an English wife, and is either imagining or carrying on an affair with another woman. The other woman is herself married, and her husband in turn is cheating openly on her. Philip's wife finds the book and assumes that her husband is carrying on and that his daily trips to his study are now unmasked for what they are, excursions to the telephone and maybe, it is unclear, visits to his lover in the flesh. Not so, protests Philip. I have imagined the woman and this relationship; you're confusing my art with my life, and my life is perfectly humdrum in order that my art can grow riotous and orgiastic. Roth has said such things before: "In my imagination I am unfaithful to everybody, by the way, not just to you. Look, think of it as an act of mourning, because it is that too—a lament of sorts for a life I did lead before you. I don't any longer, I actually happen to live as married men were once supposed to—but allow me to miss the old ways just a little." The novel, such as it is, seems to take its cues from both "The Prague Orgy" and *The Facts,* bringing the surveillance back home and having the novelist in effect spy on himself, taking notes that sound like transcribed wiretaps, and then, under interrogation, deny everything.

Roth has a history of playing fast and loose with his readers, ever since *My Life as a Man* proposed that reality might be a hall of mirrors in which one story has many tellings. The stylistic R & D of that book has become the steady production technique of subsequent books. Roth's sleight of hand and the subtle blendings of the factual and the imagined have given Roth's later novels a Kafkaesque feeling of uncanniness, of realities just beyond reach and epiphanies forever out of focus. The most vivid and believable pages of *Deception* are those from the journal, which involve "Philip" and the imaginary lover, whose name is never given. The imaginary "she" is the book's most striking character, and we know her intimately. She is married but out of love with her husband whose affair is the talk of the town. She resents his affair, but has no intention of confronting him about it, fearing the inconvenience to him. She is also growing weary of Philip and is beginning to find sex a chore. She is in group therapy, but distrusts her therapist: "I'd tell my cleaning lady more than I'd tell him." She is depressed: "I just operate on one cylinder these days." She drinks.

Philip is a man of the world, a traveler, especially to Eastern Europe, a womanizer, and a writer, but the last is the basic self, the core, and he is accused of seducing women mainly for their stories. He is, he tells her, "an écouteur—an audiophiliac. I'm a talk fetishist." Some men, charges one of Philip's friends, talk to women in order to get them into bed. "*You* get them in bed to talk to them." And you can see why Philip might cherish this affair, since "she" is highly articulate and matches him insight for insight, fantasy for fantasy, *mot* for *mot*. He plays "reality shift" with her, a game in which each pretends to be the other and carries on the conversation in the other's guise. The whole thing has the claustral, furtive, and delusional air of a folie à deux, a collusion of autistic children behind a private language. It is often hard to know when the lovers are reality shifted and when they are in propria persona, and the strength of the affair, as we hear it, is in the mutual stimulation of the talk. There is only dialogue and not so much as a "he said" or a "she said."

Deception is too much yadda yadda for my taste. While there are moments in it that have a certain aura of revelation about them—revelation about Roth's method, in the main—the book is too much the fusion of wiretap and Samuel Beckett, combining the worst features of both: the tedium of snuggly pillow talk—by phone, no less—and the distraction of cryptic fragments served up a little too reverentially, as though they were Zen koans. Roth came twenty years late to the French *nouveau roman* and its stylistic pretensions, and by 1990 had developed methods of his own that were far more original than the routines of postmodernist indeterminacy, in which life is never what it seems and the unfolding of reality is a dance of the seven veils. Philosophical and academic, that stuff tended to be taken up by academic novelists, like John Barth and Robert Coover, and was a trial to read and a headache to comprehend. The justification, so far as I can tell, was that it transformed the passive experience of reading into the active one of participating in the construction of meaning. The couch potato (bad) became a collaborator (good); the story became his or her Rorschach. Vladimir Nabokov's later novels were ponderous with that sort of thing, and other novelists came down with virulent strains of the *Ada* virus, which didn't kill them but was hell on their work. The indeterminate novel that flaunted its artificiality, its *writtenness,* paid obvious dividends in the seminar room, where professors and students needed interpretive problems—cruxes—to labor over for two hours, but it failed as bedside reading, and indeterminacy as method never really took root in America, with its national prejudice against extreme forms. Why Roth fell prey to it so late in the game is hard to fathom, except that it seemed fashionably up-to-date and in this case it lent itself to the situation in the book: as a style of alibi, of evasion. *Deception* looks at times like a natural adultery-postmodernist handshake: Bill Clinton reminding us of the slipperiness of the word *is.* This is how you operate in the land of spin: The novelist acts like the press secretary to his own life. "Philip" will complain to his wife, who has found the notebook: "I write fiction and I'm told it's autobiography, I write autobiography and I'm told it's fiction, so since I'm so dim and they're so smart, let *them* decide what it is or it isn't." He practices a postmodern form of situational ethics, complaining that "Philip" is not him. "It is *far* from myself—it's play, it's a game, it is an *impersonation* of myself! Me ventriloquizing myself." The wife of course has to care—it is her place in life—and, for the sake of the wife's legal settlement and his own fee, her lawyer might want to subpoena Philip's phone records to get to the bottom of the ventriloquism. Disinterested parties—you and I—may feel less inclined to sort it all through.

That's too bad, because in a capricious and aleatory way there are some brilliant essayistic nuggets in *Deception,* if you don't mind having to rummage through the tailings of flirtatious chitchat, postcoital crooning, and domestic alibi to dig them out. They take the form of notes for an essay on fiction that he has not yet written, though bits and pieces of it appear in his *Reading Myself and Others* and *Shop Talk.* Here are a few at random:

> There are two nightmares for a biographer. . . . One is that everybody gives you the same story, and the other is that everybody gives you a different story. If everybody gives you the same story, then the subject has made himself into a myth, he's rigidified himself, but you can sort of crack at it with an ice pick and break it down. It's much harder when everybody gives you a different story. You may be closer that way to a portrait of a multiple personality, but it's also awfully confusing.

> *Caprice* is at the heart of a writer's nature. Exploration, fixation, isolation, venom, fetishism, austerity, levity, perplexity, childishness, *et cetera.* The nose in the seam of the undergarment [a reference to James Joyce]—*that's* the writer's nature. *Im*purity, but these Lonoffs—such a suffocating investment in temperance, in dignity, of all damn things.

> What happens in history is that it's dotted with disasters, and when you study history, you go from one disaster and you look forward to the next, and you have steps into the abyss, and there are dates and concepts, you learn those, and then you pass the exam. The trouble with life is you don't really know if this is a downward process. The trouble with life is you don't really know what's going on at all.

> One of the unfair things about adultery, when you compare the lover to the spouse, the lover is never seen in those awful dreary circumstances, arguing about the vegetables, or burning toast, or forgetting to ring up for something, or putting upon someone or being put upon. All that stuff, I think people deliberately keep out of affairs. I'm generalizing from tiny, tiny experience, almost none. But I think they do. Because if they didn't it would be so unrestful. Unless you like two sets of domestic conflict, and you go from one to the other.

There is plenty more of this sort of thing throughout the book, beside which the he-said-she-said pales. When "Roth" the character collapses into Roth the author and the latter's fine radar is dopplering through the local weather, the book possesses the freshness of voice and clinical precision of thought that we associate with a Roth who, as "she" says, "love[s] [his] typewriter more than [he] could ever love any woman." Throughout the remainder of the 1990s, as his marriage to Claire Bloom dissolved, Roth would spend long, punishing hours at his typewriter, justifying to himself, and to us, the audiophilia of which he is accused and the graphomania to which he confesses.

Second Thoughts

We learn in Roth's very next book, *Patrimony,* the story of his father's death of a brain tumor, that while *Deception* was being written, Roth was constantly preoccupied with his father's deteriorating health, and for a while with his own, as a heart attack required him to have a quintuple bypass operation in 1989. It is likely that the confluence of those two health crises explains *Deception*'s lack of robustness. Through the 1990s, his books will become far more vigorous, as if Roth has been rejuvenated.

The review above of *Deception* leaves out an element of the book that Roth obviously deemed important: several digressions featuring Czech or Polish exiles in London and New York. One is about a Czech girl, a graduate of Russian literature, who came to the United States in 1968 and was seduced into becoming a highly paid party girl in Manhattan, finally falling in love with a rich Arab and living with him in Paris. She seeks out Philip to help her write her book about being a prostitute. A second involves a Czech girl who had been Philip's guide to Prague many years before—though he had treated her rudely—and was arrested and interrogated after he left, to find out if they had had sex together. She had married an Englishman in 1978, a sportsman who loved his cricket and football, and was put out by him after she had an affair. Now she is adrift, and seeks out Philip because she has a story to tell. The third is about a Czech friend, Ivan, whose wife, Olina, has taken on a Black lover with a gold necklace. At the heart of his story is the accusation that Philip too had bedded Olina, not so much for the sex as for the stories. "Other men," accuses Ivan, "listen patiently as part of the seduction leading up to the fuck. That is why men usually talk to women—to get them in bed. You get them in bed to talk to them." The final one is with a Polish woman, a translator, whom Philip has met at a party. It is the most enigmatic of them and ends with his kissing her, saying, "I'm kissing your sentences, not you. I'm kissing your English."

I wish none of this were here. I understand that copy was needed to pad *Deception* out to book length. And I understand too the compact one makes with oneself in opening any of Roth's books: check your Puritan squeamishness at the door before starting to read. Nor am I so benighted as to suppose that erotic anthropology or erotic anticommunism or erotic tourism or erotic book rescue are anything other than what we all know them to be: do good, get laid. Get published, get laid. Save a book or a civilization, get laid. We need our incentives, whatever they may be. But finally I wanted to know more about Roth's days editing Writers from the Other Europe, apart from the tenderloin of communism. The suppression of high-mindedness is an inverted Puritanism, with its own limiting fetishes and prohibitions. Call it Impuritanism. How easily last year's hot blood becomes this year's dogma. Writers from the Other Europe was a major and significant project, and there is no warrant to diminish it by admitting, or pretending, that one went to Prague for the sex and may have betrayed one's own wife and seduced another's while serving the cause of intellectual freedom. It is a false immodesty that is as damaging as false modesty, and worse in a way because we never think to probe behind the raffish mask to seek out the furtive and reclusive and blushing decency that might be hiding there.

12

You Must Not Forget Anything

Patrimony

"What a blessing for the city of Newark when they built this hospital." So he's thinking not about his tumor but about the city of Newark. *He's* the bard of Newark. That really rich Newark stuff isn't my story—it's his.

Philip Roth, from *Patrimony*

In October 1989, as Roth was recuperating from quintuple bypass surgery, his father, Herman Roth, died of a brain tumor. He was eighty-eight years old, and the tumor had been affecting his faculties and devastating his senses for something over a year, during which time he understood that he was dying and he conducted his dying as he had conducted his life, with obstinate tenacity. His son was his companion fairly constantly during that year, and in keeping with the unseemliness of his profession, was meticulously recording what he could of his father's decline and his battle to hold off what could be held off. "I must remember accurately," Roth told himself throughout the ordeal, "remember everything accurately so that when he is gone I can re-create the father who created me. *You must not forget anything.*" The book that would emerge less than two years later, *Patrimony*, a son's Kaddish for his father, though because both father and son were secular Jews, it is a

126

Kaddish outside of the Jewish liturgy, one that magnifies and sanctifies the father only, not the Lord.

It is appropriate to repeat here a note from the chapter on *The Facts*, where Roth, speaking through Nathan Zuckerman, talks about biography as being intrinsically deceptive and manipulative form. "With autobiography there's always another text, a countertext, if you will, to the one presented. It's probably the most manipulative of all literary forms." When Roth just three years later comes to tell the story of his father's last year of life, the Zuckerman kibitzing and jeerleading are dispensed with and talk about manipulative literary forms is nowhere to be found. It is well and good to take corrosive postmodern views of your own life, especially after you have endured years of psychoanalysis and learned that every motive bespeaks a shameful hidden motive and that every shameful hidden motive stands in for a yet more shameful and more hidden one, all the way on down to the bestial core. Dissolving reality and speaking only through masks is fine, when the subject is yourself, but in writing about your father, you had better get real. And this is getting it right, is it not? The "self" may be something you put together afresh every day, or every book, especially if you are a writer for whom self-consciousness is the breakfast cereal of your profession. But your father is *your father*, and postmodernism and magic realism simply won't do.

Patrimony, then, is a refreshingly nineteenth century kind of book, both in its strictness of conscience and in its subject, which recalls Victorian discourses on blood, destiny, duty, and character, the relationship between father and son, the inheritance handed down from a patriarch to his heir. It is largely a memoir of Roth and his father in the year between the discovery of the latter's brain tumor until his death on October 25, 1989. It also takes in great stretches of family history, since one year conjures up an entire life, and Herman Roth, as he moves toward death, becomes the great rememberer of the family's past, of how this one set up in business and that one failed, this one became a gangster and that one a furrier, this one spent and that one saved, this one married and that one passed away. He wrings himself dry of every last vapor of memory to whoever will hear him out: friends, nurses, kibitzers, strangers, and sons, reciting the Roth chronicles as though he were one of those ritual bards of antiquity who were elected by the clan to memorialize its collective experience in the form of memorable verses. "It was his Deuteronomy, the history of his Israel, and ever since his retirement, whether he was on a Caribbean cruise or in a Florida hotel lobby or in a doctor's waiting room, very few who wound up sitting across from him for any length of time didn't get at least the abridged version of his sacred text."

Roth knows what is being handed on to him and reminds himself time and again of his duty: *"You must not forget anything."* It is from his own memory, precise, vivid, and fringed with pain, that this book is written. Think of *Patrimony* as a eulogy or a sacrament or a Jewish rite of *yizkor* or memory. It is certainly a ceremony, a public farewell to a father he had not always understood but invariably had loved.

Herman Roth, however, was not an easy man to love, and his son does not soften the contours or sentimentalize his father into a kindly senior citizen. An insurance salesman for Metropolitan Life who worked the most difficult territory imaginable—the Black neighborhoods of Newark—Herman Roth was a man of strict judgment and granite will. A man of thin patience, he was a raconteur of other people's limitations, and "he would have told you that you can lead a horse to water and you *can* make him drink—you just hock him and hock him and hock him until he comes to his senses and does it." Hock is a Yiddish word meaning "to badger, to bludgeon, to hammer with warnings and edicts and pleas."

It was not for his sons, however, Philip and his brother Sandy, that Herman Roth reserved his most intemperate hocking, but his wife Bessie, who died in 1981 of a massive coronary, and his subsequent woman friend, Lilian Beloff—Lil—whom he would take up with a year later. With Lil, he could be merciless and unreasonable; she can't drive, she doesn't know how to use the can opener, she can't even pick out a cantaloupe. To which Philip responds with characteristic humor: nobody can. "We weren't made to buy cantaloupe." The hocking was the downside of Herman Roth's iron self-discipline, his guts, his self-education, the blunt and unshakable conviction that there was only one way to do things.

Toward his novelist son, who at one time or another had scandalized half the readers of America, there is an indulgence, and unlike the fictitious father in the Zuckerman novels—see especially *Zuckerman*

Unbound—who believes his son to be the betrayer of his people and his family, Herman Roth was "a fiercely loyal and devoted father who had never found a thing in my books to criticize." Roth describes a bond between father and son that had nothing to do with the usual American father and son intimacies about whatever: sports, manhood, women, advancement in life, though Herman Roth, during his illness, became a Mets fan under his son's tutelage, and they both talk baseball together toward the end. They talk by phone across the Atlantic. "But pitch by pitch I was enjoying it enormously, maybe even more than if I had been there. 'Go ahead, Herm. I'm a rich man. Pitch by pitch. Who's up?'" Yet Roth remembers that as a child he felt a bond of another kind, almost as if he were possessed by a patriarchal dybbuk. "Yet for many months there was nothing my reasonable self could do to shake off the sense of merging with him that overcame me in the library and in the classroom and at my dormitory desk, the impassioned, if crazy, conviction that I was somehow inhabited by him and quickening his intellect right along with mine."

There are tensions and obstacles, but they are always in the spirit of tough love, which Roth will have us believe is the only kind worth having, a love you don't snuggle up to but one that has to be fought for and won anew each time, almost as if life resembled a baseball season. You are going to lose some games. It is in this spirit that Roth reins in all that is expansive in his writing in favor of a muscular, colloquial, and unadorned style in which the prosaic facts of his father's last year speak for themselves. Herman Roth was the great teacher of the plain vision and the plain style: "He taught me the vernacular. He *was* the vernacular, unpoetic and expressive and pointblank, with all the vernacular's glaring limitations and all its durable force."

The story is a simple one: the discovery, at the end of 1988, that Herman Roth had a massive tumor at the front of the brain stem that was pressing against nerves and had already encased the carotid artery. It was the sort of tumor, a cartilaginous growth, that was unresponsive to radiation treatment or chemotherapy, and unless something surgical were done soon, physical and mental functions would deteriorate at an alarming rate and an unpleasant death could be expected. But Herman Roth was already eighty-six years old; surgery would be massive, lengthy, and possibly fatal. It was plainly out of the question. What was in store for him is a step-by-step deterioration and loss of function as the tumor pressed against yet another nerve and constricted yet another artery. First there was the facial paralysis, then the losses of hearing, vision, bowel control, and the swallowing reflex. Yet, what remained until the last were memory, people, and ferocity. The stories continued, and the fury remained unabated. What is the son's patrimony from such a father? In a sense nothing less than his own character: his humor, his stories, his own iron will, vernacular heart, and toughness of mind. As father and son walk down the corridor of a nursing home, the receptionist says to Roth: "So, you're Philip Roth. Thank you for all the laughs." And turning to the father she says, "Your son's got quite a sense of humor."

"'The jokes,' I told her, 'originate with him.'"

And so, we add, does everything else. But there is one episode in which the patrimony becomes stunningly clear. One evening, while staying at Roth's Connecticut home, Herman Roth loses control of his bowels on the way to the bathroom and fouls his pants, mires the floor, the rugs, the towels, even the window curtains of his son's bathroom. He is humiliated and his son must clean up, which he does dutifully with buckets and rags, and finally a toothbrush, to get down into the crevices between the tiles. As he walks out to the car with a black garbage bag full of soiled things, Roth understands what it has all been about.

"Why this was right and as it should be couldn't have been plainer to me, now that the job was done. So *that* was the patrimony. And not because cleaning it up was symbolic of something else but because it wasn't, because it was nothing less or more than the lived reality that it was. There was my patrimony: not the money, not the tefillin, not the shaving mug, but the shit."

At the moment, there are few writers in America who could have pulled off such a realization without tricks or gimmicks or, God help us, symbolism. Roth does it with simplicity and with dignity. And that is what is at stake for both father and son: for the father, the dignity of remaining himself until the end and dying his own death; for the son, the dignity of doing what he has to do, facing what he has to face, and remembering the savor, the feel, the burden, the pain of each moment.

In *Patrimony*, Philip Roth has written one of his finest books ever and one that should be read by anyone who thinks that the human heart still matters and is worth examining. At a time when so many American novelists are staking their claims on other grounds—stylistic grounds, political grounds, or purely commercial grounds—only a few writers appear to be committed to the novel's first premises: to deliver the news, to examine society, and to probe the human heart. Philip Roth is one of these, and if this account of his mission sounds a trifle old-fashioned, that is because it is.

Second Thoughts

With the publication of *Patrimony,* Roth launched himself, virtually flung himself, into a decade of robust, vital novels: *Operation Shylock* (1993), *Sabbath's Theater* (1995), *American Pastoral* (1997), *I Married a Communist* (1998), and *The Human Stain* (2000). If we include *Deception* and *Patrimony,* that would amount to an astonishing seven books in eleven years. The 1990s would prove to be a remarkably fertile decade for Roth, who turned fifty-seven in 1990. We needn't commit a biographical vulgarity and claim that his father's death and his own cardiac surgery provided a sense of resurrection, of renewal, out of which this creative uprising would take place. And that decade would see its own turbulence and misery, including his divorce from Claire Bloom. It was anything but smooth sailing. But something happened, and Roth gathered up his energy and began to write circles around the other writers, around, indeed, himself.

13

Let Your Jewish Conscience Be Your Guide

Operation Shylock

> For the moment, Diasporism is my own School, neither particu-
> larly unhappy practice nor proud persuasion. I would simply say it
> is an unsettled mode of art-life, performed by a painter who feels
> out of place much of the time, even when he is lucky enough to stay
> at work in his room, unmolested through most of his days. His Di-
> asporism, to the extent that it marks his paintings, relies on a mind-
> set which is often occupied with vagaries of history, kin, home-
> lands, the scattering of his people (if he thinks he may have a
> people), and such stuff. Is that not a general meaning of Diaspora?
> R. B. Kitaj, *First Diasporist Manifesto*

When *Operation Shylock* was published in 1993, I wrote to a friend,
"Philip Roth's new book, *Operation Shylock*, is a reckless, windy, overstated, improvident, and paranoid book about Israel, and therefore must
be true." That needs explaining. I was not saying that Israeli society or
politics are any more needful of such treatment than our own. In Israel,
the language of everyday life is more apocalyptic, yes; life feels more
perilous, sure; it is more propelled by memory, confounded by suspicion, and galvanized by panic, of course; life is more ideologically
driven — perhaps. Otherwise, events these days, in America and Israel
alike, are touched equally with the truly crazy, and it has long been
Roth's method to assimilate the surreal, hallucinatory, and vaudevillian

aspects of this world into his writing, because that is where a search for the truth begins.

It was not Roth, after all, who invented the Branch Davidians, the armed messianic cult that fought an entire federal assault force to a standstill in Waco, Texas, and then immolated itself (if official reports are to be believed) when the end drew nigh. Nor was it Roth who invented the story that former FBI Director J. Edgar Hoover was a transvestite who was once seen at a party in a black taffeta dress. Or, that Hoover was a sex snoop who blackmailed Jack Kennedy into selecting Lyndon Johnson for his Vice President.[1] However, it was Roth who confessed in an essay on "Writing American Fiction," that "[American reality] stupefies, it sickens, it infuriates, and finally it is even a kind of embarrassment to one's meager imagination. The actuality is continually outdoing our talents, and the culture tosses up figures almost daily that are the envy of any novelist." That observation, made over thirty years ago, has grown into Roth's theme song; he has devoted his energies to jousting with the morning headlines, which "fill us with wonder and awe." If America can do that to Roth, what about Israel?

It is common knowledge that Roth has claimed *Operation Shylock* to be, as its subtitle announces, a confession and not a work of fiction, and all that stupefies and infuriates in it is being trumpeted as "98 percent based on fact."[2] "It's becoming ludicrous to me, especially after the battle I've fought for twenty years against journalists and reviewers who insist that everything always happened to me in all these novels. This is really a terrific irony, but there's nothing much I can do about that. . . . I'm a bit astonished by the intellectual level of the response. . . . It would be interesting if one critic or journalist would say, 'What if this guy's telling us the truth?' . . . They're all afraid they're going to look silly. . . . Not one of these people has thought to talk to people who were involved in this thing and see if they corroborate my story. I actually don't care whether they believe me or not. It does not seriously disturb my composure."

What are we to make of such a claim and of the shrill and exasperated tone in which it is issued? How, if at all, does it affect our reading of the book? Of the characters and events in *Operation Shylock,* we can be certain of this much. In 1987, Roth suffered a mental breakdown, a decomposition of personality that turned out to be a result of the drug

Halcion, which had been prescribed as a sleeping pill after knee surgery. We know that within months after withdrawal, he went to Israel to conduct an interview with the Israeli novelist Aharon Appelfeld. We also know that while Roth was in Israel, the trial of John Demjanjuk, the retired Detroit autoworker who was accused of being Treblinka's Ivan the Terrible, was being conducted and that Roth attended that trial. (Only after *Operation Shylock*'s publication was Demjanjuk acquitted.)

But what of the rest? Was Roth, in Israel, confronted with a duplicate Philip Roth, with a passably similar face and identical clothing? Could such a second Roth have been a Chicago detective in Israel on a mission of prophecy and profit, author of a "Diasporist Manifesto" that promotes a Jewish return to the countries of their origin?[3] Might he have enjoyed the companionship of a voluptuous oncology nurse named Wanda Jane ("Jinx") Possesski, a founder of Anti-Semites Anonymous (a kind of AAA for anti-Semites, with its own ten-step program for recovery), whose private mission was to overcome her anti-Semitism, preferably in the beds of Jewish men? Could a second Roth have plotted to have the son of Demjanjuk kidnapped and killed? Did the second Roth have a penile implant that rendered him permanently erect, and did he masturbate on the author's bed? Did Roth meet up with an old student chum from his University of Chicago days, named George Ziad in this book, who had become an anti-Zionist agitator and a PLO operative? Are anti-Zionist Jews really bankrolling the PLO? Did a retired American and Mossad agent, code-named Louis B. Smilesburger, recruit Roth for a secret mission to Athens? Did Roth undertake it, and did Smilesburger later warn Roth that to write a word about that mission could cost him dearly? Finally, does it matter if any of this is true or not?

The answer to the last question is no and yes. No, we surely don't need to know whether Roth has given us an account of his exploits in this book, provocatively subtitled *A Confession*, or turned suggestive events over to a suggestible imagination and let it run free. We're familiar enough with the Roth sound and light show to know that both credulity and incredulity must be checked at the door upon entering his books. In another sense, however, truth is at issue, for what Roth has clearly done is embroider real circumstances, authentic issues, and genuine voices with a fanciful and cinematic plot. Roth needs to have invented little to write this book. If the other Roth (whom Roth calls

Moishe Pipik, after a character of mischief in Jewish folklore), Possesski, Ziad, and Smilesburger do not exist, their voices do, and to come up
with the unhinged monologues they deliver during the course of this
novel, their shrill arias of prophecy, grief, and doom, Roth had only to
take out his notebook and start scribbling. It is fair to say that *Operation
Shylock* commits its excesses in order to keep pace with a world in which
the excessive is the commonplace and the outrageous the ordinary. The
plot may be thickened, but the history, the politics, the intrigue, the
menace, the scheming, the charlatanry, the paranoia, and the tirades,
"the whole pungent ideological mulch of overstatement and lucidity," is
recorded from life. As for whether Roth actually did an unnamed job
for the Mossad, one might well apply the simple pragmatic test: of what
use is it to the reader to have an answer to this? For myself none; for the
Mossad, I would guess, it might matter. Let Smilesbuger write his review and we'll see. Whether *Operation Shylock* is "98 per cent based on
fact" or not is immaterial to my own reading, though my inner Bill
Clinton really wants to ask what is meant by "based" and "on" and
"fact." The more interesting question about Roth's assignment, which
has so far gone unasked, is not whether Roth actually did it, but, fact or
fiction, what it was.

Before leaving for Israel to interview Appelfeld, Roth is called by
the latter and informed of a Roth impersonator, who has been propa-
gandizing for "Diasporism," the resettlement of Israeli Jews in Europe.
He has been telling the press, "The time has come to return to the Europe that was for centuries, and remains to this day, the most authentic
Jewish homeland there has ever been, the birthplace of rabbinic Judaism, Hasidic Judaism, Jewish secularism, socialism—on and on. The
birthplace . . . of Zionism too. But Zionism has outlived its historical
function."

Keeping this news from his wife Claire (the actress Claire Bloom),
who will only try to restrain him, Roth bootlegs a phone call to the
other Roth at the King David Hotel in Jerusalem. Pretending to be a
French journalist and asking whether the Roth on the other end is the
author of *Portnoy et son complexe* (the actual French title of *Portnoy's
Complaint*), Roth provokes his double into an outlandish diatribe of
anti-Zionism, thinly disguised as a rescue mission for the Jews. "You
know what will happen in Warsaw," declaims the other Roth to the

novelist, "at the railway station, when the first trainload of Jews returns? There will be a crowd to welcome them. People will be jubilant. People will be in tears. They will be shouting, 'Our Jews are back! Our Jews are back!'" Read a line like that and you know that something perverse and diabolical is afoot. And yet, outlandish as it is, don't bet that Roth, for all his formidable powers, just made it up.

Roth takes the strange bait and finds himself at lunch with a quasi-double with "a conventionally better-looking face, a little less mismade than my own, with a more strongly defined chin and not so large a nose." The garb, however, is identical, "Same washed-out button-down open neck Oxford blue shirt, same well-worn tan V-neck cashmere sweater, same cuffless khaki trousers," down to the threads around the jacket buttons. This Roth/Pipik is a brilliant impersonator, who, with the skills of an investigator and the devotion of a fan, is the leading scholar of his novelist double. "I know your *life* inside out."

The imitation also serves his mission, to use the author's prestige to move history along. Roth/Pipik accuses Roth of having squandered his fame: "Your prestige has been a little wasted on you. There's a lot you haven't done with it that you could have done." That may be a misunderstanding of how literary fame can be used, but it does open an old wound for Roth, a self-accusation we've seen in previous books: that he has done little more with his art than soothe, cajole, entertain, and aggrandize himself, never making the responsible leap from American "I" to Jewish "we." Roth's clown alter-ego is also his conscience, one, it turns out, of many.

This meeting sets up the dialogue with conscience that is the substance of *Operation Shylock*. Pipik may be an absurdity and a comic foil, like Alvin Pepler in *Zuckerman Unbound*, but like Pepler he can be brilliantly off-the-wall. By plunging Roth into a dialogue over Israel, Pipik forces Roth to confront his choices, to define himself, and possibly to use his prestige to do some good.

Operation Shylock turns out to be a morality play of a very conventional kind: a trial of conscience, a pilgrim's progress. Philip Roth, pilgrim and innocent, his personality fully formed but his soul up for grabs, is beset by temptations, Left and Right, which make powerful and cogent appeals. Pipik represents the temptation of anti-Semitism — his Diasporism is a fiendish plan for a final Final Solution. It is no temptation at all, and Roth turns it aside with ease.

George Ziad, however, presents a serious temptation: anti-Zionism, which boasts a long and popular tradition among Jews. Except that Ziad is unmasked as a fanatic and a PLO agent, his long recital of the sins of the Zionist state touches base with reality, and the reader has to wonder just how Roth means us to take it. In the longest monologue in the book, maybe the longest Roth has ever written—he holds forth for sixteen pages—Ziad conducts a harangue about the transformation of diaspora *gemütlichkeit* into Israeli *macho,* declaiming: "There is more Jewish spirit and Jewish laughter and Jewish intelligence on the Upper West Side of Manhattan than in this entire country—and as for Jewish *conscience,* as for a Jewish sense of *justice,* as for Jewish *heart* . . . there's more Jewish heart at the knish counter at Zabar's than in the whole of the Knesset."

Ziad's indictments of "*Shoah* business" ("the mythology of victimization that they use to justify their addiction to power and their victimizing of *us*") and of Israel's behavior toward the Palestinians are not dismissible as the ravings of a man whose pride has been shattered or as the propaganda of an operative. To be sure, Ziad's diatribe, "a loose array of observations as disjointed as it was coherent and as shallow as it was deep" has all the earmarks of a Palestinian nationalist indictment. However, the temptation of Ziad is that of one who is reciting a version of the truth, in his shrill and partisan way, and appeals to one's sense of justice and fair play. What he says about Israeli attitudes toward diaspora Jews repeats what we have heard earlier, in *The Counterlife:* "What they teach their children in the schools is to look with disgust on the Diaspora Jew, to see the English-speaking Jew and the Spanish-speaking Jew and the Russian-speaking Jew as a freak, as a worm, as a terrified neurotic." Insofar as Roth the author gives Ziad's voice ample scope, we are meant to hear what he has to say.

The third temptation, to which Roth the character yields, is that of raison d'état (which has its Hebrew equivalent in *ein breira,* "we have no choice"), the needs of the state, which is nakedly presented by Smilesburger in recruiting Roth for the Mossad. Smilesburger does not argue from conscience, which he regards as a luxury he cannot afford, and he willingly grants that Ziad has both reason and justice on his side. "I speak sincerely. They are innocent, we are guilty; they are right, we are wrong; they are the violated, we the violators. I am a ruthless man working in a ruthless job for a ruthless country and I am ruthless knowingly and voluntarily." Surely Smilesburger is giving away too much; nobody in that part of the world has a monopoly on moral claims. But, as a device for steering the conversation away from the arena of conscience, with its appeals to mercy, justice, reparations, and moral duty—an arena in which there are legitimate competing claims—he appeals to what might be thought of as a deeper conscience, the conscience of survival. He presents himself as an instrument of necessity; if the Jewish state is to survive, certain things must be done.

Should there ever be a Palestinian victory, Smilesburger confesses to Roth, he will have no alibi, nor shall he wish for one. "My brutality will be measured against their righteousness and I shall hang by my neck until I am dead. And what will I say to the court, after I have been judged and found guilty by my enemy? Will I invoke as my justification the millennial history of degrading, humiliating, terrifying, savage, murderous anti-Semitism? Will I repeat the story of our claim on this land, the millennial history of Jewish settlement here? Will I invoke the horrors of the Holocaust? Absolutely not. I don't justify myself in this way now and I will not stoop to doing it then. I will not plead the simple truth: 'I am a tribesman who stood with his tribe. . . .' I will offer no stirring rhetoric when I am asked by the court to speak my last words but will tell my judges only this: 'I did what I did to you because I did what I did to you.'"

In its nakedness and absolute absence of all sentimentality, it is a remarkable speech, to which Roth the character yields, even as Roth the author stands back and distributes arguments with an even hand, if not positively tilting toward Palestinian appeals for justice. Having heard out Smilesburger, the man who will not stoop to justify, Roth the character agrees to carry out a mission for the Mossad, presumably to do what he will do because it is what he will do.

Having yielded to as pure an expression of raison d'état as you will ever hear, what precisely has Roth agreed to do? Since Roth the novelist claims to have excised the actual Operation Shylock from the book, under the guise of saving himself some unpleasantness from the Mossad, the usual supposition is that, disguised as his imitator, Roth/Pipik, and therefore accessible to the circle of anti-Zionist bankrollers in Athens, Jews presumably high in their ranks, he is sent to spy on the Shylocks and finger them for Smilesburger and his cohorts. Clearly it is not a mere fact-finding mission but the kind of selective assassination mission that has long been the backbone of Israeli self-defense. Smilesburger is not simply a spy; he is a state-employed assassin, who at one point boasts of the assistants who plucked Roth off the street for an interview: "They plays cards and they smoke cigarettes. Occasionally they kill someone." There is no ambiguity about Smilesburger's function in Israeli intelligence or what he is asking Roth to do: put the finger on certain wealthy European Jews who are bankrolling the PLO so that Smilesburger may order their killing.

Roth assents, undertakes the mission, satisfies the Mossad, but is warned later in New York, by Smilesburger himself, after seeing a draft of his novel: "It is not a quiet book you've written—it is a *suicidal* book, even within the extremely Jewish stance you assume." Roth the character caves in, excises the offending chapter, and Roth the writer appends this disclaimer to the book: "This book is a work of fiction. . . . Any resemblance to actual events or locales or persons, living or dead, is entirely coincidental. This confession is false." Then Roth the writer goes on NPR and to the press with declarations that his book is 98 percent based on fact.

Is there any wonder that a few readers are skeptical? I am myself, but then I also balk at the news that J. Edgar Hoover was seen at a Washington party in a black taffeta dress. What we need not be skeptical of is the book itself. Be it 98 percent true or only 9.8 percent, *Operation Shylock: A Confession* is a delicious performance, delicious in itself and for its provocations. I'd begun to worry that after his last three books, *The Facts, Deception,* and *Patrimony,* Roth had said farewell to all that had been reckless and unaccommodating in him. Only *The Counterlife* in the 1980s had given any hint of the old demonic imagining. And not since *The Anatomy Lesson* in 1983 had he unleashed that dybbuk-in-residence that knows no limits and is willing to risk driving his characters insane in order to unlock his own abundant and careening imagination. I'm happy to report that Roth's flirtation with sobriety has been put on hold.

Second Thoughts

I began having second thoughts about *Operation Shylock* almost immediately after writing the above. I made the mistake of adding the book to a reading list for an undergraduate American fiction class and found myself with a small intifada on my hands, though a passive one of sullen resistance and grumbling resentment. This was a savvy and attentive enough group of juniors and seniors whom I had been spoonfeeding homeopathic doses of Raymond Carver and Richard Ford and Alice Munro, easing them into contemporary fiction. I should have known better. Roth's sudden shattering of the bonds of diffidence and economy that had marked the three earlier books, which I had hailed as a return of the reckless and unaccommodating in his art, had its downside: long, tedious monologues unbroken by action, an immersion in history of a kind that I could scarcely have expected my students to keep up with, and Jews and Jews and more Jews. The other writers had approached my students on existentialist grounds: "To read my books, you need to know nothing but the English language and the infinite human capacity for fuck up and humiliation," and my undergrads, settling in with the commonplaces of private pratfall and catastrophe, plunged in, feeling themselves to be happily afloat in the alienation dramas of mid-American modernity. Then, suddenly, out of the blue, there were Israelis and Palestinians, settlers and unsettlers, Pipik and Possesski, Aharon Appefeld and Smilesburger and Ziad and Demjanjuk, the forged diaries of Leon Klinghoffer and "the whole pungent ideological mulch of overstatement and lucidity." I myself faltered on my own second reading of *Operation Shylock* and began to appreciate how windy and unfocused the book was.

Also, the reviews began to roll in, a decidedly mixed bag of congratulation, bewilderment, and seething. By 1993, the days were long past when Roth would routinely be driven out of town by reviews or need a friendly bodyguard of critics to ride shotgun for him, but in 1993, no less than in 1959 or 1969, he needed explaining, and *Operation Shylock* was an explainer's paradise. Reviewers lined up around the block to weigh in on the book: John Updike and Ted Solotaroff and Robert Alter and D. M. Thomas and Hillel Halkin and Harold Bloom and Richard Eder were just a few, and in the midst of all was Roth himself sitting still for multiple interviews. It was a full-court press, and as one review from abroad noticed with detached amusement, the publication of *Operation Shylock* was attended by more drum-beating than any of Roth's books since *Portnoy's Complaint* in 1969.[4]

My students were not alone. John Updike, reviewing *Operation Shylock* with general acclaim in *The New Yorker,* did not fail to observe that the book was an "orgy of argumentation" and that "Roth, in his furious inventiveness and his passion for permutation, has become an exhausting author to be with. His characters seem to be on speed, up at all hours and talking until their mouths bleed. There are too many of them." For one major novelist to review another is always a barefoot walk over hot coals, and Updike pulled it off without singeing his feet and had in addition shrewd things to say. Of course, not being Jewish, Updike felt no obligation to deal with the book's political content, except to note Roth's own ambiguities. His review had particular interest as one writer's estimation of another's prose: "Relentlessly honest, Roth recruits raw nerves, perhaps because they make the fiercest soldiers in the battle of truth. Moral ambiguity, Semitic subdivision, has always been his chosen briar patch. His searching out of Jewishness is of a piece with the searching out of himself that has consumed so many pages and so many pleading, mocking, mocked alter egos."

Robert Alter, more attentive to the historical and political issues raised by *Operation Shylock,* also could not help but observe that instead of dialogue Roth had written "meandering verbal extravaganzas," and native to Jewish discourse though they might be—literary derivatives of the "spritz" that had been a standby of Jewish comedians in the 1950s—in such a massive package the book was hard to keep track of. "As to the larger political questions raised by the novel, the splitting of selves and the clash of opposing performances do strike brilliant sparks; but one wonders whether the routines may not be in the end too easy a way to handle urgent and even excruciating dilemmas." The method is quintessentially Jewish and owes much to Sholom Aleichem and the Eastern European Jewish world—indeed, I can't imagine any non-Jewish writer pulling off such verbal extravagance—but for Alter too it could be vexing to read.

Ted Solotaroff, on the other hand, was undismayed by the hectic overflow. "Along with being the first international contemporary Jewish novel, *Operation Shylock* is also a brilliant novel of ideas, a distinguished genre that is practiced in the United States today about as widely as the epic poem. . . . Roth has assembled a cast that is singularly articulate and expressive. This is, after all, Israel—where an Orthodox civil defense lawyer, who is a Shin Beth agent, rolls out a mordant lecture on taqia, the indigenous code based on desert scarcity that has created a binational politics of deceit and treachery; or where an Israeli bookseller fills Philip in on the terrifying performances of Shylock on the English stage as he hands over the Klinghoffer forgery. The most articulate and expressive voice of all is the one that presents them, provokes them, endures them, fools and is fooled by them and never stops commenting keenly on what is or may be going on." Roth, he felt, "has gone deeper into his own genius than he ever had before."

Brilliant and distressing go together, and one either has a taste for Roth's spontaneous improvisations or one does not. For myself, there are spritzes so inspired that I'm bound to quote at least one of them at length. This one by the character of Philip Roth, that is, Roth 1, who at the moment is impersonating his impersonator, Roth 2 or Pipik, for George Ziad and his wife, as a way of gaining Ziad's confidence that he is indeed an anti-Zionist Jew who can be trusted.

> So, this is how its done, I thought. This is how they do it. You just say everything.
>   No, I didn't stop for a very long time. On and on and on, obeying an impulse I did nothing to quash, ostentatiously free of uncertainty, and without a trace of conscience to rein in my raving. I was telling them about the meeting of the World Diasporist Congress to take place, in December, fittingly enough in Basel, the site of the first World Zionist Congress just ninety years ago. At that first Zionist Congress there had been only a couple of hundred delegates—my goal was to have twice that many, Jewish delegations from every European country where the Israeli Ashkenazis would soon resume the European Jewish life that Hitler had all but extinguished. Walesa, I told them, had already agreed to appear as keynote speaker or to send his wife in his behalf if he concluded that he could not safely leave Poland. I was talking about the Armenians, suddenly, about whom I knew nothing. "Did the Armenians suffer because they were in a Diaspora? No, because they were *at home* and the Turks moved in and massacred them *there*." I heard myself next praising the greatest Diasporist of all, the father of the new Diasporist movement, Irving Berlin. "People ask where I got the idea. Well, I got it listening to the radio. The radio was playing 'Easter Parade' and I thought, but this is Jewish genius on a par with the Ten Commandments. God gave Moses the Ten Commandments and then He gave Irving Berlin 'Easter Parade' and 'White Christmas.' The two holidays

that celebrate the divinity of Christ—the divinity that's the very heart of the Jewish rejection of Christianity—and what does Irving Berlin brilliantly do? He de-Christs them both! Easter he turns into a fashion show and Christmas into a holiday about snow. Gone is the gore and the murder of Christ—down with the crucifix and up with the bonnet! *He turns their religion into schlock.* But nicely! Nicely! So nicely the goyim don't even know what hit 'em. They love it. *Everybody* loves it. The Jews especially. Jews loathe Jesus. People always tell me Jesus is Jewish. I never believe them. It's like when people used to tell me Cary Grant was Jewish. Bull*shit*. Jews don't want to *hear* about Jesus. And can you blame them? So—Bing Crosby replaces Jesus as the beloved Son of God, and the Jews, the *Jews go* around whistling about Easter! And is that so disgraceful a means of defusing the enmity of centuries? Is anyone really dishonored by this? If schlockified Christianity is Christianity cleansed of Jew hatred, then three cheers for schlock. If supplanting Jesus Christ with snow can enable my people to cozy up to Christmas, then let it snow, let it snow, let it snow! Do you see my point?" I took more pride, I told them, in "Easter Parade" than in the victory of the Six Day War, found more security in "White Christmas" than in the Israeli nuclear reactor.

There is a good deal more of this; Roth is only getting warmed up. But does it matter if we are listening to Philip Roth the character or Philip Roth the author? Is there a separation between them that means something? I can't see one. Here it seems is a tirade that has found its masquerade, and in Roth the character imitating his imitator for the benefit of a Palestinian who is himself doing an imitation was an opportunity for Roth the author's own sentiments to get ventilated as only they could be, as ventriloquism. "Better Irving Berlin than Ariel Sharon. Better Irving Berlin than the Wailing Wall. Better Irving Berlin than Holy Jerusalem!" Here it is, Diaspora shtick presented as Diasporist shtick. I'm not sure that, content aside, it sounds much different from a daily session of the Knesset, where vituperation and spritz are the daily fare, as if Jerusalem was an annex of Grossinger's and the struggle for existence was just a hair's breadth removed from a tummler's routine.

Nor am I certain that this isn't the deeper sentiment of the book— and I prefer the word sentiment here to message, since it is more a cast of mind than a homily—a celebration of diaspora Jewishness, the Jewishness that Roth inherited from his parents and the only Jewishness he knows: secular and English-speaking, though it vibrates with the cadences and asperities and invective of Yiddish. It is fleshy; it has appetites; it is ironic, exuberant, peformative, loquacious, agitated, noisy, and sentimental. Irving Berlin also wrote "God Bless America," "Cheek to Cheek," and "The Girl That I Marry." And then there were Lorenz Hart, Jerome Kern, Oscar Hammerstein, Harold Arlen, the Gershwin brothers, Stephen Sondheim. . . . Roth/Pipik's Diasporism ("Our Jews are back! Our Jews are back!") may be a malicious comedy, but Roth's (the author's) devotion to the diaspora culture that created him is certainly not. Listen again to Ziad, who is Roth's mouthpiece on the subject of comparative Jewries: "There's more Jewish heart at the knish counter at Zabar's than in the whole of the Knesset." There is no little irony in Roth's finding in himself a third-generation celebrant of the world of secular, Yiddish-speaking Jewry that Irving Howe celebrated in his *World of Our Fathers*.

Maybe it is prudent to call a halt to the cavalcade of book reviews here, though they represent in sum some of the best that has been written about Roth over the years. *Operation Shylock* was taken seriously, and the appraisals in themselves represent how far Roth had come from the days when it was fashionable to take him lightly. There is one, though, that needs to be highlighted in passing. It was by the *Jerusalem Post*'s reviewer, S. T. Meravi, who might have been expected to take a dim view of the book, given its politics, but who found it supple, deft, and entertaining. His review appeared late enough for him to take note of both the campaign of hype that attended the book and its failure. His observations about the book and Roth's readership cut deep and will be referred to later.

"At one time every new Philip Roth production was an event for American Jews. Today I'm afraid that, through no fault of his own, he has largely lost his audience. The vast majority of American Jews now no longer sweat over questions of Jewish identity. A new generation has arisen that often as not is comfortably intermarried (and the product of intermarriage). It has little interest in Israel, and certainly doesn't want to think about the Palestinian question. And to a large extent it doesn't read. . . . The man hasn't lost any of his estimable skill; he's just lost an estimable readership. Which may be the ultimate comment on the

Israel-Diaspora question." Here was an olive branch for Roth and a kick in the nuts for Diaspora Jewry. In 1969, American Jews might have pursued Roth all the way to the caves at Tora Bora for a book like *Operation Shylock.* Now they ignore him. This may be a consideration separate from Roth's writing, but it is one that has profound consequences for it.

14

Sabbath's Theater

Strange to think of Philip Roth's winning the National Book Award for fiction in 1995 with *Sabbath's Theater,* a nervous breakdown in the form of a novel that had some reviewers muttering aloud and tossing stink bombs when the book was published that August. The *New York Times*'s Michiko Kakutani, who may have seen herself unflatteringly cartooned as the admonitory dean of a women's college, one Kimiko Kakizaki, led the charge, calling Roth's character, Mickey Sabbath, a "loathsome narcissist" and finding the novel sour, nasty, and lugubrious.[1] The *Boston Globe*'s Gail Caldwell did a more complicated stutter step, but finally deplored Sabbath's "profligate sexual shenanigans," noting that "anything done to death gets dreary pretty quickly, whether it's art or God or the world's longest orgasm."[2] Possibly the lone four-square accolade to appear in a major American paper (the British were more amused by the barbaric yawp) was Donna Rifkind's salute in the *Baltimore Sun,* and it was a pat on the back and a knife in the ribs. Paying homage to this "deeply life-celebrating memento mori," Rifkind also took a swipe at thirty-six years of previous "literary exercises" that she found "synthetic," "full of stylistic gimmicks," and "annoying."[3]

Of course, nowhere is it written that the path to the National Book Award must be strewn with roses or prostrate reviewers, and it is refreshing to see the NBA go to a book that not only renounces the hope of ever showing up under anyone's Chanukah bush or on President Bush's coffee table, but also refuses to claim redeeming social significance for its crimes and misdemeanors. Good for Roth, and good too for the National Book Foundation in standing up for smut and refusing to douse the libido in saltpeter and get all the secretions and orifices out of sight before the adults see them. (Fiction committee chair Thomas McGuane reportedly said, "The book is beyond abrasive; it's insulting to everybody represented in it, but I think it's brilliant and really challenges people to weigh what art is in literature."[4] Now that's the spirit!) And quite apart from its timely gesture of defiance, patches of *Sabbath's Theater* are as pungent and penetrating as anything Roth has ever written. Here is our author, sixty something, quintuple bypassed, and separated from his companion of twenty years, actress Claire Bloom, and just as red in cock and claw as he was twenty-six years ago in *Portnoy's Complaint*. *Sabbath's Theater*, then, is a triumph of sorts and a vindication for an author whose previous book, *Operation Shylock*, was a windy and unfocused hopscotch through Israeli politics, whose poor reviews and spotty sales are rumored in the tabloids to have brought down the house of Roth and Bloom.

Still, *Sabbath's Theater* remains a hard book to swallow, and not only for its testosterobatics, which include street puppeteer Mickey Sabbath unbuttoning a young woman in public in one of his Indecent Theater routines; engaging in phone sex with an undergraduate at a women's college; celebrating the disappearance of his first wife by bedding a friend in just hours; stealing underclothes from a host's teenage daughter and money from the hostess; masturbating and urinating—on separate occasions—on the grave of his deceased lover, the Croatian earth-mother Drenka Balich. It also, for all its sodomy, fetishism, voyeurism, water sports, and all purpose whoopie, refuses to justify itself, to claim its outlawry to be more than outlawry, its naked psychic spillage more than naked psychic spillage. In a little vignette at the end of *Portnoy's Complaint*, Alex Portnoy imagines himself surrounded by police and ordered to come out with his hands up for the crime of tearing off the mattress tag, "Do Not Remove under Penalty of Law." It is delightful, and one wonders how much of *Sabbath's Theater* is a reprise of that scene and its battle cry, "Up society's ass, Copper!" *Sabbath's Theater* is an "up society's ass" book that declines the moral square-up of blaming society for its own obstinate defiance. The defiance simply is! For all its winking and capering before the reader, *Sabbath's Theater* is a relentlessly private performance that keeps its reasons for being locked away. No doubt domestic stresses figure among them, as do fears about health and aging. Sabbath's book-long suicide preparations make it clear that the book is a tract on mortality. "The fear of death is with you forever and a shred of irony lives on and on, even in the simplest Jew," thinks Sabbath toward the end, and death is certainly a piece of the book's home base. Another piece, though, is Roth's abiding myth of himself as the renegade and unassimilable Jew, and *Sabbath's Theater* is a restatement of his alienation, after preceding books had raised expectations that Roth was poised to relent and join the congregation.

Immediate tensions aside, it is Roth's myth of Roth that powers *Sabbath's Theater*, as it had powered other books. Roth himself, from time to time, has given a name to it, in the epigraph to *Portnoy's Complaint*, for instance, where he defined Portnoy's malady as "a disorder in which strongly felt ethical and altruistic impulses are perpetually warring with extreme sexual longings, often of a perverse nature." Elsewhere, in essays in *Reading Myself and Others*, he confessed to high culture/low culture, paleface/redskin oscillations and a divided nature, Jewish Boy and Jewboy, the one bookish, retiring, neurotic, the other greedy, libidinous, and world devouring. Over the years, Roth has exploited these bipolar images of himself and worked them up into shtick in scenes like the one in which Nathan Zuckerman, in *The Ghost Writer*, eavesdrops on the bedroom hijinks of writer E. I. Lonoff and his paramour Amy Bellette, while standing atop Lonoff's desk on a volume of Henry James. Roth's fiction is full of this comedy of the high, the low, and the horny, and a very Jewish brand of comedy it is.

The paleface/redskin routine is all very clever and schematic, but it doesn't go far enough. There is something more basic going on, which I have come to think of as Roth's war with the normal in an era of rehabilitation. *Sabbath's Theater* would appear to be the latest word—maybe even the last word—on Roth's romance with illness, his shot across the bow of an age that is all gung ho for "healing" and "wellness." From health club to support group to ashram, Americans are lining up to get physically hard and emotionally sturdy. This is the age of the stairmaster, the sweat lodge, the five-bean salad and the tofu stir-fry, the personal zone and the personal trainer. Roth himself has flirted variously with the temper of the time ever since Alex Portnoy poured out his heart on Dr. Spielvogel's couch, twenty-six years ago. "Oh to be a center fielder, a center fielder, and nothing else," cried Alex, invoking a classic American symbol of health, and Mickey Sabbath calls back from across the years, oh to be a satyr and a wicked old man.

Through the intervening years, we have seen the other Roth heroes, the Zuckermans, the Tarnopols, the Kepeshes, the fictional Roths, trying on the masks of the normal, hoping to find one that felt natural. Alex Portnoy implores Spielvogel to punch his ticket to Wellville, while in *The Breast,* David Kepesh tries to chat himself out of monstrous breasthood with Dr. Klinger. *My Life as a Man*'s Peter Tarnopol has failed in analysis and has only his storytelling to save him. Nathan Zuckerman in *The Ghost Writer* has his daydreams of settling down with Anne Frank and outflanking his assailants by hitching his wagon to a Holocaust star. *The Anatomy Lesson* finds Zuckerman wanting to cash in the writer's life and become a doctor, only to wind up stoned and senseless in a Chicago cemetery on the way to medical school, while *The Counterlife*'s visions of the normal include being a husband, a dentist, and a family man in suburban New Jersey, a militant Zionist on the West Bank, the responsible brother/writer, and the husband of a well-bred English shiksa, whose everyday speech is right out of Jane Austen. In *Patrimony,* Roth cast himself as a devoted son to a dying father, and in *Operation Shylock* normality is nothing less than Philip Roth doing cloak and dagger work for the Israeli Mossad. In one way or another, these fictions are parables of rehab, in which peace of mind or reconciliation or just the common life goeth before a pratfall, though not before being longed for, worried over, and taken provisionally to heart.

The crucial difference between Mickey Sabbath of Philip Roth's *Sabbath's Theater* and previous Roth heroes who have found themselves either overstimulated or overwrought or overcome is that the former wanted to be relieved of their afflictions whereas Sabbath wants only to be perfected in his: to be perfectly perverse, perfectly humiliated, perfectly defeated. At sixty-four, so crippled by arthritis that he can no longer perform the Indecent Theater that used only fingers for puppets, Sabbath has made his illness his art in order to plumb the secrets of shame: to learn how it feels to be isolated, alienated, and without justification. Ethical conflict is now out the window and capricious appetite rules. I've heard it suggested that the book's antinomianism—what was proscribed is now mandatory—explains its hero's name: Sabbath after Sabbatai Sevi, the seventeenth-century false messiah who proclaimed a sybaritic millennium before leading a band of Jews on a Quixotic crusade to free the Holy Land from the Turks. Maybe, though if so, it is no longer the restraints of Halakah, the law, that are being challenged but the Torah of Normality and the wholeness and wellness industries that have sprung up to serve it. Roth spells that out sharply, when Sabbath provokes his wife Roseanna into tossing him out of the house.

Roseanna, who has drunk her way through a dry marriage, in which her lecherous husband has remained only for her paycheck, has gotten herself turned around in AA and comes home from meetings sporting a new confidence along with jargons of "sharing," "honesty," "humility," "coming into recovery," and "being honest with yourself": a grab bag of New Age sound bites for recovering addicts. Her husband is "in permanent relapse." Sabbath goes nuclear when she nails him with this therapeutic maxim: "You're as sick as your secrets." Sabbath, who has been waiting for a banality to sink his teeth into, pounces: "Wrong. . . . You're as adventurous as your secrets, as abhorrent as your secrets, as lonely as your secrets, as alluring as your secrets, as courageous as your secrets, as vacuous as your secrets, as lost as your secrets."

She persists, "You can't have secrets and achieve internal peace," and he parries, "Well, since manufacturing secrets is mankind's leading industry, that takes care of internal peace." Is there any doubt that this is Roth stepping out from behind the Sabbath mask and speaking for himself? Away with internal peace; it isn't worth a moment of a grown man's time. Surely this is where Roth comes out: not just in a romantic rebellion à la *Portnoy's Complaint* or *The Anatomy Lesson*, but in a dark Hobbesean funk that concedes nothing to sentimentality, let alone "repentance" or "redemption." It is as breathtaking as it is nasty, as gusty as it is vivid.

In *Sabbath's Theater* as elsewhere, internal peace is antithetical to seeing all the way to the bottom, and Mickey Sabbath's unrepentant wickedness is Philip Roth's own way of maintaining his personal baseline, his obstinate I AM: the road of excess that leads to the only palace of wisdom he will permit himself.

Second Thoughts

Not all the book reviewers rent their garments over *Sabbath's Theater*, and it is only fair to note that the *Times*'s Michiko Kakutani had good and sufficient reason to find it offensive, since on occasion the Japanese are the subject of foul tirades by Mickey Sabbath, who remembers a brother who was shot down and killed in the war. He tells his wife why he hates the Japanese so much: "Because of what they did to Alec Guinness in *The Bridge on the River Kwai*. Putting him in that fucking little box. I hate the bastards. . . . When I hear the word Japan, I reach for my thermonuclear device." Having lived in Japan and having many Japanese friends, I could have done without that; it transforms Sabbath from someone who is merely Rabelaisian, devious, lecherous, larcenous, lying, untrustworthy, and desperate—all of which fall under my umbrella of tolerance—into something a tad more loathsome than that. It would seem that Roth was out to challenge the sympathies of even his strongest of admirers, the literary liberals who take long views and have shed, at least for literature, all remnants of sexual Puritanism. And now that I've written that, I do find it strange how easily I can extend sympathy through the page to characters I would rather not give spare change to in person. There is the power of literature: widened, and entirely abstract, tolerance. The racial invective removes some of the glamour from Sabbath's sly public disrobings of innocent young girls and his defiant acts of masturbation over his lover's grave. There, surely, Roth can be seen drawing out the logic of Kafka's remark, quoted in *Zuckerman Unbound,* "I believe we should read only those books that bite and sting us. If a book we are reading does not rouse us with a blow to the head, then why read it?" In that spirit, Frank Kermode wrote in a wholly laudatory review of *Sabbath:* "If nobody is outraged, then the whole strategy has failed."[5] In other words, this fulmination on race is calculated. "It is essential to Roth's achievement that he can startle hardened readers, make them pause to remark that they cannot remember having seen such language in print before; and to reflect that further outrage now seems close to impossible, the future charges on Roth's imagination almost unthinkably high."

James Wood, observing in the *New Republic* that in more recent novels Roth had had his dangers caged and obsessions routinized, was similarly taken with the book.[6] "*Sabbath's Theater* is wild, but its nihilism is disciplined and generously subsidized by philosophical tradition—we might expect as much from a novel whose hero has been working on a puppet adaptation of Nietzsche's *Beyond Good and Evil,* and who wants to kill himself because he has seen that life is 'stupid. . . . Anyone with any brains understands that he is destined to lead a stupid life because there is no other kind.' We recognize the ring of that hammer, hear Nietzsche in it, and those wild uprooters Louis-Ferdinand Céline and Thomas Bernhard. It is the sound of a voice stinging itself in trances of negation, the sound of logical vandalism. Sabbath is a creature of this tradition, and Roth uses it with considerable philosophical precision." It is noteworthy here that Roth has gone a long way toward creating the climate of taste in which his books could be understood and appreciated. How surprising, and bracing, to read someone like Wood's disappointment with earlier books whose tirades and agonies were merely shtick, his characters "parlor soldiers," as he put it, "and the novel simply the piano around which they gathered to sing their little rages." Here, Wood, Kermode, and others agreed, was a rending of the soul, a bottoming out on despair, a Prometheus unbound but no less heartbroken for it.[7]

However, in a marvelously witty review in the New Criterion, where Roth would not be expected to be a favorite, James Wolcott complained, "The novel is so narrow in its obsessions, so petty and overwrought, that its author seems to be wringing himself dry, choking off his last drops of juice. His flashlight gets stuck in the hole. Yet it's too early to consign Roth to the remainder bin. These days, sixty-two isn't so old. He's managed to stretch his midlife crisis this far. He may mature yet!"[8]

Final observation. It became a commonplace of reviews to observe that Roth had modeled his character, or at least named him, after Sabbatai Sevi, the seventeenth-century false messiah who turned Judaism on its head, preached the counter-Torah of redemption through sin, and led thousands of Jews off to the Holy Land to liberate it from the Turks. And when captured, he converted to Islam, an apostasy that left some followers undeterred, since, under redemption through sin, that was just another redeeming act. Possibly Roth did have him in mind, but even if so we can hold that as nothing more than a curiosity, a resort to symbols for the delight of the symbol hunters. Finding the Sabbatai figure in a novel—unless the novel is by Isaac Bashevis Singer—is about as helpful as finding the Christ figure, that old expedient of readers from another era who, praying to turn up hidden symbols, could uncover a crucifix faster than you can say "Eli Eli" as a sign that a character had been "redeemed." The last thing we can expect of Roth is either to grant indulgences to his characters or to attach his meanings to any liturgical system: Hasidic, Gnostic, Christian, Hindu, Jain, or Jubu—Jewish Buddhist. To the end he will be loyal to his own brands of *mishegas*. Mickey Sabbath is a creature of nature, not religion or history, and he appeals to us in terms of tumescence, not of Torah. Don't bother looking for his prototypes in Gershom Sholem; try the police blotter. And anyway, Mickey Sabbath is an American and a madman of his time. In the old country, Jews didn't urinate on the graves of their Croatian lovers, did they?

15

American Pastoral, or The Jewish King Lear

The intelligence was intact and yet she was mad.

Nathan Zuckerman, from American Pastoral

The monotonous chant of the indoctrinated, ideologically armored from head to foot—the monotonous, spellbound chant of those whose turbulence can be caged only within the suffocating strait-jacket of supercoherent dreams. What was missing from her un-stuttered words was not the sanctity of life—missing was the sound of life.

Nathan Zuckerman, from American Pastoral

> Is it the fashion, that discarded fathers
> Should have thus little mercy on their flesh?
> Judicious punishment! 'twas this flesh begot
> Those pelican daughters.
>
> King Lear, act 3, scene 4

Philip Roth is our man in hell, who has devoted his life as a writer to re-porting back from all the circles, slums, caves, dungeons, wormholes, and ratholes he has found there: the circle of love and that of no love, the brimstone of marriage and the dungeon of loneliness, the wormhole of ego and the rathole of other people. Roth hell has rooms for Jews and non-Jews, Israel and America, literary fame and writer's block, life as a child and life as a man. At the end of *Sabbath's Theater,* a suicidal Mickey Sabbath steps back from his own graveside and reflects: why should he take his life "when everything he ever hated was here"? In

American Pastoral, hell is called New Jersey, and it is the most sulfurous pit of despair Roth has uncovered so far. At dead center is Newark, after the Jews have moved out and the riot of 1967 has gutted it, though the suburbs are infernos after their own fashion. Roth bottoms out here on misery, and in a final chapter that is one of the most electrifying tableaus he has yet concocted, he stages a dinner scene as spellbinding and remorseless as any I know.

To open *American Pastoral* to any page is to find oneself in classic Rothland. First and foremost there is the high consciousness: a radar of awareness that dopplers in on everything within range and is spring-loaded with aperçus. Like the Hubble telescope, it can resolve microscopic objects at astronomical distances. Add to that a dogged encyclopedism, devoted here to glove manufacturing: the tanning and stretching of leather; the soaking, dehairing, pickling, sorting, and taxing of it; the stitching of fourchettes, thumbs, and tranks; the calfskin and buckskin; the grain finish and the velvet finish. Where does he get this knowledge, and why? And glove manufacturing is as nothing compared to consciousness manufacturing, about which Roth, a soldier of introspection and martyr to subjectivity, knows as much as anyone.

And there is always the sense of wonder at how strange the ordinary life can be. Roth gets off on the freak show of desire; nothing is too strange to be true; nothing can be true unless it defies all reason. *American Pastoral* has it all: the consciousness, the hysteria, the fulmination, and the off-the-wall research, all simmered down into a scalding, pungent sauce, the patented Roth compote of the raw and the cooked.

⌁

American Pastoral is a return to the turf of Roth's 1959 novella, *Goodbye, Columbus,* Newark, New Jersey, and its surrounding suburbs, symbolized in this book by a mythic rural paradise called Old Rimrock. The hero, or he-who-gets-flattened, is Seymour "Swede" Levov, one-time star athlete for Weequahic High School, "the neighborhood talisman, the legendary Swede," who marries the former Miss New Jersey of 1949, Dawn Dwyer, takes over his father's business, Newark Maid Gloves, moves out to Old Rimrock, and inherits the fiery destiny of Newark itself and American life in the 1960s. With everything going for him and a life as meticulously patterned as a Newark Maid glove, Levov gets swept up in the maelstrom when his daughter Merry (Meredith) puts aside her Audrey Hepburn scrapbook for anti-Vietnam War literature, hangs out with Weathermen types in New York, and bombs the Old Rimrock post office, killing a local man who just stopped by to pay his bills. Later on she will kill three others in Oregon. She becomes a fugitive from her family and the law for five years, while the Levovs descend into the most dreadful of circles that Roth-Dante can dream up for the unreflective: tormented self-reflection. Their lives are ripped apart by questions. How did this athlete and this beauty produce this urban terrorist, this teenage guerrilla? And after Newark is laid waste and all their work—business, family—are in shambles, how will they live?

Roth never stoops to answering big questions. Rather, he turns them over to a gang of talking heads who perform a Grosse Fugue of opinions. Roth populates his New Jersey with characters in gridlock, and *American Pastoral*'s prickly brilliance is spun out of their operatic arias of ego and self-will. The cast includes the bewildered Swede—decorous, smooth, modulated—who has to learn the magic phrase: "I want"; the fashion-plate Dawn, who raises cattle, gets a facelift, and takes a lover; a hotheaded brother, Jerry Levov, a heart surgeon with a scalpel for a tongue; a father, Lou Levov, who knows only rectitude and gloves; daughter Merry, the fourth-generation's perverse reward for three generations of upward mobility; one Rita Cohen, a libidinized spokeswoman for the cult of Mao or Never; William Orcutt, Morristown architect and failed surrealist painter with a corrosive vision, an alcoholic wife, and a poacher's heart; Marcia Umanoff, an English professor and "a difficult person" who lives to see the middle class take it in the chops; and Sheila Salzman, a speech therapist who had treated Merry's stutter and was once Swede's lover.

Nothing much happens in *American Pastoral* except that Merry reappears after her five-year absence as a Jain, veiled and penitential and so worshipful of life that she refuses to kill even the bacteria on her body. The book otherwise has no plot, just encounters along the way to set the Swede on the path to learning "the worst lesson that life can teach—that it makes no sense." Roth's *port-parole* here, as elsewhere, Nathan Zuckerman, who daydreams the entire story, informs us from the get go that getting things wrong is what life is all about, "so ill-equipped are we all to envision one another's interior workings and invisible aims. . . . The

fact remains that getting people right is not what living is all about anyway. It's getting them wrong that is living, getting them wrong and
wrong and wrong and then, on careful reconsideration, getting them
wrong again. That's how we know we're alive: we're wrong." Jerry
Levov, one of the book's most corrosive voices, adds: "My experience is
that personal philosophies have a shelf life of about two weeks." We
may not be comfortable with a Jewish author touting the void like this,
but Roth, here as elsewhere, has not set up shop as a Maimonides or
Vilna Gaon.

Maybe that and that alone explains Merry Levov, who runs through
teenage infatuations, from Audrey Hepburn to astronomy to the 4-H
Club to Catholicism to antiwar activism, and grows into an All-
American cultist for whom ordnance is as ordinary as cheerleading. It is
the floating world that Roth captures brilliantly here, a world in which
nothing can be explained, though it is teeming with emperors of explanation and little commissars of accusation. Perhaps none of these is
more inspired or more exasperating than Swede's father, Lou Levov, a
stubborn businessman and iron-willed teacher of good conduct, whose
advice about getting on in life is simple: "You work at it." He is the
book's eccentric moral center, his voice, dyspeptic, nostalgic, unstop-
pable, crazed after its own fashion. And while Lou Levov counsels
"work at it," Jerry remembers angrily "a household tyrannized by gloves,
bludgeoned by gloves, the only thing in life—ladies' gloves! . . . Oh
where oh where is that outmoded America, that decorous America
where a woman had twenty-five pairs of gloves?" William Orcutt
presses the case that "the grotesque is supplanting everything commonplace that people love about this country," and moments later is seen
pressing Dawn Levov into the kitchen sink while showing her how to
peel a carrot. And Newark, the great Jewish paradise lost, lies smolder-
ing in the background. Is this hell or is it suburbia?

American Pastoral is a longer and more diffuse book than it needs to
be, going into triple overtime with rant and grievance, as though Roth
had no conception of how to shut it off. And one has to ask why, at this
late date, thirty years later, we need an anti-sixties book? Is this a piece of
unfinished business, snatched from the drawer and sent into the world
scarce half made up? And yet, in the midst of all the posturing and verbal artillery, Roth stages a final grand masque with all hands assembled

and allows the demonic in his art a last-second victory over some very wearisome blah blah bah. *American Pastoral* is a novel that worms its way, sinuously and through much muck, toward revelation, in a demonstration that Roth, though he has lost his patience for the well-made novel and is now going in for all-out psychic spillage, has lost none of the raw nerve that has kept him in the limelight since *Goodbye, Columbus,* almost forty years ago.

Second Thoughts

I've come back to this book at length because I find it haunting, as it had to have been for Roth as well. It rattles such heavy chains: the sixties, the fanatical flip side of liberalism, fatherhood, Newark, and in its urgency it sounds like a reprise of a venerable piece of theater that was transplanted successfully from Shakespeare to the Yiddish stage in the 1920s, *The Jewish King Lear.* Roth's version makes do with just one daughter, but how many daughters does it take to bring a father to his knees? Couldn't Goneril have done the job on her own?

A review of the kind I initially wrote leaves all the big questions up in the air. What is it that we are supposed to understand about the book, about Roth, about life? It is such a thunderous cloudburst of grief that we have to wonder what to do with it. What does Roth want us to know? How does he want us to feel? Not only about Merry Levov and her multiple conversions away from the ease and security of Old Rimrock, but about the middle-class life, the life of hard work and striving and the kicking back that comes with success? Has Merry Levov seen through an elaborate ruse to the radical core of things—capitalist exploitation, white domination, American "hegemony"?—or has she herself been taken in by the monotonous platitudes of romantic revolutionism? What do we wind up knowing, *from* Roth and *in spite* of him? What does it all add up to?

An obvious property of the book, if not the most obvious, is its focus on the great Newark riot of 1967 and the Weatherman bombings of 1968 and after, when some elements of the anti-Vietnam War movement took a revolutionary turn and a splinter of SDS went in for violent guerrilla action. It gives the book the appearance of being a screed against the sixties. And so I take it to be. In many of its particulars the book sounds remarkably like Saul Bellow's novel-cum-diatribe of 1980, *Mr. Sammler's Planet,* which, like *American Pastoral,* takes a jaundiced view of youth culture, of revolutionary romanticism, and of libertine sex as a manifestation of a permissive and self-aggrandizing Zeitgeist. Howe's psychology of unobstructed need? But then, Bellow's book was the expression of an emerging politics on his part, which he expressed often outside the novel, and the novel-as-broadside was consistent with the main currents of his intellectual life. And, besides, that was 1970, when the insurrection was fresh, we were still at war in Vietnam, and there was a live audience for expressions of post-sixties shell shock. Has Roth belatedly jumped on an empty bandwagon? Is he a NeoCon at last? Or is that club itself now in Chapter 11? By 1997 the issue would seem to have lost its freshness and its power to provoke, though consider the venerable David Horowitz, a former red diaper baby and author of *America: Free World Colossus,* who has made a career of denouncing all he had ever done and been in the sixties. So Roth has a drummer to march to. Of course, to be from Newark, New Jersey, that devastated city, and to take a drive through the Weequahic section is to feel keenly the pain of paradise lost. That neighborhood is as ruined and as bleak a cityscape as there is in America, and what the riots didn't destroy, the Garden State Parkway finished off. The book's passages about Newark, indeed, strike home with hurricane force, and it is hardly anti-sixties or even anti-Black to remind the rest of us that there are some places in America where nobody would choose to live given the freedom to move elsewhere.

That doesn't explain why at the book's center, where there should have been a character whom we could believe, if not necessarily approve, we get these cartoon insurrectionists in Merry Levov and her comrade in firearms, Rita Cohen. You can see Roth working mightily to anoint Merry with a distinctive profile. There is her stutter, for example, and her childhood Audrey Hepburn scrapbook. (Audrey Hepburn! Has Roth no pity on this poor child whatever?) She even undergoes a phase of extreme Catholic devotion, moving up, it seems, from adoration of the soubrette to worship of the Madonna. But as a revolutionist she is Brand X, utterly without the sharply observed particulars of life. Now, to treat revolutionism as an adolescent "phase," like the 4-H Club or religious devotion or ballet, is not entirely reductive, but the novelist's job is to bring even banality to life. Possibly Merry's failure to become human is the point: you join The Movement and you cast off your bourgeois individuality to become a soldier and to enter completely into the spirit of whatever fundamentalist manifesto has become your bible: Maoist, Taoist, Leninist, Islamist, Jainist, Hasidic, Koreshian, Raelian. The complex, layered self is useless once you've exchanged sensibility for a checklist of imperatives, for the monotonous chants of ideological armor. There are such people and they are as much a challenge to the fiction writer as they are to their families and the civil order. They defy what we normally consider the province of fiction: intricate consciousness. How does the novelist bring to life someone who has taken the oath to deny all the superfluous debris of the middle-class life that goes into the formation of personality? Is not personality—self questioning, the interior monologue, the interior dialogue, the quirky and elaborate accretions of manners and habits, memories and ideas—an impediment to action, to "revolutionary praxis"? Roth is too keen a recording instrument to have met anyone like Merry and not come away with something more than the mantras: the telltale trace of something else around the mouth, the eyes, the physical gait, the turn of phrase. That especially. As a sixteen-year-old revolutionist in the making, while still living at home, the surly Merry Levov is all teenage bluster and subarticulate resentment. "[President Johnson is] an imperialist dog. . . . There's no d-d-d-difference between him and Hitler." It may be authentic, but it is off-the-shelf. Compare with Pepler, with Lonoff, with Nathan Zuckerman playing the pornographer, Milton Appel. The banality of evil gets a new life in *American Pastoral.* As for Rita Cohen, the emissary from Merry who peppers Swede Levov with revolutionary clichés and crude sexual taunts, the less said the better. Both would appear to be a violation of Roth's dictum, which he announces at the beginning of *The Facts,* that "the facts have always been notebook jottings, my way of springing into fiction. For me, as for most novelists, every genuine imaginative event begins down there, with the facts, with the specific, and not with the philosophical, the ideological, or the abstract."

It is not that the Merry Levovs and Rita Cohen's were not stunning figures in the news in the 1960s. By blasting their way into public consciousness with homemade explosives, they were spectacularly central to their time and periodically make the news even today. Roth had his choice of models to work from, and Merry Levov might be thought of as a composite of incendiaries: Kathy Boudin, Cathlyn Wilkerson, Bernardine Dohrn, Linda Evans, and Kathy Soliah, this last a member of the Symbionese Liberation Army who went underground in 1974 and surfaced in 1999 as a Minnesota soccer mom named Sara Jane Olson. Those at least were the ones who survived, unlike the SLA members who died in a shootout with police in Los Angeles in 1974 or Boudin's Bryn Mawr classmate Diana Oughton, who was killed in 1970 when a bomb exploded in the basement of Wilkerson's father's Manhattan townhouse.

What all had in common with one another and with Merry Levov is that they were granola terrorists, well-loved children of the middle class who grew up in relative ease, even Park Avenue luxury, as the children of successful professionals. Their sense of oppression and need to rebel violently did not come from the material circumstances of their lives; they imagined themselves warriors for the dispossessed: the poor, the Black, the Vietnamese. Kathy Boudin was the daughter of Leonard Boudin, an activist civil-rights lawyer who raised her in a comfortable left-wing environment, where dinner-table companionship included Julian Bond, Pete Seeger, the Berrigan brothers, Alger Hiss, Paul Robeson, and Dr. Benjamin Spock. The father of Weatherman leader Bill Ayers was a high executive at Commonwealth Edison, Chicago's electric company. It was Ayers, author of a recent book, *Fugitive Days,* who coined one of the rallying cries of the Weather Underground: "Kill all the rich people. Break up their cars and apartments. Bring the revolution home, kill your parents—that's where it's really at." (Could the Doors' Jim Morrison, whose song "The End" includes the line "father, I want to kill you," have been any more nakedly parricidal than that?) Roth needn't have invented a line of Merry Levov's: it was all there for the taking. Indeed, when Rita Cohen tells Swede that Merry "thinks you ought to be shot," she is speaking well-scripted lines.

It isn't to the point here to be asking at this late date what drove any of the dynamitards to their desperate acts of violence, which included the 1981 robbery of a Brinks armored truck (Boudin), in which a hapless Brinks guard and two police officers were killed. That any of them actually believed themselves to be the vanguard of a popular uprising is doubtful, but then, who knows what delusions people live with? Those questions have been worried to death, and at least one book has been written about them: Midge Decter's *Liberal Parents, Radical Children* (1975), which argued that permissive child-rearing practices gave rise to youngsters who could not take their place in the adult world. The question rather is why Roth chose to dust off that history when he did and write a book that would seem to be, on the face of it, a delayed response to the sixties, as if a time bomb of horror that had been set a quarter century earlier had suddenly gone off in him. There are, it seems to me, three possible ways of understanding this, none of which necessarily rules out the others.

⁓

In the original review I had asked, "Is this a piece of unfinished business, snatched from the drawer and sent into the world scarce half made up?" We tend to assume that books are written just before they are published, though the reality is often quite different, and parts, maybe sizable chunks, are likely to have been on the shelf for years, before the authors feel ready to bring them to completion. My guess would be that Roth had drafted parts of *American Pastoral* a good many years earlier and then shelved it in order to take up some of the urgent and immediate issues that surface in *Deception, The Facts,* and *Patrimony.*

Then again, one can't discount Roth's smarting over old wounds and deciding to put the sixties behind him once and for all. Old heart wounds grow scar tissue and can fester and fester for a lifetime, and lashing out, as Roth had done so vehemently in *The Anatomy Lesson,* had failed of its purpose—if its purpose was to ease the pain—and had, if anything, reinforced Roth's image as a literary saboteur. Finally, the moment had come for saying, "I, too, recall the sixties as an abomination, and I am no longer, if I ever was, a White Panther, let alone the 'Laureate of the New Class.' Norman, Irving, Bruno, Marie, Midge, Mom, Dad, my family, my people, my tribe, my congregation, all you good burghers and burgherettes whom I have so long misunderstood and injured grievously with my words, *I've come home!*" Far-fetched? Near-fetched is more like it. Roth had rehearsed just such a scene years before as theater of the absurd, when in *The Ghost Writer* he has Nathan Zuckerman dream of marrying Amy Bellette, whom he has cast in his daydreams as Anne Frank. "This is my Aunt Tessie, this is Frieda and

Dave, this is Birdie, this is Murray . . . as you see, we are an enormous family. This is my wife, everyone. She is all I have ever wanted. If you doubt me, just look at her smile, listen to her laugh. Remember the shadowed eyes innocently uplifted in the clever little face? Remember the dark hair clipped back with a barrette? Well, this is she. . . . Anne, says my father—the Anne? Oh, how I have misunderstood my son. How mistaken we have been!"

There is a maniacal and bold comedy in this imagined scene: a majestic and dangerous self-impaling. But the feeling of isolation behind it comes from a deep enough place: homecoming, the secret dream of the self-exiled, if only he can find a way that is not an abject admission of error, of defeat, of having gotten it all completely wrong. I think it may be here somewhere. Damage control. "Enough of this sixties *mishegas:* the world in revolt, the city in flames, the old verities overthrown, the revolt of the masses, the cars and apartments broken up, the parents killed, rambunctious Alex Portnoy, the Bill Ayers, nay, the Che Guevara, of cunnilingus, calling shots in the new morality. Time to get back down to basic values: hard work, long hours, thrift, caring for loved ones, raising families, supporting the United Jewish Appeal. I shall henceforth be the David Horowitz of the novel. Off with that red diaper; off with all diapers, and down to the honest sweat of a busy, productive life." Only, you know, it ain't Roth.

Finally, *American Pastoral* is not a social drama being played on the broad stage of history. The Roth canvas is always vertical, in portrait mode, not horizontal, in landscape. It is a family drama, played out on a stage no larger than Northern New Jersey, and we don't need to know much about Merry Levov as the incarnation of Kathy Boudin et al., but Merry Levov as the daughter of Swede and Dawn Levov and granddaughter of Lou Levov. There are reasons why we know more about the manufacture of gloves than we do about the manufacture of bombs or revolutionists. Because Roth finds glove manufacturing more interesting. And we hardly need to look beyond the history of Roth's own career to tune in on the essential drama here. Did Flaubert say, "Madame Bovary, c'est moi?" Well, could Roth not say, "Merry Levov c'est moi?" The book suddenly clicks into place like a piece in a jigsaw puzzle, and we are revisiting for the nth time the theater of rebellion and atonement that has been Roth's personal theater ever since he started writing and since he found himself, or got himself, singled out as a literary terrorist. This drama would have been sharpened for Roth by the death of his father in 1987, which would have occasioned his taking the book off the shelf and taking one last look at the entire business of insurrection and how solid middle-class families with decent values produce mutinous children like himself. How, indeed, at certain historical junctures, the middle class becomes a factory for mass producing insurrectionaries.

The novel opens with Nathan Zuckerman's forty-fifth high school reunion and his reflections on his childhood hero worship of one of the great athletes Newark ever produced: Seymour "Swede" Levov, who was a magician at all sports for Weequahic High School in the early 1940s who might well have signed with the New York Giants after the war were it not for pressure to go into the family business of glove manufacturing. Swede would marry Dawn Dwyer, Miss New Jersey of 1949, and settle down to be a businessman, a father, and a pillar of the community. At the school reunion Zuckerman meets up with Swede's younger brother, Jerry, who had been Zuckerman's high school classmate and is now a surgeon in Florida, and learns from Jerry that the Swede's life had been hell. His sixteen-year-old daughter has been the Rimrock Bomber, the young woman who had blown up the post office at Old Rimrock, killing a doctor who had gone out to mail a letter. With that story in mind, Nathan Zuckerman, "Skip" to his high school crowd because he had skipped two grades, finds himself toward the end of the reunion in the arms of Joy Helpern, who had once refused to let him unhook her bra on an October hay ride, dancing to the strains of Johnny Mercer's song "Dream." While "Dream" is playing and Nathan is dancing with Joy, he slips into a reverie and daydreams Swede Levov's life, "not his life as a god or a demigod in whose triumphs one could exult as a boy but his life as another assailable man." The remaining 350 pages of the book are Nathan Zuckerman's daydream, much as he had daydreamed in *The Ghost Writer* that Amy Bellette was Anne Frank and his wife-to-be. I don't supposed that Zuckerman is still dancing with Joy Helpern 350 pages later; "Dream" wasn't that long a song. But wherever Zuckerman may be, the rest of the book is entirely a product of his reverie, and if Roth is true to his premise here, the book is really about how Nathan Zuckerman, taking the plunge into his own knowledge of the world and imagination of reality, might conjure up a tragic life for Swede Levov. It is Nathan Zuckerman calling upon his own world knowledge who invents all that comes next: Merry's stuttering and her speech therapist, the psychiatrist, the massive eating binges and weight increases that turn Merry from a petite child into an overweight adolescent, the antiwar sentiments, the Marxist slogans, the parricidal outbursts, the terrorism, the killing of four people, the conversion to penitential Jainism, the bleak exile in industrial Newark.

Maybe that accounts for the sixties premises of the book being both politically urgent and yet politically thin. So little about Vietnam; so much about gloves. For Roth, the sixties became a fetish without being an experience. Not in any way that we normally think of it, either politically or culturally. Did he march against the war? Maybe, but whatever he did it was a far cry from the kind of involvement that got Norman Mailer arrested and resulted in *Armies of the Night.* Did he ever do acid or abandon himself to the fluxions of eternity at a Grateful Dead concert? I bet not. He'd have told us long ago. To ask what Roth was doing in the sixties we need only read the books that are about that decade in his life—*My Life as a Man, The Facts,* and even *Portnoy's Complaint*—and it is apparent what Roth was up to: marriage, misery, divorce, women, analysis, casting off the analyst, and busily, feverishly, desperately, and finally gleefully finding his voice as a writer.

In other words, the weather underground plot of *American Pastoral* is the MacGuffin, the term invented by film director Alfred Hitchcock for the device or plot element that catches the viewer's attention or drives the logic of the story but is also a diversion. It is indeed where the eye goes and where Roth wants us to look, but it is not, I think, what the book is about. The water isn't deep enough, and while an overpowering sense of grievance and loss animates the story of Merry and her devastated father, it is draped so loosely around the figures of Bernardine Dohrn, Kathy Boudin, and the Weatherman Left that it can't possibly fit them. Not like a Newark Maid glove. There are other things that rattle the emotional seismograph more powerfully.

One is the imagination of fatherhood as devastation. Where Roth gets this from the biographers will have to tell us, but wherever it may be he knows something of what transpires between a father and a daughter, what tenderness can be aroused and what terrible shocks go off when the relationship fails. Some of the book's most touching sequences involve Swede Levov's recollections of moments of tenderness with his very young daughter, before everything comes crashing down. The final coda of the book, with its Molly Bloom–like soliloquy racing through Swede Levov's shattered mind, recalls his walks across the field with Merry as they identify flowers together and she points out, "See, Dad, how there's a n-notch at the tip of the petal?" Sure, that delicacy is set up against her later fulminations, but that isn't as important as the way it takes us right to the heart, the father's heart, of Levov, and exposes the core of tenderness at the dead center of his unquenchable pain.

American Pastoral is the lament for Newark. As the Jews once lamented Jerusalem, Roth laments Newark. Only here it is not so much residential Newark, that domestic paradise from which all subsequent life events proved to be a fall, but industrial Newark, which worked and manufactured and had dynamism and muscle. Newark Maid is a stand-in for industrial North Jersey, that concentration of foundries and factories and mills and banks and department stores and corporations and retail shops of every kind that flourished and gave life to the city. The long sequences about the Newark of Swede Levov's childhood are virtually biblical passages. Not just the Weequahic section, the cradle of Zuckerman's recollections, but the Italian neighborhoods, "Down Neck," where immigrant families from Naples worked together in tenements doing piecework for Newark Maid gloves. "The old Italian grandfather or the father did the cutting on the kitchen table, with the French rule, the shears, and the spud knife he'd brought from Italy. The grandmother or the mother did the sewing, and the daughters did the laying off—ironing the glove—in the old-fashioned way, with irons heated up in a box set atop the kitchen's potbellied stove. The women worked on antique Singers, nineteenth-century machines that Lou Levov, who'd learned to reassemble them, had bought for a song and then repaired himself; at least once a week, he'd have to drive all the way Down Neck at night and spend an hour getting a machine running right again."

Now, the ruin is total.

> On the east side of the street, the dark old factories—Civil War factories, foundries, brassworks, heavy-industrial plants blackened, from the chimneys pumping smoke for a hundred years—were windowless now, the sunlight sealed out with brick and mortar, their exits and entrances

plugged with cinderblock. These were the factories where people had lost fingers and arms and got their feet crushed and their faces scalded, where children once labored in the heat and the cold, the nineteenth-century factories that churned up people and churned out goods and now were unpierceable, airtight tombs. It was Newark that was entombed there, a city that was not going to stir again. The pyramids of Newark: as huge and dark and hideously impermeable as a great dynasty's burial edifice has every historical right to be.

The collapse of Newark and the hole left in the heart by its passing calls forth an extraordinary sensuousness from Roth, who draws life, if only a life in prose, out of the ruins. Seldom has Roth written better than this. He laments the fall of Newark as though it were the Third Temple itself fallen to the barbarians. But there will be no next year in Essex County.

Finally, though, I think *American Pastoral* is about fanaticism, Jewish fanaticism, making it consistent with almost everything Roth has written since the story "Eli the Fanatic." The mystery of Merry Levov's turn to revolutionism, having grown up in so decorous and cheerful a home, is hardly mysterious at all once we have spent time with Swede Levov's father Lou, the glove manufacturer, and met also the brother Jerry, grown up from being an awkward boy to a heart surgeon who seems always in a rage of resentment. Merry a genetic anomaly? A mystical self-creation? A creature of the Zeitgeist? A dupe of Herbert Marcuse and Frankfurt School dialectics, in violent revolt against "repressive tolerance"? A victim of her father's blandness, her mother's blindness, her family's stolid and unreflective bourgeois comfort out there in stolid Old Rimrock? If the book shows us anything, it is that Merry's politics and her obstinacy are bred in the bone. The line of fanaticism runs straight from grandfather to granddaughter, skipping only Swede, which singles him out as the anomaly, since his brother Jerry, with his fulminations and his four wives, has contracted it in full. Listen to Lou Levov, the intemperate man with the skull of a brawler, carry on when President Nixon appears on television during the Watergate hearings.

> "That skunk!" the Swede's father said bitterly. "That miserable fascist dog!" and out of him, with terrifying force, poured a tirade of abuse, vitriol about the president of the United States that absent the stuttering that never failed to impart to her abhorrence the exterminating

adamance of a machine gun, Merry herself couldn't have topped in her heyday. Nixon liberates him to say anything—as Johnson liberated Merry. It is as though in his uncensored hatred of Nixon, Lou Levov is merely mimicking his granddaughter's vituperous loathing of LBJ. Get Nixon. Get the bastard in some way. Get Nixon and all will be well. If we can just tar and feather Nixon, America will be America again, without everything loathsome and lawless that's crept in, without all this violence and malice and madness and hate. Put him in a cage, cage the crook, and we'll have our great country back the way it was!

It would be strange indeed if Merry Levov came out of nowhere. Given the combustible emotions of her family and Lou Levov's blast furnace of a heart, one wonders where Swede came from. Maybe the baseball bleached it all out of him, having to learn patience and balance in waiting for his pitch. It takes focus and patience and your weight slightly back on the rear foot to hit the slider down and away. All in all, I've had preferred to see Merry become a Miryam and wind up performing her penitential drudgery with the Hasidim, tending kitchen perhaps for the Lubovitchers in Brooklyn. I understand that Roth has already done the radical, sacrificial kibbutz mentality in *The Counterlife* and wanted to break new ground here, and yet that is where Merry comes from. She is an Essene at heart, and it is to Essene asceticism and zealotry that she returns.

American Pastoral finally possesses a brawling, rambunctious, quarrelsome, kvetching magnificence. Sure, Roth carries on for too long with everything, and you want to put a cork in him. Intemperate? That's middle C in Roth's range, from which he ascends the octaves of jarring, unstanched emotion. But you don't always want the plot to advance. There is so much line-by-line shrewdness about the world that if you can steel yourself to the bludgeon of grief, grief, and still more grief you begin to hear the sawing and hammering of Roth's mind, as the mighty phrase book rustles its pages and gives forth these marvelous aperçus that you'd only miss by rushing. About William Orcutt's Hawaiian shirts. "According to Swede's interpretation, all of the guy's effervescence seemed rather to go into wearing those shirts—all his flamboyance, his boldness, his defiance, and perhaps, too, his disappointment and his despair." About Swede's mother. "He didn't even have to be in the same room to know where his mother was—he'd hear her laughing and could pinpoint her on the map of the house that was not so much in his brain as it was his brain (his cerebral cortex divided not into frontal lobes, parietal lobes, temporal lobes, and occipital lobes but into the downstairs, the upstairs, and the basement—the living room, the dining room, the kitchen, etc.)" And finally, on being alive and being wrong. "The fact remains that getting people right is not what living is all about anyway. It's getting them wrong that is living, getting them wrong and wrong and wrong and then, on careful reconsideration, getting them wrong again. That's how we know we're alive: we're wrong." About that at least, Roth has never been more right.

Third Thoughts: Can't Get No Satisfaction

One day soon a film will be made of *American Pastoral,* and the film will need to have what the book conspicuously lacks: a soundtrack. Roth is no stranger to soundtracks, and has indeed orchestrated early pages of *American Pastoral* as well as sections of *Portnoy's Complaint, I Married a Communist, The Human Stain,* and *The Dying Animal* with appropriate background, and sometimes foreground, music. With the exception of the very last, however, which finds David Kepesh serenading his Consuela Castillo with a medley of European classics from Hayden trios to Dvořák string quintets, and, after the roof falls in on him, hammering out at the keyboard one desperate Scarlatti sonata after another, the soundtracks never get out of the 1940s. In *American Pastoral* we find Nathan Zuckerman at his forty-fifth high school reunion dancing with Joy Helpern to the strains of "Dream" by the Pied Pipers, one of those confected lullabies that Tin Pan Alley cooked up during the war years to divert Americans from thoughts of battle. Released in May 1945, "Dream" was a perfect song for VE Day. And since Nathan Zuckerman, momentarily in Joy Helpern's arms, begins to dream, the reverie segues into his book-long dream of the life of Swede Levov.

Elsewhere at the reunion, Zuckerman encounters Mendy Gurlick, "the Weequahic boy with the biggest talent for being less than a dignified model child, a personality halfway between mildly repellent shallowness and audacious, enviable deviance, flirting back then with indignity in a way that hovered continuously between the alluring and the offensive." It was Mendy Gurlick who had taken Zuckerman to shows downtown and introduced him to the other music of the 1940s, Duke Ellington, Sarah Vaughan, "Mr. B.," Billy Eckstine, and Louis Jordan, whose "Caldonia, Caldonia, what makes your big head so hard" he would run around singing to his buddies, "free of charge."

In *Portnoy's Complaint*, where 1940s radio culture makes its first spectacular debut in Roth's fiction, it is not so much the music that provides the soundtrack but baseball, as heard on the radio, and the broadcast dramas of the day from *Henry Aldrich* and *The Great Gildersleeve* to Fred Allen and Jack Benny and the poetic free verse dramas of Norman Corwin, including "On a Note of Triumph," a VE Day special that Roth would return to in *I Married a Communist*. The texture of this radio experience in *Portnoy's Complaint* is so thick and so pervasive as to be more than just background: it is nothing less than the culture itself, the fabric of American pop culture that was so instrumental in assimilating young Jewish boys from insular, parochial neighborhoods into the common language of American life. It overpowers the Jewishness of the home, which, though a bastion of tribal solidarity and old world vulnerability, lacks entirely a devotional content and is no match for the robustness and daily presence of radio and film and the sunny social attitudes they broadcast. The family dinner? But Jack Benny is on! Rosh Hashanah? But Mom, the World Series!

In *I Married a Communist,* radio again is foregrounded, but with the exception of a song by the Russian Army Chorus, it is radio drama rather than music, in the form of the program, *The Free and The Brave,* in which Ira Ringold, under his *nom de radio,* Iron Rinn, impersonates Abraham Lincoln and other icons of patriotic adoration. Among the inspirations for this use of radio to boost national morale was Norman Corwin, whose dramatized odes to democracy and the nobility of the little man had a profound impact on the young Nathan Zuckerman and were instrumental in attracting him to the person of Ira Ringold. Since Norman Corwin and the Russian Army Chorus's rousing rendition of "Dubinshka" are discussed in great detail in chapter 16, I'll defer any longer discussion of postwar Popular Front rhetoric until then.

It is in *The Human Stain,* however, that Roth returns, shyly I think, to the music of the 1940s, where it is apparently the deeper, personal theme music of Dean Coleman Silk, who, in the throes of a professional and personal crisis, restores his sanity in the sanctum of his home by tuning in to a Saturday night FM program that plays big band music and jazz from six until midnight. During a visit to Silk's cottage one evening, Nathan Zuckerman is treated to the strains of Doris Day singing "It's Magic" ("You sigh, the song begins. You speak, and I hear violins . . ."), Helen O'Connell and Bob Eberle delivering the verses of "Green Eyes," Dick Haymes singing "Those Little White Lies," and the young Frank Sinatra singing "Everything Happens to Me" and "Bewitched, Bothered, and Bewildered." Some of this is standard-issue wartime musical embalming fluid, though Sinatra has held up over the years. Indeed, when "Bewitched" starts to play, Coleman Silk asks Nathan Zuckerman to dance, and awkwardly they do, as Silk reveals to Zuckerman that he is having an affair with the college janitor. That should ease Zuckerman's homophobic panic, as the two men dance to Sinatra, their arms around each other.

The reader might well be led to believe that we are being taken behind the scenes of Dean Silk's emotional life here to gaze at last at the primal codes of a soul that had depths beyond the classical Greek texts that he teaches, or taught before his ignominious retirement from Athena College. However, by this time in the book the reader knows, though Zuckerman does not, that Coleman Silk is a Black man who has made a career for himself in the academy by passing for white, or at least passing for Jewish. Zuckerman observes that he seems "the small-nosed Jewish type with the facial heft in the jaw, one of the crimped-haired Jews of a light yellowish skin pigmentation who possess something of the ambiguous aura of the pale blacks who are sometimes taken for white." He only learns later that Silk is a melanistic anomaly from a family far darker than himself. It is only natural to wonder how such a man, who grew up in East Orange, New Jersey, and spent the postwar years in Greenwich Village, came to embrace the likes of Doris Day, Helen O'Connell, Ray Eberle, and Dick Haymes and can confide to Zuckerman that "everything stoical within me unclenches and the wish not to die, never to die, is almost too great to bear. And all this from listening to Vaughn Monroe." That's exactly what he says. And not a syllable does he utter about what we might expect him to cherish from his Village days: the bebop greats, Charlie Parker, Miles Davis, Dizzy Gillespie, and the early blues singers of the forties, like Jimmy Rushing, Amos Milburn, Wynonie Harris, or Big Joe Turner. This is not even to mention the successful crossover singers, whom all Americans knew: Louis Jordan, Billy Holiday, Sarah Vaughan, Billy Eckstine, Cab Calloway.

There is something wrong here, and it is a problem that segues right into *American Pastoral*. It is possible that Coleman Silk's letting Nathan Zuckerman know that he clings to the straw of life by listening to Vaughn Monroe, a forties-era bandleader and lead baritone singer best known for his "moon" songs—"Moonlight and Roses," "Moon of Manakoora," "It's Only a Paper Moon," and in particular "Racing with the Moon"—tells us either that Coleman Silk is laying on the whitewash extra thick for a credulous Nathan Zuckerman or that he has no taste. Or, that Roth himself draws a blank about what someone growing up Black, more or less, in New Jersey and spending the postwar years in Greenwich Village is likely to have immersed himself in. It is comforting to imagine that Roth, the Godlike artist up above his work paring his fingernails, is in control here, that Coleman Silk is doing a sly shuffle for yet another small town white dude—sure do love that Vaughn Monroe!—and that the other songs we hear, "Those Little White Lies," "Everything Happens to Me," and "Bewitched, Bothered, and Bewildered," are all choruses in the personal theme music of a man who has indeed been telling little white lies and is about as bewitched, bothered, and bewildered as anyone we are going to meet in a Roth novel. It is comforting to think this, but I wouldn't put my money on it.

I wouldn't put my money down because Roth has missed the musical boat once before, in *American Pastoral*, where he was handed a golden opportunity to give Merry Levov an extra dimension of reality by giving her a soundtrack of her own as a radical during a decade that was galvanized by music. Nathan Zuckerman is given his cue when, in his conversation with the Swede's brother, Jerry, he is told: "But it's one thing to get fat, it's one thing to let your hair grow long, it's one thing to listen to rock-and-roll music too loud, but it's another thing to throw a bomb." Zuckerman takes most of these cues and runs with them, except the one about rock-and-roll, and that omission flattens out not only the picture of Merry Levov but of the sixties as well, a decade that is as unimaginable without its music as the forties are without Ellington and Sinatra. When the genie of insurrection popped out of its bottle in the 1960s, it was playing an amplified Fender Stratocaster. What was Merry Levov listening to in her room, with the doors closed and her parents shut out? It wasn't likely to have been the Top-40 tunes of the day, like, say, "Daydream Believer" by The Monkees (remember them?) or

"Windy" by The Association or "Ode to Billy Joe" by Bobby Gentry. If music was in any way implicated in her 1968 bombing, it could have been almost anything out of the tangerine trees and marmalade skies of 1967 that had licks, kicks, and a back beat: any music with a short fuse and a detonator. She might have been listening to "Light My Fire" by the Doors; any of the songs from the Jefferson Airplane's *Surrealistic Pillow* album, including that anthem of anthems to LSD, "White Rabbit"; Jimi Hendrix's *Are You Experienced?* album or, of course, the Beatles' *Sgt. Pepper's Lonely Hearts Club Band*, which the *Times of London* critic Kenneth Tynan had called "a decisive moment in the history of Western Civilization." Throw in almost anything at all by Bob Dylan ("The Times They Are A-Changin'"), the Rolling Stones ("Street Fighting Man"), Buffalo Springfield, Cream and Eric Clapton, Frank Zappa, the Fugs, the Velvet Underground and Nico, and you have the back beat to Merry's turbulence, even a partial explanation of it. You can bet that whatever she was doing in her room prior to the bombing, she wasn't merely reading Frantz Fanon and stewing over the wretched of the earth. She was also tuning into the Rolling Stones as they got no satisfaction or Jim Morrison and the Doors as they tried to set the night on fire. She was trying to break on through to the other side.

The point of this lengthy digression is not to demonstrate an exemplary musical erudition, though the sixties did leave an indelible impression on me, and its music continues to evoke scenes of vivid experience. Clearly, it did not do the same for Roth. It seems, moreover, that Roth's personal sound card, that circuit of neural connections that puts any of us at one with the music of our time, crashed on him at the end of the 1940s, while he was still in his teens. Everybody's shuts down sooner or later; nobody remains a musical sponge through an entire lifetime, and even most of what appears in this section I've had to research, as Roth would have had to as well. I add this mainly in the hope that it just might be read by those people, whoever they may be, who will make the film of *American Pastoral* and will be mindful to restore some of the crucial details that Roth omitted, in order to bring Merry some credibility as a creature of her time, and not simply as a symptom of suburban anomie or of growing up absurd. To default to a soundtrack by, say, Randy Newman, would only compound the damage.

16

Take a Bow, Little Guy
I Married a Communist

"Revenge," announced Murray. "Nothing so big in people and nothing so small, nothing so audaciously creative in even the most ordinary as the workings of revenge. And nothing so ruthlessly creative in even the most refined of the refined as the workings of betrayal."

Murray Ringold, from *I Married a Communist*

"All those antagonisms," Murray said, "and then the torrent of betrayal. Every soul its own betrayal factory. For whatever reason: survival, excitement, advancement, idealism. For the sake of the damage that can be done, the pain that can be inflicted. For the cruelty in it. For the *pleasure* in it."

Murray Ringold, from *I Married a Communist*

So why'd she do it? She being Claire Bloom and it being her 1996 memoir-cum-disemboweling of ex-husband Philip Roth, *Leaving a Doll's House*. Didn't she know that when payback time rolled around—and a good working novelist can easily turn around a betrayal in two years—he'd recite his lines ever so much more cunningly? Did nobody warn her that next to her meat cleaver of a verbal arsenal, his filleting knife, sharpened on decades of settling scores in fiction, would slice her into strips so transparent that prosciutto would look like brisket alongside her? Didn't she remember how he savaged a far more formidable adversary, Irving Howe, in *The Anatomy Lesson*? Well, she did it and now he's done it, and Roth has produced a striking novel in the bargain,

I Married a Communist in which the pathos of a marriage gone south is scotch-taped onto the history of the red scare and the assault on the entertainment industry that took place in the early 1950s. Despite a clunker of a plot, most of which is narrated to the listening Nathan Zuckerman, Roth's venerable alter-ego, *I Married a Communist* contains some gems of character analysis and a high-amp prose that draws us in no matter what indecencies Roth happens to be committing. The combustible cocktails of muscle and delicacy, panic and rhapsody, indecent exposure and quivering sensitivity, moral nuance and appetite red in tooth and claw, are way over critical mass in this book, and there are shattering explosions throughout.

The storyteller is Murray Ringold, who was once Nathan Zuckerman's high school English teacher at Newark's Weequahic High School and is now, at the age of ninety, a guest in the rural Connecticut hideaway where Nathan has retreated to strip back to essentials and decontaminate himself of striving. Murray Ringold has not yet been decontaminated of the past; he is infected with it, especially with the 1950s in which his kid brother Ira played a minor, tragic role. It is a history too that implicates Nathan, who had been for a brief spell Ira's political protégé. The unhappy marriage in this book is that between Ira Ringold, aka Iron Rinn, and Eve Frame, née Chavah Fromkin, and the long dying fall of the relationship takes place between 1948 and 1952, between, that is, Henry Wallace's failed campaign for President under the banner of the Progressive Party and the rise of Senator Joseph McCarthy and the anticommunist witch-hunt. Ringold, a Jewish laborer from Newark, New Jersey, with a heroic physique and a hot temper, has recently become a radio actor, starring on the program *The Free and The Brave*, where, under the name of Iron Rinn, he impersonates Abraham Lincoln and other icons of national adoration. By 1948, Ringold/Rinn, who had once worked in the New Jersey zinc mines and took up the persona of Lincoln in union hall fundraisers, is a radio celebrity married to Eve, a silent-film actress whose career has been on the skids since films began to talk.

Ira and Eve are mismated. Ira is a man of the Left, a Communist Party member, a righteous pontificator, a justice-making machine, and a believer in art as a weapon. "His mind moved all right," remembers his brother, "but not with clarity. It moved with force." Murray elaborates,

"Remember, Ira belonged to the Communist Party heart and soul. Ira obeyed every one-hundred-eighty-degree shift of policy. Ira swallowed the dialectical justification for Stalin's every villainy. Ira backed Browder when Browder was their American messiah, and when Moscow pulled the plug and expelled Browder, and overnight Browder was a class collaborator and a social imperialist, Ira bought it all—backed Foster and the Foster line that America was on the road to fascism."

We are, I think, supposed to take pity on Ira's passionate naiveté without taking him into our hearts, but we pity him as we do Othello, wishing mightily that he'd wise up to that Iago of Iagos, Stalin, and see what was clear to everyone else. His character is a problem for the book, since Roth cuts him no slack, slicing him down to the size of the prefabricated ideas he had picked up from an Army buddy, a Party functionary named Johnny O'Day, who combined revolutionary asceticism with muscle and Marx. Ira is the most unreflective of all Roth's unreflective characters—Swede Levov is Proust in comparison. Ira had come of age politically during the era of the Popular Front, when the Moscow party line was that Communism was Twentieth Century Americanism and consistent with the democratic sentiments of men like Tom Paine and Lincoln. Ira's own formula for action is muscle and Marx, Tom Paine and Lincoln and their heir in progressive thinking, Henry Wallace. In his absolutism he reminds us of the teenage incendiary of *American Pastoral.* In these novels, Roth takes swipes at two generations of Leftists, whom he portrays as victims of their own agitprop vocabularies and dogmatic temperaments. Ira's liberationist's handbook, like Dawn's, is a prison house of language, and when once, during a dinner party, he berates the black maid about the Negro community's failure to support Henry Wallace, the reader joins in praying for his fall to come swiftly. When Ira finally does go down, undermined by his own delusions, his infidelities, and by the book his wife has had ghostwritten for the occasion, *I Married a Communist,* he is a tragic figure in the Shakespearean mold: self-betrayed by a blind and obstinate will. Like Othello, he strikes us as hopelessly stupid, which becomes a problem as the book goes on, because you can't extend sympathy, the reader's version of credit, to someone who is so doggedly clueless.

Ira has another side, and though humanizing it is no more reflective than his politics. It is a weakness for women, and this being a Roth novel, after all, infidelity comes with the territory of marriage. The first is a flutist from London and a friend of Eve's daughter Sylphid named Pamela Solomon, who has a perky sense of adventure and a youthful urge to cast off English decorum for American licentiousness. It doesn't take much for her to vamp Ira, whose marriage has run dry, and they carry on for six months while Ira begs her to run off with him and have his child. Shortly after Pamela calls it off—the strain of being Sylphid's friend and Ira's lover is too much for her—Ira is seduced by his Estonian masseuse, the gold-toothed Helgi Pärn, who is maybe ten or twelve years older than Ira, and, as it will turn out, as larcenous as she is licentious. As Murray tells it, "[She] had that worn, twilight look about her, the sensuous female, rumbling downhill, but her work kept her in shape, kept that big, warm body firm enough." When as part of her massage of Ira, who is badly arthritic, she administers a blow job, Ira discovers yet another wonder of existence that had gone unmentioned by Johnny O'Day, probably because it was missing from Lenin on State and Revolution. Hello!

Eve Frame is not cut out for Browder or Foster or Wallace, let alone Pamela Solomon or Helgi Pärn, both of whom eventually confess their trespasses to Eve under different circumstances. She is a mechanical ingenue, "a spiritual woman with decolletage" and a fastidious aversion to Jewishness, her own in particular. She has a distaste "for the Jew who was insufficiently disguised." Murray Ringold, the Tiresias who saw it all with the compound eyes of a great fly on the Ringold/Frame wall, remembers her to Nathan with a cruel and unsparing intelligence. "She could go along parallel to life for a long time. Not *in* life—parallel to life. She could be quite convincing in that ultra civilized, ladylike role she'd chosen. The soft voice. The precise locution. . . . She knew all the moves, the benign smile, the dramatic reserve, all the delicate gestures. But then she'd veer off that parallel course of hers, the thing that looked so much like life, and there'd be an episode that could leave you spinning."

Like Ira, Eve is masked and inaccessible, but if his mask is the square-jawed face of the earnest proletarian, the Yankee Stakhanovite, acting out a predestined role in the WPA mural of his life, hers is that of the overstated bourgeois, the sea captain's daughter, the lady. Eve Frame despises the Chava Fromkin in herself and has thrown up theatrical disguises to shield herself from the one identity she finds insupportable: the *shayne maydel* from Brooklyn. She had gone to Hollywood not only to seek her fortune but also to do a complete makeover, that sort of de-Judaizing that others would achieve with Ivy League educations. There she married a fellow actor, a silent film star with a pedigree and a noble profile named Carlton Pennington, a member of the polo set who just happened to have more passion for boys than he did for her. And wanting to be rid of her Jewish past, she took Pennington for a social model as well. Only Pennington, as a homosexual, was overplaying the role, camping it, so that Eve learned to pretend a gentile's social graces from a pretender at gentile social grace. So here they are, Ira and Eve, the raw and the cooked, the bohunk and the diva, bound together at first by a desperate sensuality, then by illusion, perplexity, and deception, and finally by the logic of the mortal feud: to strike hard and strike decisively.

Ira, then, is Roth's stick to beat the old Stalinist Left, while Eve Frame is his stick to beat Claire Bloom. And both are Roth's stick to beat the fifties. But what a difference! Although Roth encountered Stalinism sans bullets in Prague and knew its repressions through the lives of his friends, American Stalinism is only a reflex of a history that Roth knows as a bystander and a reader of the liberal anticommunist journals of his time, like *Partisan Review.* The fifties material in this novel may be deeply felt, but it comes across as canned history. Marriage, by contrast, resides in the marrow. Which is why when nitty meets gritty in *I Married a Communist,* it isn't the Red scare that bubbles to the surface like swamp gas, not *Red Channels,* not HUAC, but Eve's daughter with Pennington, Sylphid, who emerges as the Iago of this book. Or, rather, as Goneril and Regan rolled into one, in a version of *King Lear* without a Cordelia. This is the second novel in which the daughter is a bad seed, and we know what this is about.

Sylphid Pennington is an overweight, sardonic, ruthless, and domineering young woman who refuses to leave the maternal nest so long as by staying she can make her mother wretched. She refers to Ira as "the Beast" and accuses her mother of having destroyed her childhood by leaving Pennington, who, despite being gay and parading a string of boys through the house, was a good father! There is no more chilling scene in the book than the one that finds Ira going to Sylphid's room only to find mother and daughter in bed together, "Eve on her back screaming and crying, and Sylphid in her pajamas sitting astride her, also screaming, also crying, her strong harpist's hands pinning Eve's shoulders to the bed. There were bits of paper all over the place—the floor plan for the new apartment—and there, on top of his wife, sat Sylphid, screaming, 'Can't you stand up to *anyone*? Won't you once stand up for your own daughter against him? Won't you be a mother, *ever? Ever?*'"

Do we want to see this? Is something shameful taking place here? If the ex-wife is fair game, especially after she has gone in for the preemptive first strike and failed to knock out her target, is the daughter a fair target as well? It is bootless to ask this of Roth, for whom turning aside wrath is a crime worse than McCarthyism, and the reader either stays on as a guilty coconspirator or puts the book down in a spirit of affronted decency. Privacy? What privacy? In tabloid America, where all is material, closed doors are open invitations, and what is the envious writer of serious fiction to do but press on with the illicit pleasures of exposure and revenge, with all the bile he can muster. In the end, Eve is undone as her book is exposed in *The Nation* as having been ghostwritten and she is revealed to be a Jewish girl from Brownsville, not the sea captain's daughter from New Bedford.

Where does all this go? What does it do? What is it worth? All this furious striving and star-crossed destiny does not lead, I think, to revelation, either for the characters or for the reader. Neither Ira nor Eve at any point stops to conclude: "So that was it all along." The story has the implacability of a tragedy without the flash of insight that usually comes with horror. The novel is resolved in a vision of Nathan Zuckerman, up in rural Connecticut on a starry night, lying on his deck, looking up at the stars, content to not have a story of his own. Contemplating the stars and their great flames of hydrogen, he imagines a place where there is no betrayal. "There is no idealism. There are no falsehoods. There is neither conscience nor its absence. There are no mothers and daughters, no fathers and stepfathers. There are no actors. There is no class struggle." One might be skeptical and say that this is only Roth running his scales, trying out a five minute moderato at the end of his six day furioso, if only to demonstrate that he can do it and that he is not maddened with revenge. And what are we left with at the end of any Roth novel anyway but the prose, a feverish patter that can gear up from Jackie Mason to Henry James or slip into James Joyce overdrive at the drop of a comma? And the rancor. Stars or no stars, that tincture of rancor is the fuel that has always driven Roth's writing. *I Married a Communist* is all prose and rancor, cooked in a fine, clear vitriol, every phrase measured by the milliliter, by the drop, by the atom. Writing well IS the best revenge. Philip Roth has been our resident maestro of rancor since *Goodbye, Columbus* in 1959, and it might seem from this book that he spent the first thirty-eight years just warming up. The starry coda of *I Married a Communist*, with its vision of "the vast brain of time, a galaxy of fire set by no human hand" is a bit spacy compared to the bracing last line of *Sabbath's Theater* where Mickey Sabbath decides not to commit suicide because "Everything he hated was here." Now that's the spirit, but that is the resident spirit of *I Married a Communist* as well: the heat and the turbulence, the pain and the lunacy down here beneath the orbit of the moon.

Second Thoughts

I found *I Married a Communist* a headache to reread. It is among the noisiest of Roth's books, and the uninterrupted rant grows quickly monotonous. The plot disappears, not under the weight of Ira Ringold's tragic destiny or the pile driver of his relentlessness, but drawn under by the concrete shoes of fulmination. Every character hauls around a soapbox, which he puts down anywhere, on the radio, in the union hall, on the corner, in the parlor, in the bedroom. Recall the word "hock," a word associated with Herman Roth in *Patrimony*. *I Married a Communist* is the Mount Everest of hock, the great Himalaya of hock. The waves of indignation that sweep through the novel eventually become the novel. Johnny O'Day fulminates at Ira Ringold; Ira fulminates at anyone in earshot; Nathan Zuckerman's English instructor at Chicago, Leo Glucksman, fulminates at Nathan and Nathan fulminates at his parents; Sylphid fulminates at her mother; her mother fulminates at Ira; Murray Ringold fulminates for six nights at Nathan in the latter's Connecticut retreat, and Nathan passes it on to us, raw, unedited, a juggernaut of woe. Only the Wailing Wall has heard such lamentation, and it is fortunately made of stone. We are less fortunate.

There *are* nuggets to be picked up: this is a Roth novel, and you have to drop your pan into the muck and sluice them out. *I Married a*

Communist may not be Roth's most readable book, but it is among the most quotable, on the subjects of lying, betrayal, revenge, recrimination, power, the daily theater, language, pretense, on talk itself. A wilderness of miscalculations, it is a forest of epigrams. "Occasionally now, looking back," muses Nathan Zuckerman, "I think of my life as one long speech that I've been listening to. The rhetoric is sometimes original, sometimes pleasurable, sometimes pasteboard crap (the speech of the incognito), sometimes maniacal, sometimes matter-of-fact, and sometimes like the sharp prick of a needle, and I have been hearing it for as long as I can remember: how to think, how not to think; how to behave, how not to behave; whom to loath and whom to admire; what to embrace and when to escape; what is rapturous, what is murderous, what is laudable, what is shallow, what is sinister, what is shit, and how to remain pure in soul. Talking to me doesn't seem to present an obstacle to anyone." It is the cacophony of these voices, bearing down not only on Nathan Zuckerman but on us also that is the book's primal music, its ground note, and whatever is appealing in it can't be disentangled from what is infuriating.

It was natural enough to read this book, upon its appearance, as the divorce novel, with all that that entails, from payback to exorcism. Given the circumstances, not to say the story itself, it was impossible not to. But there is a lot more going on in this crepuscular kingdom of Roth's. As always, there is language, and not just language as Roth's elegant and extravagant way of moving the story forward and keeping us riveted to the page, but as the subject itself. It usually is in a Roth novel, though he has taken more and more to calling it to our attention. Nathan Zuckerman hovers between being the audience for Murray Ringold's epic of Ira and recalling the walk-on role he himself played, in his teens, in Ira's life. Nathan had been recruited to liberalism by radio. As a boy he had been enchanted by a radio play, *On a Note of Triumph* by Norman Corwin, who was one of the major innovators in the field of radio drama during radio's Golden Age: wartime and the immediate postwar years. Written to celebrate the allied victory over Germany in 1945, *On a Note of Triumph* was a versified ode to democracy and the common man, the "little guy" who had whipped the German *Übermensch* at his own game: war.[1]

So they've given up.
They're finally done in, and the rat is dead in an alley
      back of the Wilhelmstrasse.
Take a bow, G.I.,
Take a bow, little guy.
The superman of tomorrow lies at the feet of you com-
      mon men of this afternoon.

It was rousing language, and the young Nathan Zuckerman, at the age of twelve, was roused enough to begin writing patriotic radio plays as his first attempts at literature. Late in life he would reflect on that language and its appeals: "It was written in the high colloquial, alliterative style that may have derived in part from Clifford Odets and in part from Maxwell Anderson, from the effort by American playwrights of the twenties and thirties to forge a recognizable native idiom for the stage, naturalistic yet with the lyrical coloration and serious undertones, a poeticized vernacular that, in Norman Corwin's case, combined the rhythms of ordinary speech with a faint literary stiltedness to make for a tone that struck me, at twelve, as democratic in spirit and heroic in scope, the verbal counterpart of a WPA mural." Such language was, Zuckerman goes on, the liturgy of World War II, and as an American child he had been recruited to the American ethos, its democratic idealism, by this poetry of solidarity and manly endeavor.

Lord God of trajectory and blast . . .
Lord God of fresh bread and tranquil morning . . .
Lord God of the topcoat and the living wage . . .
Measure out new liberties . . .
Post proofs that brotherhood . . .
Sit at the treaty table and convoy the hopes of little
      peoples through expected straits . . .

Corwin was the bard of fresh bread and the living wage who brought the dithyrambs of Whitman to the aspirations of the street. "The power of that broadcast!" Zuckerman thinks years later. "There, amazingly, was *soul* coming out of a radio." Later on, when Zuckerman finds himself at the age of sixteen a protégé of Ira Ringold and writing verse dramas, including one about a Catholic family encountering bigotry in a small Protestant town, they are in the form of Corwinized protest drama. "I'm Bill Smith. I'm Bob Jones. I'm Harry Campbell. My name doesn't matter. It's not a name that bothers anyone. I'm white and Protestant, and so you don't have to worry about me." Not until, of course, after sundown when the white sheets and pointy hoods come out.

It was the availability of writing such as Corwin's on radio that aroused Nathan Zuckerman's, and presumably Philip Roth's, infatuation with the spoken word, and of course that brand of verbal impressionism is gone from radio and television forever. Indeed, the window of opportunity for Corwin and the other radio poets was fairly short anyway. Corwin's muse was Popular Front patriotism—behind which stood dogmatic Proletarianism—and the many others who wrote in that tradition of high demotic poetry would never have made it to radio, where a Nathan Zuckerman might encounter them. 1945 was not only the end of the World War but also the twilight of Popular Front camaraderie, when the United States and the Soviet Union were lend-lease allies against the Nazis, and Corwin could write, without looking over his shoulder "This is It, kid, this is The Day, all the way from Newburyport to Vladivostok." By 1946 that camaraderie was in intensive care, and its funeral would be Henry Wallace's run for president on the Progressive Party ticket in 1948.

Behind Corwin lay poets like Edwin Rolfe and Kenneth Patchen and possibly the best of them, Kenneth Fearing, who had all of the makings of a popular writer except access to a public. But, to add a personal note here, the frisson that Nathan Zuckerman feels upon hearing Norman Corwin's *On a Note of Triumph* is more or less what I experience in rereading some of Fearing's more popular and available poems, such as "Dirge" and "Denouement."

Ira Ringold had appealed to Nathan initially through his susceptibility to stirring cadences, by giving him a record of the Soviet Army Chorus and Band singing "Dubinushka," a Russian folk song in praise of the working man. Its words, in English, go like this:

> Many songs have I heard in my native land—
> Songs of joy and sorrow.
> But one of them was deeply engraved in my memory:
> It's the song of the common worker.

Ekh, lift up the cudgel,
Heave-ho!
Pull harder together,
Heave-ho![2]

Sure, this is propaganda, a stirring Comintern-distributed hymn designed to inspire workers to exceed production quotas, and you have to wonder if they played it in the gulags across Siberia. But it was also American depression-era effort-optimism, our own democratic ethos and spirit of Heave-ho! and pull harder together.

Much of the book's appeal as entertainment takes the form of writing that judges its writers. Consider Katrina Van Tassel Grant, a society matron and hostess of the radio program *Van Tassel and Grant* and also a novelist of historical bodice rippers, including one called *Eloise and Abelard.* "His hands clasped about her waist, drawing her to him, and she felt the powerful muscles of his legs. Her head fell back. Her mouth parted to receive his kiss. One day he would suffer castration as a brutal and vengeful punishment for this passion for Eloise, but for now he was far from mutilated." It gets zanier. She cries out, "Now teach me, please. Teach me, Pierre! Explain to me your dialectical analysis of the mystery of God and the Trinity." This he does, after which he takes her as a woman for the eleventh time. Heave-ho! We don't need an editorial by Murray Ringold to tell us that this is a homegrown American *poshlust* that reveals a politics of its own: one as far from Ira Ringold's Proletarianism as Peter Abelard's dialectics are from Nikolai Lenin's.

As for Eve Frame's "as told to" denunciation of Ira, ghostwritten by Bryden and Katrina Van Tassel Grant, it is written to rule.

How can I possibly consider it my moral and patriotic duty to inform on a man I loved as much as I loved Iron Rinn?

Because as an American actress I have sworn myself to fight the Communist infiltration of the entertainment industry with every fiber of my being. Because as an American actress I have a solemn responsibility to an American audience that has given me so much love and recognition and happiness, a solemn and unshakable responsibility to reveal and expose the extent of the Communist grip in the broadcasting industry that I came to know through the man I was married to, a man I loved more than any man I have ever known, but a man who was determined to use the weapon of mass culture to tear down the American way of life.

He was my man, but he done America wrong. Anyone who was around in the 1950s would recognize that as the prose of countless testimonies drawn up in law offices by the attorneys of frightened clients who had been called to testify before the House Un-American Activities Committee. Its tragic survivor was Elia Kazan, its canary was Harvey Matusow, its Flaubert Whittaker Chambers, its fallen soldiers the Hollywood Ten. Chambers alone would not have stooped to a phrase like "fiber of my being."

The protagonists die: Eve in a drunken stupor in a Manhattan hotel room; Ira of heart failure in Zinc Town, where he has wound up in a rock shop, selling minerals by the bag. Murray Ringold's wife is murdered on the streets of Newark, where they are the last white couple on a Black street, and Murray himself does not long outlast his disburdening to Nathan Zuckerman. Only Zuckerman remains, cocooned in his cottage monastery in the Connecticut countryside. Roth offers no consolations here, least of all the consolation of human attachment. This is beyond the "hell is other people" of Sartre's *No Exit;* hell is also oneself. And is that not also a fanaticism, the fanaticism of retreat, decontamination, self-absolution, and self-reliance? "What are you warding off?" Murray asks Zuckerman as he leaves. "What the hell happened?" Roth, it would seem, is not yet finished with fanatics, only fanatics with dreams, with hope, with blueprints for self-improvement and social reform. A fanaticism of disillusionment is still a live option, and *I Married a Communist* is its "Dubinushka," its *On a Note of Triumph.*

17

The Psychopathology of Everyday Life

The Human Stain

The inauthentic Negro is not only estranged from whites—he is also estranged from his own group and from himself. Since his companions are a mirror in which he sees himself as ugly, he must reject them; and since his own self is mainly a tension between an accusation and a denial, he can hardly find it, much less live in it. . . . He is adrift without a role in a world predicated on roles.

Anatole Broyard, "Portrait of the Inauthentic Negro"

So here is a man who passed for white because he wanted to be a writer and he did not want to be a Negro writer. It is a crass disjunction, but it is not his crassness or his disjunction. His perception was perfectly correct. He *would* have had to be a Negro writer, which was something he did not want to be. In his terms, he did not want to write about black love, black passion, black suffering, black joy; he wanted to write about love and passion and suffering and joy. We give lip service to the idea of the writer who happens to be black, but had anyone, in the postwar era, ever seen such a thing?

Henry Louis Gates, "The Passing of Anatole Broyard"

Philip Roth's next novel of cultural crisis and human dysfunction, *The Human Stain,* carries his ongoing exploration of will-as-tragedy into the country of "race, class, and gender," the politically correct American academy, where the most hideous collisions are known to take place over the most trivial provocations—where, as Woodrow Wilson is supposed to have said, the battles are so vicious because there is so little at stake. This novel fills out a trilogy of tragic America that he kicked off with *American Pastoral* and continued with *I Married a Communist.* Roth specializes in the jaundiced eye and the sour cud and extends the line of H. L. Mencken, Mark Twain, and P. T. Barnum in depicting America as the land of the booboisie and the realm beyond good and evil that pretends to be the embodiment of the moral life it has lost. Only he doesn't play this situation these days for laughs. There is a comedy to *The Human Stain* but few laughs. The *comédie humaine* that Roth is dealing in, the inexhaustible human capacity for humiliation and damage, can be decidedly bleak.

This is old territory for Roth—his burned-over district. It was forty years ago, in an essay titled "Writing American Fiction," that he confessed to being stupefied by reality. "The daily newspapers," he wrote, "fill us with wonder and awe (is it possible? is it happening?), also with sickness and despair. The fixes, the scandals, the insanity, the idiocy, the piety, and lies, the noise." The fiction writer may be horrorstruck by the day's headlines, but can he compete with them? Forty years later, Roth has come back to the headlines, to the media thunder of Bill and Monica and the telltale stain, in a world grown savage with piety. *The Human Stain* carries his perennial astonishment at the national capacity for idiocy, piety, and lies into the halls of poison ivy, the American academy, which has swallowed whole the apple of political correctness.

Roth's victim-hero this time is a classics professor and dean, one Coleman Silk, a pedantic and tight-assed administrator who also teaches Greek literature at Athena College, somewhere in New England. To all appearances he is a success and a man of substance: a dean, a husband, a father of four children, and a figure of distinction in an otherwise lackluster college. His achievements at Athena, so far as we are told, consist of having weeded out academic deadwood on the way to becoming deadwood himself. Of his publications or intellectual convictions, we haven't a clue. He's Mr. Chips. He also lives something of a half-life, harboring a secret from not only his colleagues and students but also from his family. Silk is a Black man—whatever that can possibly mean in the case of someone whom all see as white—who has spent his adult life passing for Jewish. His children are indeed curious about their lack of relatives on their father's side, but he has covered his tracks so cunningly that nothing ever comes out to embarrass him on that score. (And what was Silk in the Old Country? Silberzweig, he tells his family.) *The Human Stain* is pretty much a moral romance, a *Scarlet Letter* about race, and all we can do is grant the premises and see what Roth does with them.

What Roth does is blow his man sky high for the sin of passing. In taking roll in class one day he remarks on two students who have never appeared for class, and asks, "Does anyone know these people? Do they exist or are they spooks?" "Spook" is one of the magic words, and everybody knows that, except perhaps a man who has grown so remote from his origins—unto complete separation from his own mother—that he has forgotten which taboos can't be violated. Silk writes and stars in his own Greek tragedy, and the furies that hound him from the college are all rolled into one Professor Delphine Roux, a self-exalted feminist, a French poststructuralist, and a distracted woman who writes personals ads to *The New York Review of Books* and accidentally e-mails them to her colleagues. (Talk about Freud's "psychopathology of everyday life"! Couldn't Spielvogel get an article out of her?) In short, she's a bitch. Coleman Silk is denounced as a racist and is obliged to retire from Athena College. At seventy-one, he should have been easing into retirement anyway, without having to walk the gangplank. The crisis kills his wife Iris, and in his vexation he turns to the local novelist—Nathan Zuckerman—in the hopes of getting his story told and the record set straight. So, the man gets his first scarlet letter, which he has to wear across campus: a red "R" for Racist.

The reclusive Zuckerman, now hors de combat from life, impotent from prostate surgery, and living an asocial and womanless life, has lately become an ear on life for those who seek him out to tell their stories of woe and betrayal. He's become a kind of backwoods Ann Landers. Zuckerman takes a liking to his stricken informant, with whom he shares a fondness for the music of the 1940s and with whom he dances one lonely night in his cottage in the Berkshire countryside. Zuckerman becomes the Greek chorus to Silk's downfall, which is nudged along by Delphine Roux and by Silk's own inner furies. Rejuvenated by Viagra, Silk takes up with a woman half his age, a janitor at the college and a part-time farmhand, Faunia Farley, who comes equipped with her own blues in the night: she is illiterate to the point of being unable to read a menu, and her children died in a fire while she was outside giving someone a blow job in the front seat of a truck. It takes no time for Delphine Roux to unleash a venomous memo: "Everyone knows you're sexually exploiting an abused, illiterate woman half your age." Second scarlet letter: "E" for Exploiter. Nor does it take long for Faunia Farley's ex-husband, Les, a crazed Vietnam vet and a helicopter door gunner for whom every day is a firefight, to vow to kill the Jew who is dating his ex. His third letter: "J" for Jew. Move over Hester Prynne; you're only a novice at infamy. This is Hawthorne country, and this New England community has street corner transgression alarms the way some towns have fire alarms. They're on this guy like white on rice.

In the background is the daily Bill and Monica extravaganza. Indignation has become to the nation's emotional life what day trading is to its economic life. It is the summer of 1998, the summer of impeachment, and America is on "an enormous piety binge, a purity binge." The president has been getting blow jobs by a Jewish intern from Beverly Hills, and the bill has come due. Get blown and get blown away. It's all remarkably biblical.

Roth has dealt himself a full hand here, and the success of the novel depends on how he plays it. Roth goes Sophocles to the max and plays it dark, dark, dark, and agonistic. Looking for plot, for characters, the reader has to machete his way through rain forests of woeful beseeching and violent denunciation in voices that sound uncommonly alike. They're all Nathan Zuckerman's puppets after all, and he, of all people, can "do" injury and indignation. He's the Mel Blanc of piss-off. Coleman Silk rages, Delphine Roux rages, Les Farley rages, and America rages over the president's self-indulgence. There is a line—a none-too-fine one—between making indignation your subject and making it your muse, so that reprimanding and pontificating are all your characters can do. Roth can occasionally make it work. His send-up of Delphine Roux's "all encompassing chic" and "École Normale sophistication" will delight anyone who has spent five minutes in the academy, if only because Roth has been around universities and can easily mimic the languages of academic flim flam. But he hasn't a clue about Les Farley, who is Brand-X Vietnam Vet, all shattered nerves and tripwire aggression, or Faunia Farley, who is generic lower class, complete with childhood molestation, adult abuse, and goatish sexuality. Of course, overscale

eroticism is a Roth trademark, and everybody is either Priapus or Vo-
luptas, unless a gland is missing, as turns out to be the case with Nathan
Zuckerman.

As for Coleman Silk, Roth tries earnestly to model him from the inside: to show how his life is propelled by his traumas. He is given a history and a résumé of significant moments, with his parents, his boxing
coaches, and with women in the Village. But there isn't enough inside
to give him the ridges and contours of a full character. He has a Ph.D.
in classics and he reads Greek and Latin, sure, but what does he think
about with his gigawatt powerplant of a brain? He begins, and remains,
a reflex of his history, a man devoted mainly to denying, reversing, pro-
jecting, sublimating, blaming, erupting, and general amnesia. He is a
walking compendium of the mechanisms of defense, and the reader is
left wondering how this banality rose to such a station in life and then
deserved all this persecution and grief on the way down. The academic
in me wants to say that his vacancy is in keeping with his station: you
become a dean by going through the motions, keeping your head down,
and keeping your passion and originality on a short leash. Do that for
twenty years and you'll rise to the level of your incompetence. But Roth,
I suspect, sees the deanship as a genuine merit badge.

Roth modeled Silk in part on former *New York Times* book editor
Anatole Broyard, who also passed and kept his family at a distance,
though to read a line of Broyard and a line of Coleman Silk's interior
monologues is to know what is the matter with Silk.[1] "Broyard's col-
umns," wrote Henry Louis Gates about him after his death, "were suf-
fused with both worldliness and high culture. Wry, mandarin, even self-
amused at times, he wrote like a man about town, but one who just
happened to have all of Western literature at his fingertips. Always, he
radiated an air of soigné self-confidence: he could be amiable in his
opinions or waspish, but he never betrayed a flicker of doubt about what
he thought. This was a man who knew that his judgment would never
falter and his sentences never fail him."[2] Not only was Broyard a sea-
soned and passionate book reviewer, but in his late books, *Intoxicated by
My Illness* and *Kafka Was the Rage,* he wrote with pungency and wit
about those things in his own life that he could openly acknowledge.
Coleman Silk knows his own life only through the fogs of indignation
and grief, the fog of self-intoxication, the fog of self-loathing, the fog of

self-misunderstanding, the fog of occluded desire, the fog of self-forgetfulness. Lacking the benefit of Roth's own perceptual sniper scope and Broyard's omnivorous intelligence, Coleman Silk comes across as a pasteboard college professor, clever enough to teach literature but not interesting enough to be literature.

Second Thoughts: The Resurrection of Deadwood Dick

As I was writing this, I learned that a friend at another college, one that bears a resemblance in size to Roth's Athena College, had gotten himself into hot water by assigning one of Roth's novels, *The Dying Animal,* for a junior qualifying exam. That novel, about faculty-student sex, disturbed some of the female students, who complained to sympathetic women faculty. "Do they secretly wish to sleep with their female students?" asked one student of the all-male committee that made up the exam. This being a more forgiving environment than Athena College, and my friend being on better terms with his colleagues than Coleman Silk is with his, nothing came of it. But when I told him of the coincidence of my writing about *The Human Stain* when I heard about his brush with feminist vigilantism, he responded, "I think *The Human Stain* may be Roth's best novel, along with *American Pastoral.* I especially loved his hit on the 'Normalienne.' He gets that just right. I was amazed he has such a discerning nose for the academic stench."

I found *The Human Stain* a perplexing book, even stranger on a second reading. Roth, it seems to me, is onto things that cut far deeper than the academic stench or the American piety binge, but they get lost in the bombast and soapboxing. One is the utter elusiveness of Coleman Silk himself, who is as responsible for his own catastrophe as Ira Ringold is for his, only he has something that Ira lacks: the rough contour of an inner life that compels him to make a late-life botch of all that he has painstakingly built up to hide himself from himself. It would not have been lost on Roth, that old Freudian, that in uttering the word "spooks" when he did, Silk meant just what everyone thought he meant. If ever there was a classic return of the repressed, there it is. (Broyard, we learn from Gates, was prone to making remarks about "spades.") Why? Silk was dying to be found out, and if he had to smash his life to do it, well, at his age, with the children gone and alienated, his wife indifferent to him if not outright hostile, his sexual potency in the deep freeze, his colleagues whispering in corners, his lies grown rank and horrible in his own ears, and with himself become the Deadwood Dick of his college, wasn't it time to step out of the shadows and kill off the old life? The book makes scant sense unless Coleman's Silk's self-demolition is undertaken with a pure and burning will. With a raging fire in the belly. The game is pretty well given up at the moment when his lawyer gives him the perfectly sensible advice to stay away from Faunia Farley, and Silk responds, "I never again want to hear that self-admiring voice of yours or see your smug fucking lily-white face." Lily white? Some reflective narrative voice—is this Zuckerman?— drops the clue: "How one is revealed or undone by the perfect word. What burns away the camouflage and the covering and the concealment. This, the right word uttered spontaneously, without one's even having to think." And so after leaving the lawyer's office, Silk decides to take a last look at Athena College, thinking, "One last look at Athena, and then let the disgrace be complete."

That's part of it, the Schadenfreude: the strategic slip of the tongue in a time of weakness and need. But Coleman Silk also wants to be restored to the last vital time, when he was most himself, Silky Silk, the smart, tough cookie from East Orange, New Jersey, and the star pupil in Doc Chizner's boxing class at the Newark Boys Club, who went 11–0 as an amateur before his father made him stop. He had sweet moves: he could slip a punch and control the ring and he could bang. It was the high time of his life, and to the dismay of his parents, he took on the toughest of Newark and beat them. He remembers visiting the University of Pittsburgh with Doc Chizner to fight a college boxer, whom he creamed with a hook to the gut, to "the labonz," folding the guy up like a suitcase. It was the last honest time as well, when he could float like a butterfly and sting like a bee; everything since has been holding and grabbing, masquerade and manners, and Silk has elected to reclaim as an old man what he gave up at seventeen.

Later, after the war, while living in the Village and taking classes at NYU, he turns pro and wins four fights, before hanging them up. His promoter wants him to carry an opponent and give the fans their money's worth: "You could have stopped the nigger in the fourth round instead of the first and gave the people their money's worth." Asked why, Silk answers, "Because I don't carry no nigger." The mask is already being fitted for size; the dishonesty is becoming routine; the illness is in the blood stream, and he obeys the rule laid down by Doc Chizner: "If nothing comes up, you don't bring it up." At first, studying, picking up women, passing for white, and making his own life is all so easy for him. "What was supposed to be hard and somehow shaming or destructive was not only easy but without consequences, no price paid at all." Until, that is, he takes his deception right into marriage with Iris Gittelman and has to go home to tell his mother that he will never see her again and she may not see her grandchildren, unless she agrees to sit silently at the zoo or the train station while he parades by with them. His brother phones him afterwards and orders him to never show his "lily-white face around that house again."

What goes on, then, between Coleman Silk and his students, between him and his lawyer, between him and Delphine Roux, and between him and Les Farley follows the inexorable unraveling of his own rage and self-loathing. He wants to come roaring out of his corner and deliver a shot to the labonz, he wants to be Silky Silk again: the Sugar Ray Robinson he might have been. His legs are gone and his reflexes are shot, but what the hell? What goes on between himself and Faunia Farley is no less primal. He wants to get laid. Viagra has restored him to life as a man, and nothing will stand in the way of his sexual rejuvenation. And who, outside of Athena College and the small gossipy town in which it exists, can fault him for that? The man wants energy, and he is heedless of the cost.

Is Roth too quick in turning this situation to tragedy? From what we know, Broyard carried off his masquerade, though his background wasn't exactly secret to those who knew him in his Village days. Nevertheless, he kept his children in the dark and it was not until after his death in 1990 that his children learned their father's secret.[3] Broyard's early life conforms in many of its details to Coleman Silk's, including his denial of his family in order to forge a separate identity, having been a boxer and a womanizer in his youth, and wanting to step outside of the "we," the prison house of race, to spring afresh from his own brow, to be, as he put it in *Kafka Was the Rage,* an orphan of the avant-garde. Broyard's chances of becoming a freelance intellectual at liberty to write as he chose, at the time he began his career as a writer, would certainly have been blocked by his race: he would have had to be a "Negro writer," a James Baldwin or Ralph Ellison, and been expected to reflect on the "Negro experience," something he did not wish to do. Could Coleman Silk, starting out in the 1940s, have become a professor of classics in an America hysterical about race? I know of no instances of that, and it is plain that a man with a calling to teach Homer or Virgil or the great Greek tragedians during an era when the one-drop rule was as firm in the North as anything Jim Crow had devised in the South, had to choose, either to surrender his ambitions or dissemble his identity, grateful that the unpredictable lottery of melanism among people of mixed blood gave him the opportunity to live out his dreams. The word "passing" carries with it a moral implication of illegitimacy and deviousness, even selling out, while "living out one's dreams" carries a different moral weight, implying courage, fearlessness, guts. That Roth plays Coleman Silk's choice as both a social tragedy and a tragedy of character is hardly out of bounds: what is this but a tragic situation?

Yet there is no simple equivalence between Coleman Silk's repressing his past and Ira Ringold and Merry Levov's signing up to become ideological dray horses for anti-American crusades. There is a world of difference. Silk's real world prototype, Broyard, got away clean professionally. And he was trying to be an American, an ordinary American, living up to his full human potential. We can't know what price he paid personally for his imposture, though the stories told by Gates of his touchiness on the subject of race do not suggest that he was entirely easy in his skin. Or rather, in the fictions he created about his skin. And yet, for all that, the possibility of breaking free of your past, making your own destiny, and claiming your unique "I," unbounded by the demands and expectations of a "we," is still the great American myth, and for that reason, among many others, Broyard's story holds more fascination than Coleman Silk's. It has layers to it, dimensions; there was a real intellectual life, a formidable social presence, and a lifetime of essays and reviews that made a mark on their time. Broyard whitewashed his past in order to join the ranks of the downtown intellectuals, the Village avant-garde, and he made good on this awesome gambit. He was anything but Mr. Chips, and *New York Times* editor M. L. Rosenthal once complained, "The trouble with Broyard is that he writes with his cock!" Gates shows us, in a spirit of astonishment, just how intellectual passing can work: how high the bar is, what sacrifices are required, and how much tenacity is demanded. The difference between his portrait and Roth's is not one of holding out hope, but of seeing the situation without pity and terror, either Aristotle's or Roth's.

Finally, a word about Delphine Roux and the academic stench. There is no mistaking the Eve Frame/Merry Levov figure of this book—that is, the consummate Lilith. It is Delphine Roux who lowers the boom on Coleman Silk, who sends him a menacing note, and who finally, on the night of his death, fakes an office break-in to explain her personals letter being sent to the department listserv. Yet she is more vivid than either of her predecessors and more fascinating, at least to this reader, than Colemen Silk. Roth devotes considerable attention to her intellectual life, which he regards as of a piece with her malice and skullduggery. Delphine Roux is French born and French educated, right up through that elite of elites, the École Normale Supérieure, from which she graduates to Yale and a Ph.D. With such a background, and a Ph.D. dissertation on Georges Bataille ("Self-Denial in Georges Bataille"), she is mortified to have landed in a backwater like Athena, where there are neither colleagues nor students to challenge her nor interesting men to satisfy her socially and sexually. By the time she is chair at twenty-nine and brimming with intellectual self-conceit, she has identified Coleman Silk as *her* version of deadwood, and a sexist to boot. When a student complains that the plays of Euripides taught by Silk, *Hippolytus* and *Alcestis*, are "degrading to women," she takes up the student's case with Silk. As they talk, Silk sizes her up in elaborate detail.

> It isn't difficult to understand what she intends for him to understand, especially as Coleman knows something of Paris from being a young professor with family on a Fulbright one year, and knows something about these ambitious French kids trained in the elite lycées. Extremely well prepared, intellectually well connected, very smart immature young people endowed with the most snobbish French education and vigorously preparing to be envied all their lives, they hang out every Saturday night at the cheap Vietnamese restaurant on Rue St. Jacques talking about great things, never any mention of trivialities or small talk—ideas, politics, philosophy only. Even in their spare time, when they are all alone, they think only about the reception of Hegel in twentieth-century French intellectual life. The intellectual must not be frivolous. Life only about thought. Whether brainwashed to be aggressively

Marxist or to be aggressively anti-Marxist, they are congenitally appalled by everything American.

There is a sexual forcefield around Coleman Silk and Delphine Roux, but it is played out in intellectual terms, whose latest moves Roux has down cold: that we all speak in gendered language and that the undergraduate, Miss Mitnick, has been affronted by Silk's masculinist perspective. "Coleman," offers Roux, "you've been out of the classroom for a very long time."

"And you haven't been out of it ever. . . . I've been reading and thinking about these plays all my life."

"But never from Elena's feminist perspective."

"Never from Moses's Jewish perspective. Never even from the fashionable Nietzschean perspective about perspective."

If her pedagogical feminism is just old-fashioned careerism, Silk tells her, it's fine with him. That's human and he can understand it. "But if it's an intellectual commitment to this idiocy, then I am mystified, because you are not an idiot." Meanwhile, she has him pegged as a bland and tedious humanist, and she warns, "If you insist on taking the so-called humanist approach to Greek tragedy you've been taking since the 1950s, conflicts like this are going to arise continuously."

Yes, there is a subtext, and it will turn out that Roux's feminism is infused with sexual jealousy, that her vicious turn against Coleman Silk over his affair with Faunia Farley seems to contain no small bit of pettiness and injured vanity. And gendered language.

If there is a parallel to the Stalinism of *I Married a Communist* and the Maoism of *American Pastoral*, it is here, in the French-fried feminism of *The Human Stain*. Not only does it contribute petulant and opaque interpretations of literature—imposing on it the intransigent party line of the historically aggrieved and theoretically armored subaltern—but it also is not hesitant to strike hard at men who rise to object, since, after all, millennia of domination back to the days of *Australopithecus* cry out for payback, and Coleman Silk is merely the poor doofus who gets socked in the labonz for hauling around that threadbare banner of the broad and tolerant humanism in whose name he had given up half of his life and in whose defense he lost the rest as well.

18

Death and the Maiden
The Dying Animal

People think that in falling in love they make themselves whole?
The Platonic union of Souls? I think otherwise. I think you're
whole before you begin. And the love fractures you. You're whole
and then you're cracked open.
George O'Hearn, from The Dying Animal

Gib deine Hand, du schön und zart Gebild,
Bin Freund und komme nicht zu strafen.
Sei gutes Muts! Ich bin nicht wild,
Sollst sanft in meinen Armen schlafen.
Franz Schubert, "Death and the Maiden"

Think about it. Think. Because if you go, you're finished.
The Dying Animal

There was no way to predict this book; there were no warning signs.
Just as there had been no way to foresee, in 1969, that Philip Roth, author of two leaden novels and a volume of precocious stories, would
drop *Portnoy's Complaint* on us. There was no way to know that the
writer of the last three novels—*American Pastoral, I Married a Communist,* and *The Human Stain*—would, at age sixty-seven, come forth with
a scamless little book. The others could generate ferocious heat, but
they could also be saturnine and pontificating for long stretches. Over
the course of a long and illustrious career, Philip Roth has produced five
books that I regard as essential reading for anyone wanting to know

what a modern writer can do with intelligence, tender nerves, a mutinous heart, a profound seriousness about life, art, and sex, and a fascination with bedrock experiences. They would be *Portnoy's Complaint, The
Ghost Writer, Patrimony, Sabbath's Theater,* and now *The Dying Animal.*

Sex is Roth's home territory, and for over forty years he has hoisted
its flag over his own private Iwo Jima, plumbed its obsessions, and
struggled to domesticate it for fiction, though as he demonstrated in
Sabbath's Theater, sex is not made for domesticity. And as he concedes in
The Dying Animal, in a voice both insurrectionary and disconsolate, sex
won't be domesticated. *The Dying Animal* is a distillation of all he has
learned about sex and freedom, and it is a long way from being a sunny
communiqué on how blessed we would be if only we could have more
and better. *The Dying Animal* does for Wilhelm Reich and *The Function
of the Orgasm* what *I Married a Communist* did for Karl Marx and the
workers' paradise, for "Dubinushka." The hero of *The Dying Animal,*
David Kepesh, may be the rabbi of more and better, but he is also a prisoner of sex, chained up for life in the foulest dungeon of eros.

If Nathan Zuckerman is Roth's alter-ego as a storyteller, Kepesh is
the alter-id. We first met him in the novella *The Breast,* in which a college professor, in a parody of Franz Kafka's "The Metamorphosis," is
transformed overnight into a man-sized female breast. He later appeared as a neophyte of eros and culture in the novel *The Professor of Desire.* In *The Dying Animal* he is the Ancient Mariner of heartache, plying us with the story of his fall from erotic grace. A typically Rothian
sort of pushme-pullyou, he is the discriminating id: a culture pundit on
New York televison and a university professor, whose course on Practical Criticism packs in the female students. Kepesh's intellectual glamour and celebrity attracts them, and being vulnerable to female beauty,
he will mutter to himself about one of them, "You are my meat, young
lady," and often enough she is. Here we have the dynamic Roth dual-
ism: a thick personal culture and the psychology of unobstructed need,
the standard paleface-redskin package.

That life seems idyllic enough until the sixty-two-year-old Kepesh
falls for Consuela Castillo, the daughter of Cuban émigrés, who, at
twenty-four, has a haute-monde bearing that sets her apart from fellow students. "She has a cream-colored silk blouse under a tailored
blue blazer with gold buttons, a brown pocketbook with the patina of

expensive leather, and little ankle boots to match, and she wears a slightly stretchy gray knitted skirt that reveals her body lines as subtly as such a skirt possibly could. Her hair is done in a natural but cared-for manner. She has a pale complexion, the mouth is bowlike though the lips are full, and she has a rounded forehead, a polished forehead of a smooth Brancusi elegance." And, oh yes, "The silk blouse is unbuttoned to the third button, and so you see she has powerful, beautiful breasts." She is his meat, and soon after the semester's end the professor of desire and his "masterpiece of volupté" are locked in a stealthy affair. She doesn't want to appear a groupie or to show up before graduation on page six of the *New York Post,* and he has another woman. What's in it for her? All that awesome culture. He shows her Kafka manuscripts, the paintings of Velázquez. From his CD collection he courts her with Beethoven and Dvořák. At his own piano, he serenades her with Chopin preludes. For him? Those breasts. Fair exchange? I've heard of worse deals.

When has age not been infatuated with youth? Recall Gustav von Aschenbach's infatuation with the gorgeous Tadzio in Thomas Mann's *Death in Venice* and Professor Unrat's hopeless love for his Lola in Heinrich Mann's *The Blue Angel.* It brings unbearable torment, and at the age of seventy, Kepesh laments, "From the evening we first went to bed eight years back, I never had a moment's peace. . . . I was all weakness and worry from then on." The affair continues for a year and a half, until graduation. Then, because he has bailed out on her graduation party, this contemporary woman announces her farewell by *fax.*

It is the special magic of Roth's writing at its most intense that the jealousy and humiliation, the helplessness and fear, trigger storms of self-reflection, and Kepesh, true to his profession, spins out brilliant summaries. He courts us with stirring lectures on masculine helplessness, on marriage, on the insolent anarchy and gleeful debauchery of the sixties, on aging, on Thomas Morton, the presiding spirit over the seventeenth-century settlement at Merry Mount, where sexual license was the rule; on his own forty-two-year-old son, captive to both a sterile marriage and to the next wife, whom he is already out recruiting. Kepesh becomes that most pitiable and engaging of male figures: the clown of vanity. As the walking handbook of libertinism, he can out Polonius Polonius, though his outpourings of intellectualized grief are razor-sharp and desperation-vivid. A martyr to sexual obsession, he is also a virtuoso of self-exculpation. He is the Yo-Yo Ma of alibi. He eats his heart out and makes intellectual canapés of the leftovers.

We slowly become aware that there is another in the room, to whom he is brilliantly justifying this shambles. The analyst? The Dr. Spielvogel of *Portnoy's Complaint*? And he hammers away at his self-celebrating and self-mortifying recollections precisely as he hammers away at the piano: with an obstinate and mechanical zealotry. After Consuela has decamped, "I played all thirty-two Beethoven sonatas during those years, every note of them to drive Consuela out of my thoughts. . . . I played the Mozart sonatas. I played Bach's piano music. I played it, I'm familiar with it, which is a different thing from playing it well. I played Elizabethan pieces by Byrd. . . . I played Purcell. I played Scarlatti. I have all the Scarlatti sonatas, all five hundred and fifty of them. I won't say I played all of them, but I played a lot of them." When all that culture is not needed for seduction, then it is available as an anodyne for heartbreak. There is something decidedly scary about a fellow who pours out his heart obsessively in music and testimony for almost seven years, until the day Consuela calls again, in distress.

At a certain point with such a book, one lets go of the plot, which for Roth these days is only a means to his end anyway: to grab us by the sleeve. Sometimes his panhandler's insistence can be frightening, as it was occasionally in the previous books, but here, Roth makes an art of the lecture. "I'm a critic, I'm a teacher—didacticism is my destiny," protests Kepesh to his silent listener. "Argument and counter argument is what history's made of." I find myself not very interested in how the love story turns out, since it was never really there except as misery. But Kepesh has a decision to make, and a nameless interlocutor, to whom Kepesh is speaking at two in the morning, pipes up at last: "If you go, you're finished." We too have a stake in his decision: the possible end to these stirring arias by this Don Giovanni emeritus. But hey, the guy is seventy, and at that age, who needs prudence? So go, Bubbele, go. At worst she'll break your heart again, and you've got all that Scarlatti left to play.

Second Thoughts

I've had trouble believing in the reality of the busty Consuela Castillo, perhaps because I have enough Cuban friends whose lives are so highly particularized for me that Roth's rendition of one struck me as little more than a pair of sensational breasts—generic for the human species—and a compliant Latin nature out of 1940s pop music. Remember the Andrews Sisters' "Rum and Coca Cola," in which both mother and daughter are "workin' for the Yankee dollar"? So I was hardly surprised that Cuban friends have told me that Consuela is not a proper Cuban woman's name at all and that it should have been Consuelo. It may seem strange to those of us with enough high school Spanish to know that masculine nouns end in -o and feminine ones in -a: hijo, hija, hermano, hermana, etcetera. And so it seems that in this case that Roth was working out of his Spanish grammar books rather than his actual knowledge of Cuban women since, indeed, Consuelo is the common Spanish female name. If you doubt this, ask a Cuban, or, lacking that, log onto your web browser and do a Google search for Consuela, and you will be prompted, "Did you mean to search for *'Consuelo'*?"

ᷱ

The Dying Animal was not the book that most book reviewers wanted Roth to write. They were expecting another of his acid dissertations on the American heart of darkness and were dismayed to find in this book a backsliding into the merely personal. I read these chiding reviews with a certain malicious amusement, since the book seems designed to elicit them. Michiko Kakutani, in the *New York Times:* "In this slight and disappointing novel, [Kepesh] has been reduced to a shallow, sex-obsessed narcissist who 'took a hammer' not just to bourgeois covenants but also to his own life and the lives of those around him. As a result, it's difficult for the reader to ratify his sudden apprehension of mortality, much less sympathize with his loneliness and isolation."[1] Gail Caldwell, in *The Boston Globe:* "Why must brilliant men sometimes be so stupid about women? It's hard to know whether this charge should be leveled at Kepesh or his creator, since Roth provides little authorial distance from his miserable character. But the failure is really one of the imagination: If women are simply fallow fields to be claimed, then sown, how compelling can that story finally be?"[2] Noting all this, Ronald Bush, reviewing the book for *Tikkun*, wrote, "Philip Roth must have known he would be pummeled for this brief, ambiguous, and disturbing sequel to his acclaimed three-volume social history of post-war America—*American*

Pastoral, I Married a Communist, and *The Human Stain. The Dying Animal'*s reversion to private, male sexual preoccupations goes out of its way to reinforce public stereotypes about Roth's previous work."³

I have the sense the Roth's own publisher, Houghton Mifflin, was taken by surprise, to judge from the blurbs selected for the dust jacket. They are worth quoting, because of their attempt to spin Roth in a way that a publisher with a heavy investment would want him spun. "A master chronicler of the American twentieth century"—*Commonweal.* "Beginning with *American Pastoral* in 1997, them moving on in 1998 with *I Married a Communist* and continuing [in 2000] with *The Human Stain,* Philip Roth has engaged himself in a patriotic literary project that has no contemporary match in any field: not in the movies, not in music, certainly not in the work of any other novelist. . . . With political sympathies that could not be more different, Roth's project has in a sense emerged from the wreckage of the Gingrich revolution: a rediscovery of what it means to be American, an exploration of what it means both to invent a country and, as a moral citizen who in some way embodies the country, to invent oneself. . . . [The trilogy is] Roth's version of Dos Passos' *U.S.A.*"—Greil Marcus, *Threepenny Review.* A moral citizen who in some way embodies the country! Roll over Irving Howe, tell Podhoretz the news! And not a word anywhere about breasts or how a grown man might squander his life for them. One might well guess what is going on here: damage control, a makeshift grooming of Roth in the event that his name comes up in Sweden, in nomination for the Nobel Prize. After the American trilogy, Roth indeed stood in peril of being taken for an exemplary nationalist and patriot, a keeper of the moral flame: a Twain, a Dos Passos, a Steinbeck. Only Roth, having laid out the terms for adulation of this kind, clearly wasn't having any of it. If the Nobel was going to come his way, the King of Sweden was going to have to swallow some bitter pills first. How much easier it was for the committee to award the prize to V. S. Naipaul, *Sir* V. S. Naipaul at that! It may yet come to Roth; it should, but not at the price of his being Steinbecked, Twained, and Dos Passosed, face-lifted to look like an avuncular old curmudgeon who went through a bad insurrectionary patch in his youth but got it turned around in the end. Roth may yet become a poster boy for intellectual rehab—that crowded field—but I'm grateful for the moment that he discarded that script to play instead the dirty old man. He isn't ready just yet to sell War Bonds. Roth still writes with his cock and he's not ready to tuck it away.

But then, what is more American than sex? Roth does make sure that getting laid can claim both the Declaration of Independence and the Constitution and at least a smattering of the founding fathers, if only the history books could get it right. Kepesh, in a history lecture that he can't give on public television, recalls the impact that the sexual revolution of the 1960s had upon him as a college teacher (at some institution decidedly more cosmopolitan than Athena College), where one Janie Wyatt, the college's "dirty diva" and ringleader of a group that called itself Janie's Gutter Girls, wrote her senior thesis for him, titled "A Hundred Ways to Be Perverse in the Library." Its opening sentence reads, "The blow job in the library is the very essence of it, the sanctified transgression, the sanctified black mass." He doesn't risk telling us how he graded it, or what his marginalia were. He is not likely to have been strict about the footnotes or punctuation under such moral pressure. He might well, in addition, have forgotten to go home that night to his wife and son. Janie herself? "She stood in front of you, small as she was, with her legs slightly apart, planted, lots of freckles, blond short hair, no makeup except bright red lipstick, and her big, open confessional grin: this is what I am, this is what I do, if you don't like it, it's too bad." Indeed, the carefree sexual conduct that subsequent students have taken for granted, certainly in their dealings with Professor Kepesh, was pioneered by the Janie Wyatts of the 1960s and are now taken for granted, as if it was always and obviously in harmony with the pursuit of happiness as conceived in Philadelphia in 1776.

Professor Kepesh ("I'm a critic, I'm a teacher—didacticism is my destiny") follows with a lesson on American history, about the English fur trading settlement of Merry Mount in New England in the seventeenth century, which, under the leadership of Thomas Morton, was to license what Plymouth was to prohibition. Its inhabitants drank, hung around with the Indians (whose women preferred to offer themselves dog style), and danced around the maypole in animal masks. Merry Mount horrified the Puritans, who did everything they could to stop Morton, including send him off to England twice for trial, only to have him acquitted by English authorities who had no use for the Puritan separatists. The sexual libertines of the 1960s, Professor Kepesh instructs us, are the spiritual children of Merry Mount, and he in turn is their avid student. His bedding down with generations of students, right into his seventh decade, has Yankee tradition behind it: spacious skies and amber waves of grain. Had things turned out differently in America, we'd be marching every year in an equinox parade. Irving Berlin would have written a song for it and Bing Crosby would have recorded it.

So, what went wrong? What was the fly in the libertine ointment, for a man who could have the women he chose and chose the juiciest who enrolled in his classes? Sex has an ancient underside here, beyond pregnancy, AIDS, or any of the other STDs. It is obsession, jealousy, the terrible involvement of the unstable ego that makes a slave of the ostensible master. Kepesh is hooked through the gills like a fish. From the moment he makes love to his Consuela the nightmare begins: he is bound hand and foot—and heart. "The jealousy. The uncertainty. The fear of losing her, even while on top of her. Obsession that in all my varied experience I had never known before. With Consuela as with no one else, the siphoning off of confidence was almost instantaneous." *The Dying Animal* is yet another of Roth's updates from hell, and it is the particular hell set aside for those who follow their dreams into the pornotopia of sexual liberation only to discover that there is no such thing. They have simply exchanged the dungeon of marital fidelity, the dungeon of family, the dungeons of mortgage and nine-to-five, and the dungeon of all things in moderation for the black hole of their own careening emotions. What he discovers is something that Thomas Morton and the pagans at Merry Mount never spoke of, that Janie Wyatt and the Gutter Girls never told him about: that the heart is vulnerable to extremes of pleasure. "People think that in falling in love they make themselves whole? The Platonic union of Souls? I think otherwise. I think you're whole before you begin. And the love fractures you. You're whole and then you're cracked open." And what he falls in love with is not Consuela herself, who scarcely exists in this book besides her perfect breasts. He is a slave to them; they are all he can think of, and he remembers a moment when he is playing the Mozart Sonata in C Minor for her, while she sits undressed before him. She walks forward to examine the metronome, "and when she advances to examine the dial, her breasts pitch forward to cover my mouth and to stifle, momentarily, the pedagogy—that pedagogy that with Consuela is my greatest power. My only power."

Yes, of course, we have come down through all these years with Roth only to find his latest icon to be none other than Alex Portnoy's dream woman, Thereal McCoy, with her galumptious breasts and nipples the size of tollhouse cookies. And David Kepesh even ingests this dream, takes in the poison, if you like, by kneeling down to lick her menstrual blood one night. "She was a foreign body introduced into your wholeness. And for a year and a half you struggled to incorporate it. But you'll never be whole until you expel it. You either get rid of it or incorporate it through self-distortion. And that's what you did and what drove you mad." Dismiss this if you will: a grizzled author reaching back for ancient material and shopworn metaphors because he has run dry of new ones, but I don't quite see it that way. In the progress from Portnoy to Kepesh we are given a portrait of hedonism at the end of its rope, in which the old Marxian paradigm of historical repetition is turned on its head. The first time was farce; the second time is tragedy. Since Roth is always playing variations on Roth, we can see here a certain somber fulfillment of the excess that runs through the American trilogy, only for the excess of incendiary terrorism (Merry Levov), the excess of Stalinism (Ira Ringold), and the excess of feminism (Delphine Roux) we have the excess of freedom, which does not lead David Kepesh to the palace of wisdom but to the catacombs of dependency. And then to his keyboard, to discharge his frustrations with his fingers. Kepesh's libertinism in this book justifies Nathan Zuckerman's isolation in *The Human Stain:* the cordon sanitaire he has built around his cottage to keep life at bay. Yes, indeed, this is very bruising stuff, and if Roth is going to get on to his Shakespearean late comedies, he is going to have to move quickly.

Either in the original review or in these second thoughts, I've neglected to say that it is Consuela who is the dying animal and that her affliction is breast cancer. And the call Kepesh gets is to visit her in the hospital on the eve of her surgery. Of course he will go. If his therapist warns him that he is finished if he goes, well, then it is a man's way to be finished.

In 1824, Franz Schubert completed what would prove to be one of his most powerful and mournful compositions, his string quartet in D minor, which he called, after one of his earlier Lieder, *Der Tod und das Mädchen*, "Death and the Maiden." Death has come for a young woman, and she cries out:

> Vorüber! Ach, vorüber!
> Geh, wilder Knochenmann!
> Ich bin noch jung, geh, Lieber!
> Und rühre mich nicht an.

"Pass by, oh, pass by, leave, savage man of bones! I'm still young, please, leave, and do not bother me." Death replies:

> "Gib deine Hand, du schön und zart Gebild,
> Bin Freund und komme nicht zu strafen.
> Sei gutes Muts! Ich bin nicht wild,
> Sollst sanft in meinen Armen schlafen."

"Give me your hand, you lovely and frail creature; I'm a friend and do not come to punish you. Be of good cheer. I am not savage. You will sleep gently in my arms."[4] It is a piece of music that Kepesh makes a point of not playing for Consuela when she comes to announce her illness.

We can't know precisely what Roth is responding to in this book—and let's drop a curtain on such speculations anyway—but *The Dying Animal* is his "Death and the Maiden," and it extends and completes his American tragedy quartet just as surely as "The Prague Orgy" completed the Zuckerman quartet sixteen years earlier. *The Dying Animal* is a book about love and death, matters that Roth knows in the plasm of his cells. There is honest grief here, deep and lasting grief, and Roth composed this compact and mournful little envoy to love with the fullness of his being and the pathos of his advancing age and kept it short so as not to diffuse its poignancy.

19

Third Thoughts
The Blind Men and the Elephant

No, one's story isn't a skin to be shed—it's inescapable, one's body
and blood. You go on pumping it out till you die, the story veined
with the themes of your life, the ever-recurring story that's at once
your invention and the invention of you.
Nathan Zuckerman, from "The Prague Orgy"

I'm sorry and excited to be so difficult and unpopular.
R. B. Kitaj, First Diasporist Manifesto

So how, finally, does this all get put together, in five thousand words or
less? Is there a synthesis? A conclusion? A big picture of Roth that lets
us fit all the books, stories, essays, shop talk, and editorial work on
Writers from the Other Europe into a singe frame of reference? I feel
like the six blind men who are commanded by the raja to describe an elephant, each by touching a different part—a tail, an ear, a side, a tusk, a
leg, a trunk—and individually decide that the elephant is in actuality a
rope, a fan, a wall, a sword, a log, or a huge snake. Well, I'm all six rolled
into one: I've touched parts but I don't see exactly what the whole adds
up to. Instead, I'm going to let my blind men talk, each in his own voice,
and tell what he has felt. It is the best I can do.

Self and Community

Roth's writing through twenty-five books is as full of the experiments and surprises, detours and reversals that we expect of a major writer, and yet for all its variety it calls to mind and sometimes even openly confronts a single overriding issue. It is one, moreover, that shows Roth to be a typical product of the Jewish American synthesis in the middle of the twentieth century: the struggle to reconcile the competing claims of the individual imperative—the American theme—and the group imperative—the Jewish theme. The former is the optimistic triad of individual happiness, personal freedom, and self-reliance that comprises the secular liturgy of America, from the Declaration of Independence down through the recent marketing campaign of the United States Army: "Be all that you can be." The other is the belief among Jews at large, a belief both naive and profound, that Jewish writers are "their" writers and are heirs to the common history, partners in the common destiny, and spokesmen for the common will. They are agents of the Jewish folk spirit and therefore, like the early masters of secular Yiddish fiction, Mendele Moykher Sforim (S. Y. Abramovitsh), I. L. Peretz, and Sholom Aleichem, inseparable from the people about whom they wrote. The claim is naive for the obvious reason that it is founded on an expectation that any modern writer will reject as an infringement on the right of self-expression. It is naive also in its assumption that the classic Yiddish writers always wrote from firmly within the confines of community sentiment, as if, in effect, Sholom Aleichem waited for a poll or a vote or permission from the rabbi before putting pen to paper. They too took critical stances toward the Jewish community and worked at one remove from their subjects. (Yes, of course, Roth can work at up to ten removes from his Jewish subjects. Sholom Aleichem he is not.) There is the added problem that among Jews the common will is notoriously hard to find. Two Jews, three opinions. Three Jews, the Knesset. And yet the belief that "our" writers are *our* writers is also profound in that the dream of an ideal collectivity based on common destinies and shared responsibilities is lodged somewhere in the heart of so many Jews, even the most unyielding of its rebels, of whom Roth is one. In struggling with community, the renegade artist of the high modernist tradition, perennially flying by the nets of nationality, language, and religion, is also wrestling with him or herself.

Roth came on the scene in the late 1950s at about the time that the American Jewish community's sense of itself as a collectivity was all but shattered. While the Jews of America, from the beginning, did not share a unified identity or will—the breakup of the Ashkenazic community had begun to take place in Europe—it did have to a degree in America an experience of life that was unified enough to constitute fertile ground for a literature to express it, so that when Abraham Cahan published *The Rise of David Levinsky* in 1917, its notes of disillusionment and even alienation were submerged in the larger drama of social and economic advancement and the conflicts it aroused and the losses it entailed. However Cahan may have intended it, *The Rise of David Levinsky* was received by Jews at large as a book about themselves. It had the general good will and the literary credentials to be read as "we" fiction, rather than as "I" fiction, even though the portrait of its central figure as a conniver and a neurotic was anything but complimentary. That generalized good will toward "our" writers left a long trail, such that when Saul Bellow and Bernard Malamud began publishing after the war (and Arthur Miller and Paul Goodman and Isaac Rosenfeld and Meyer Levin and Tillie Olsen—let's stop there) they inherited this diffuse good will that contained the expectation that "our" writers speak generally for "us," despite their professed alienation (Bellow, at times) or incomprehensibility (the poetry of Delmore Schwartz) or restlessness or ignorance of Talmud and Torah and, in some cases (Malamud) a far more detailed knowledge of and affectionate identification with Italian art than with the legends of the Jews.

It was understandable that when Roth appeared on the scene and began to use his formidable gifts to mark the differences between himself and the Jewish middle class, a middle class that he would later learn to care for, it would turn sour on him, or worse, bitter, vindictive, even murderous. James Joyce, let us remember, left Ireland because he feared he would be killed there. Henrik Ibsen had to go into exile from Norway in order to develop as a playwright. Less understandable would be the choruses of intellectuals who followed suit and who, in the full knowledge of the necessary tension between writers and their communities—the very charter of aesthetic modernism itself—would run with the pack and put the weight of their authority behind it. With the history of the murder of Jewish artists still fresh in their minds, they could not resist in joining the choruses of indignation, and Roth was quite right to be not only stung but to feel betrayed. It was over his defense of his right to express himself free of community pressures and even to openly face them down that Roth's career and the public perception of it took its initial and lasting shape.

When the furor over Roth finally died down, as it has, what is left is a permanent detente between writers who prefer to go their own way and the collective Jewish sense of constituting a "we" on whose behalf writers will speak as a matter of course. The present climate of relations between Jewish writers and the Jewish community is much more fluid than it used to be. Writers who refuse the expectation of speaking for a community are now treated with a benign American neglect: everything goes and nothing matters. Although Roth is now a far different writer than he was at the start—except that the libido has not been tempered any—the social tensions and the clerical supervision of secular art that had led to his excommunication are also no longer there. Jews leave that sort of thing now to communism and Islam, which retain a proprietary view of what art may do and a punitive vigilance over what writers and artists are up to.

And yet, one can't help but feel that the flattening out of the response to Roth among Jewish readers has something to do with the erosion of both Jewish community and Jewish literacy in America. It was the general failure of *Operation Shylock,* a book about Israel that gave all the moral arguments to the Arabs, that one began to suspect something beyond the wearying of the audience: rather its disappearance. The reviewer of that book for the *Jerusalem Post* put his finger on it. "A generation ago a rude joke like that by Philip Roth would inspire a firestorm of response from American Jews. Today it seems to draw no response whatsoever. To most American Jews, Philip Roth and his concerns must seem dated, quaint, irrelevant. . . . Which is a sad commentary indeed. Roth has obviously poured tremendous effort into this book, and the result is a remarkable piece of work. Although *Operation Shylock* is a playful extravaganza, it is also deeply felt and deeply Jewish—a classic *Purimspiel.* The man hasn't lost any of his estimable skill; he's just lost

, an estimable readership. Which may be the ultimate comment on the Israel-Diaspora question."[1] What we see then, is not so much a maturing of Roth's relation to the Jews but his disappearance from their radar screens, a commentary it seems not on him but on them. Roth is now, willy-nilly, an American writer, Jewish variant, and he shares a readership not with Amos Oz or David Grossman but with John Updike and Richard Ford. Provoking, outraging, and delighting them is now his job, and the tools he developed as a renegade Jew engorged with sex and spiky with resentment are standing him in good stead with the rest of America.

Love and Sex

That conflict with the Jews isn't enough to constitute a full and complex body of work over forty years, and Roth's writing is sufficiently thick with overlays, dizzy with detours and epiphanies, rowdy with voices, and packed with closely observed particulars of contemporary life to give it the density and profusion of a major literature. The thickest of those overlays is the romantic/sexual, which, from *Goodbye, Columbus* in 1959 to *The Dying Animal* in 2001 remains remarkably constant: epics of longing punctuated by bursts of hedonism and failures of heart and will. Whether Roth will in the end be accounted the most sexually obsessed of American Jewish writers remains to be seen: Saul Bellow, Norman Mailer, and the late Isaac Bashevis Singer have also coveted that title and worked heroically to get it, as though to lose oneself in the fleshpots of America were to discover an alternative Zion in the daughters of Babylon. Singer usually performed his rites of unbridled eros as quasi-liturgical acts, finding sanction in Kabbalah and Jewish mysticism construed as lubricous counter-Torahs; Bellow performed his under the guise of dialectical satyrism, approaching women as though they were arcane philosophical texts—the wife as will and idea—and Roth has unzipped his libido ostensibly to gather material for the next book of desire and disappointment. From Neil Klugman's shattered romance with Brenda Patimkin in "Goodbye, Columbus" to Mickey Sabbath's mourning for Drenka Balich in *Sabbath's Theater* to David Kepesh's sodden longing for the breasts of Consuela Castillo in *The Dying Animal,* the drama of love and loss and the terrific pressure of pent up sexuality that drives it has been a constant in Roth's writing, expressing itself, indeed, as ever more urgent, ever more uncontrollable, ever more anarchic and dangerous as the years have gone by.

Although there is always the bustle of coming and going in Roth's writing—it is a very busy fiction—much of its meaning clusters about the intersection of these two themes: the loyalty/independence tug-of-war and the romantic/erotic rough melodrama where sex is a cultural weapon and romance is usually a form of erotic anthropology. Roth's imagination is powerfully activated at that intersection, and it is there that most of the more inspired fictions originate: *Portnoy's Complaint, The Ghost Writer, The Anatomy Lesson, The Counterlife, Operation Shylock, Sabbath's Theater, American Pastoral.* And here it is too that some of Roth's most vivid characters can be found. Not only Alex Portnoy, Mickey Sabbath, and the many versions of Nathan Zuckerman who pop out of the Zuckerman dressing room like rabbits out of a magician's hat, but also their inevitable consort, the *shiksa,* in all her stupefying variety: the Pilgrim, the Pumpkin, the Monkey, and the imaginary Thereal McCoy of *Portnoy;* man-eating wives named Lydia and Maureen in *My Life as a Man;* the Maria of the many flavors in *The Counterlife;* the Jenny, the Diana, the Gloria, and the Jaga who queue up to minister to an afflicted Nathan Zuckerman in *The Anatomy Lesson;* Olga Sisovsky of "The Prague Orgy," who shows everyone her cunt; the nameless "she" of *Deception;* the treacherous Jinx Possesski of *Operation Shylock;* the polymorphously perverse Drenka Balich of *Sabbath's Theater; American Pastoral*'s Dawn Dwyer Levov, Miss New Jersey of 1949; the tragic janitress Faunia Farley of *The Human Stain;* and Consuela Castillo of the golden globes in *The Dying Animal.* She is the one and the many, the breast and the beast, the milchig and the fleishig, the totem and the taboo, the perplexity and guide to the perplexed, the great cupcake and the poisoned apple all in one. I once wanted to title this book, *Getting Laid.* How far off the mark would that have been? Yet there too, at that junction of identity and appetite (I lust, therefore I am), we find her countertype, who may be the most inspired and risky of all Roth's female inventions: the Anne Frank of *The Ghost Writer,* whom a young Nathan Zuckerman dreams Amy Bellette might be.

Tenderness? Between men and women? It is virtually as hard to find as a Bar Mitzvah. It makes cameo appearances in *The Professor of Desire,* in the idyll between David Kepesh and his Claire, in *Deception,* between Philip and the other woman, perhaps in *Sabbath's Theater,* between Sabbath and Drenka, in *The Human Stain,* between Coleman Silk and Faunia Farley, and in *The Dying Animal,* between David Kepesh and Consuela Castillo. And there largely at the end, when Consuela comes to announce her cancer to David and have her breasts photographed for the last time, and rather than make love, he just holds her in his arms. It is there, and yet it is always a setup for a fall. Tenderness may sneak in around a corner and take us by surprise, but it never drives the plot, as do disappointment, disillusionment, longing, rage, shame, guilt, atonement, deception, betrayal, and, of course, raw appetite.

Crash and Burn

There is also the anguish of being oneself and the intense concentration on the afflicted ego that has occasioned the charges of narcissism and self-indulgence leveled at Roth by readers who find his particular brand of auto-analysis repellant. It is true that Roth's central male characters are more unremittingly introspective and more persistently tormented than most others in American literature. If this is to be accounted a shortcoming, it is one in which an entire literary culture is complicit, insofar as the main avenue of Jewish fiction writing in America, from Abraham Cahan to the present, had dedicated itself to the project of creating a Jewish persona that could detach itself from the restraints of Old World tradition and submit itself to the self-reliance, the uncertainty, the desublimation, and the commercialism of American life, but would also distinguish itself from the Jewish middle class by the nature and severity of the obstacles it set in its own path to self-realization. To disaffiliate from both cultures while at the same time exercising one's right to the pursuit of happiness was the intricate and Sisyphean enterprise to which these writers applied themselves. A composite Jewish persona that evolved in American fiction, from David Levinsky in Abraham Cahan's novel through Sara Smolinsky in Anzia Yezierska's *The Bread Givers,* David Schearl in Henry Roth's *Call It Sleep,* the personae created in fiction and poetry by Delmore Schwartz and Isaac Rosenfeld, and the assorted heroes in extremis of Saul Bellow's novels, to virtually every "comedian of alienation" (Irving Howe's slashing phrase)

Roth ever created as a stalking horse for his own conflicts, expressed a consistency of anxiety, self-absorption, disorientation, and neurosis that identified him as a typical product of the Jewish American synthesis. In America, this countertradition of alienation developed its own tradition, for which Roth is the last champion and Mickey Sabbath of *Sabbath's Theater* and Merry Levov of *American Pastoral*, who finally cross the line from insubordination to criminality, are the final, dazzling incarnations.

If Roth exploits the ceremonies of alienation that a prior literature had handed to him, however, he does amp up the level of panic, creating characters who invent themselves by dismantling themselves, enduring such grievous self-affliction at times that their dramas of transgression and atonement assume ludicrous and surreal proportions. "I implode, therefore I am." Thus the gruesome ending of *The Anatomy Lesson*, in which Nathan Zuckerman lies speechless in a hospital room, his jaw broken and his wagging tongue silenced by an intoxicated fall against a tombstone; thus too the end of *Sabbath's Theater*, in which a roguish and depressed Mickey Sabbath steps back from his intended suicide, uttering this marvelous last line: "How could he leave? How could he go? Everything he hated was here." Roth's truculent will to outrage, to transgress, and to suffer echoes through all the books in which Alex Portnoy, Peter Tarnopol, David Alan Kepesh, Nathan Zuckerman, Swede Levov, Ira Ringold aka Iron Rinn, Coleman Silk, and characters named Philip Roth wind up in hospitals, on couches, in their brothers' apartments, blubbering like infants, in divorce courts, inside the skin of a gigantic female breast, in Old Rimrock amid life's ruins, at the keyboard playing Scarlatti to ward off the blues. The bleak conclusion of *Zuckerman Unbound* is typical of this dismantling and dispossession. It finds Nathan Zuckerman, estranged from his brother, separated from his wife, and bereft of a father, who had cursed him with his dying words, returning to his old neighborhood in Newark, now a Black neighborhood, to stand before his old house in a moment of grief and vertigo. "A young black man, his head completely shaved, stepped out of one of the houses with a German shepherd and stared down from the stoop at the chauffeur-driven limousine in front of his alleyway, and at the white man in theback seat who was looking his place up and down."

"'Who you supposed to be?' he said.

"'No one,' replied Zuckerman, and that was the end of that. You are no longer any man's son, you are no longer some good woman's husband, you are no longer your brother's brother, and you don't come from anywhere anymore, either." The Roth male gets utterly disassembled in this 1981 novel, and in no subsequent book does it ever become satisfactorily reassembled. It is as if Roth had turned the nineteenth-century novel on its head and taken up its modern anti-form: the *Unbildungsroman*. Two thousand years of the Jews pining away for Jerusalem seems positively hopeful compared to Roth's pining away for Newark. Roth is a practitioner of what his friend, the painter R. B. Kitaj, in trying to define a "diasporist" aesthetic, calls "homeless logic." It is a logic that tends toward the depressive. "Diaspora history has its ups and down. I suspect a depressive connection which formulates its own aesthetic. Typical figures here would be Primo Levi, Soutine, Kafka, Celan, Bomberg, Benjamin, Jean Améry, Rothko, painters X, Y, and Z."[2] Does Roth belong in this camp? I would think so.

Why take an interest in any of this, since in summary it sounds claustral and disappointing and substantially lacking in shareable, public meaning? To that question there is a five word answer that sums up Roth's importance to us as a writer: *because it is utterly brilliant.* What matters in Roth is the dazzling self-awareness: the all purpose sensing equipment that is as delicate as the Hubble telescope and like it looks both out into space and back into time. Add to that an increasing mastery of the choked and littered terrain of contemporary culture and of the postmodern and incurable self. It is a balancing act to deal with this culture without, as many writers do, succumbing to it, and Roth handles that with as much balance and poise as any writer of our time.

The Voice

Roth's severest critics never fail to concede the qualities that send us back to his books time and again, no matter how distressed we may have been with the last performance. Roth is a master stylist, whose ear for speech is the most finely calibrated among living American writers and whose own sentences show a composer's ability to range freely among the registers and tonalities of the speaking voice. In *The Ghost Writer*, E. I. Lonoff speaks admiringly of Nathan's own voice, "the most compelling voice I've encountered in years, certainly for somebody starting out." And, in a memorable phrase, he distinguishes voice from style. "'I mean voice,' he tells Zuckerman, 'something that begins at around the back of the knees and reaches well above the head.'" In an essay on Jewish stylistics, Robert Alter notes how Roth gets "some of his liveliest effects by playing one linguistic register against another," and observes that the strength and weakness in much of Roth's writing are in "the energy of its verbal improvisations; so that instead of character, event, and moral or conceptual development, we get a series of shtiklach, the best of them displaying stylistic and attitudinal fireworks, many bearing the signs of self-indulgence."[3] That is a grudging way to put it, since in some of those bouts of self-indulgence we find Roth's most inspired comedy, and to miss Roth's comedy is to miss Roth. But surely he possesses the most distinctive voice in American fiction, compounded of gripe and attitude, bombast, declamation, complaint, and seduction, a molten interior, an operatic self-consciousness, a diasporic vertigo, a stunning alertness, a fitful clairvoyance, a congenital suspicion, a monumental self-indulgence, the pungency of the particular, and an ear for phrasing that marries audacity and insolence, bluster and provocation, to flawless syntax.

Having said all that I do need to hedge and footnote it just a little. Starting sometime in the mid-1990s, possibly with *I Married a Communist,* though there were signs of it earlier, the figures began to blur and the voices became less individualized, to sound like Roth talking to Roth. The voice of, say, Murray Ringold in *I Married a Communist* fades into that of Coleman Silk in *The Human Stain,* and Consuela Castillo in *The Dying Animal* is distinguishable only by her breasts, not by her speech. Only on occasion, when Roth is juiced on the rocket fuel of malice, does a separate, pungent voice emerge: Delphine Roux of *The Human Stain* and her prototype, literature professor Marcia Umanoff of *American Pastoral.* A walk-on character with a bit part in that book, Marcia Umanoff is one of its most vivid inventions. "There was nothing she did or said that didn't make clear where she stood. She had barely to move a muscle—swallow while you were speaking, tap with a fingernail on the arm of her chair, even nod her head as if she were in total agreement—to inform you that nothing you were saying was correct. To encompass all her convictions she dressed in large block-printed caftans—an extensive woman, for whom a disheveled appearance was less a protest against convention than a sign that she was a thinker who got right to the point. No nonsense, no commonplace stood between her and the harshest truth." When academic villainy is on stage, Roth's writing is on full alert and everyone has a rousing bad time.

Heart and Masquerade

As a creator of character, Roth works comfortably with a dual conception of character as both heart and masquerade, drawing on the one or the other according to his needs. From the one he derives his instinct for what is lasting in human relations, like the son's feelings for his father, out of which he gets the touching, sometimes grueling encounters like those between himself and his father in *Patrimony* or between Nathan Zuckerman and his dying father in *Zuckerman Unbound* or David Kepesh and his father in *The Professor of Desire*. Despite the differences between these relationships, each draws on a depth of feeling, a legacy of recollection, and a heartstring stretched to the breaking point that identifies Roth's attachment to his father as one of the cornerstones of his own personality. *Patrimony* stands out among Roth's fictions of life in crisis and the world in flux as a testament to the piece of his own heart that is as durable and tough-minded as his father was.

From the conception of character as disguise Roth gets the brisk theatrical effects of *The Counterlife*. A novel in five free-standing episodes, it plays variations on a pas de deux of two brothers, Nathan and Henry Zuckerman, as they wrestle with their heart problems (amorous and medical), their Jewish identities and beliefs, and their brotherhood, in the company of Henry's wife Carol, a libidinous dental assistant named Wendy, a troupe of mad Israelis—including a militant rabbi, a terrorist wannabe, and members of Israel's Shin Bet or internal security—and the usual chorus line of delectable shiksas, all going by the name of Maria. Characters refuse to stay fixed in this floating world, as Henry and Nathan trade lives and predicaments, even heart surgeries and deaths, as easily as actors change wardrobes, and Nathan may even submit to an interview from the grave, as he does in the final story. An elegant performance, *The Counterlife* traces an elaborate counterpoint between the inertia of history and the agility of the imagination and would appear to be evidence that a novel may contradict itself repeatedly without losing its unity of purpose, and that by keeping its fragments in suspension it can keep its readers in suspense.

Roth's maneuverings and fusions of the factual and the imagined lend this novel, much like *The Counterlife,* a Kafkaesque—or is it Kunderan?—aura of the uncanny, of actualities just beyond consciousness and epiphanies just out of focus. The most realistic pages of *Deception* are those from the journal, involving "Philip" and the "imaginary" though nameless lover, whom we know more intimately than any of the "real" parties—and notice the necessity of putting "real" and "imaginary" in quotes. "Philip" is a traveler, especially to Eastern Europe, a womanizer, and a writer who is accused of seducing women for their stories. He is fundamentally a man of the book, where friends, lovers, wives, parents, and brothers wind up as his creations, his property, and his puppets, for which their real-life models resent him for his hits and his misses. If he gets it right they feel exposed; if he gets it wrong they feel maligned. His defense, which turns into his craft, is to get it right and wrong together: to literalize and to improvise, to offend by exactness and offend by invention. He even claims to have invented the "I" of his journal, the nameless male whom perhaps we should call Philip, or should that be "Philip"? Whatever his name, protests "Philip" to his wife, "he" is not him. Likewise, he is not "him." "It is *far* from myself— it's play, it's a game, it is an *impersonation* of myself! Me ventriloquizing myself." However, one needs a taste for this sort of thing, and *Deception* strikes me as too unsubtle in its maneuvers, too much the fashionable text: a gaudy and belated avant-garde.

This flirtation with the masquerade of identity, the "me ventriloquizing myself," spilled over into *The Facts,* which plays off against *The Counterlife* by having Roth submit a draft manuscript of the book to Nathan Zuckerman, asking his advice on whether the book should be published. Zuckerman fires off this reply: don't publish it. "You are far better off writing about me than 'accurately' reporting on your own life."

Zuckerman's case against *The Facts* is that it is only one slant on the facts among many, designed in particular to cast a halo over a childhood that appears to be far more tense and dramatic in Roth's fiction. "You try to pass off here as frankness what looks to me like the dance of the seven veils—what's on the page is like a code for something missing."

And, "Are you not aware yourself of [*The Facts'*] fiction-making tricks? Think of the exclusions, the selective nature of it, the very pose of fact-facer. Is all this manipulation truly unconscious or is it pretending to be unconscious?" By this time, however, the counterlife gambit had ossi-fied into mannerism, and *The Facts* lacks the vitality and direct, clean force of *Patrimony*, in which the weight of the actual possesses more traction and thrust than the blatantly invented. Nathan Zuckerman himself at the end of "The Prague Orgy" had already pointed the way back from the masquerade in remarking, while being hustled out of Czechoslovakia by Czech security: "No, one's story isn't a skin to be shed—it's inescapable, one's body and blood. You go on pumping it out till you die, the story veined with the themes of your life, the ever-recurring story that's at once your invention and the invention of you."

Raw Nerve and Raw Nerves

The English poet William Blake wrote, "The road of excess leads to the palace of wisdom," and Roth has taken that axiom to heart. Certainly few American writers in recent times have been more devoted to excess, and no writer has come through the indulgence of it with more genuine wisdom, unless it be Norman Mailer and the late Allen Ginsberg. Sim-ilarities between the three are striking. They are Jewish writers who, early on—Mailer with *Advertisements for Myself,* Ginsberg with "Howl," and Roth with *Portnoy's Complaint*—took aim at the manners and mor-als, the platitudes and nostrums, the Torahs and phylacteries, of Amer-ican propriety and Jewish prohibition in order to say the unsayable. They are problems; they stir things up. They did all they could to be singled out, to be difficult and cause distress, and though they did it for themselves, they posted gains for others, and American literature owes them all a debt of gratitude. The freedom of Americans to write openly about sex, about rage, about turmoil and embattlement, to provoke au-thority, to be a contaminant, which is now taken for granted, was made possible by those writers who, among others, challenged the prevailing culture that took decency as a literary baseline and that odd American archetype, the great guy, as a model of temperament.

But there is a major difference. Whereas the bluster and anarchy in Mailer's books and Ginsberg's poetry was lived as well as written, Roth's anarchism has been substantially mental. Roth is an *homme de lettres,* whose life has been spent in the study, hunched over the typewriter, conjuring up dangerous liaisons, recalling injuries and losses, day-dreaming rages and tantrums, remembering Newark, imagining Israel, hallucinating his marriages and his martyrdom, and improvising his Kafkaesque and improbable life as a man. Something of a cross between Ginsberg and Marcel Proust, who spent his adult years in a cork-lined room writing the long memoir of his life, Roth steps out of his burrow in Connecticut just long enough to test drive his emotions, collect his experiences, give interviews, interview others, take blows, gather his disappointments, and take his feverish notes. Then he scurries back to compose his turbulent sentences, to turn them over and over until they sound plausibly like life. Or better, like literature. Which is not to say that Roth hasn't lived or lived profoundly; only that he didn't write twenty-six books without making a fundamental commitment to being alone much of the time. In *The Ghost Writer,* Roth created the novelist E. I. Lonoff, "the old master," whose life consisted of turning sentences around unto the twenty-seventh draft, until everything was exactly as he wanted it. Early readers of that book thought Lonoff possibly a por-trait of Bernard Malamud or Anton Chekhov or Isaac Babel, and all three are undoubtedly implicated, but plainly it was also Roth himself as he might become, not only a literary ascetic or a fractious depressive, but the old master of American letters. At seventy, Roth's claim to that title is credible, as is the counterclaim to being a lifelong Young Turk. Éminence grise and enfant terrible all in one is a counterlife that any author might aspire to and Roth may have achieved.

20

Epilogue
Up Society's Ass, Copper!

"You're Jewish, aren't you? Answer me!" "Sure." "Well, you're shit-
ting on my personal torah, kid." "What? You've not exactly led a
Talmudic life these years—" Suddenly he had seized my leg, throwing me off balance to the side, and he began biting for the bone. Like
being caught in the jaws of a bear. Instinctively I pummeled his back
and side with the pistol—then tore him off me (the two of us howl-
ing) and in one swift motion put my pillow to his anus and fired. As
I myself fell backward, he let out a horrible groan and jolted forward, the blood pouring out torrentially. Dazed, I raised myself and
saw his flushed face lying peacefully on the sky-blue carpet.
Alan Lelchuk, American Mischief

We leave a stain, we leave a trail, we leave our imprint. Impurity,
cruelty, abuse, error, excrement, semen—there's no other way to be
here.
Faunia Farley, from The Human Stain

You're going to feel dashed by this, Norman, but on top of everything else I don't have, I don't have a pitch. . . . I am flowing swiftly
along the curbs of life, I am merely debris, in possession of nothing
to interfere with an objective reading of the shit.
Mickey Sabbath, from Sabbath's Theater

The title of this book is taken from the very last page of *Portnoy's Complaint,* where Alex Portnoy is reliving a moment when he had become
impotent in Israel with a red-haired Israeli girl whom he had picked up
as she was hitchhiking. There is the usual sex skirmish, during which

Alex Portnoy throws a flying tackle on her and hauls her to the floor, not only to rape her but also to give her a stiff dose of diaspora clap. "Socialism exists, but so too do spirochetes, my love!" Alas, in the Promised Land he can't keep his promise. Offering an alternative, "At least let me eat your pussy," he gets a swift kick in the heart and a parting word: "Pig." In Yiddish that would be "Chazer." After a lifetime of eating chazerai, he finally hears from a woman who looks uncannily like his mother: you are what you eat.

Alex Portnoy dredges up this latest humiliation on his analyst's couch, where he has been recalling each and every bruise to the heart with a vividness that borders on hallucination, and the memory of his failure in Israel sends him into an elaborate and hilarious recollection of his childhood in Newark during the war and his many good deeds as Assistant Commissioner of Human Opportunity in New York. Everything moves with lightning speed to this final scenario of being cornered by police for having removed a tag from his mattress.

> God forbid I should tear the tag from my mattress that says, "Do Not Remove Under Penalty of Law"—what would they give me for that, the chair? It makes me want to scream, the ridiculous disproportion of the guilt! May I? Will that shake them up too much out in the waiting room? Because that's maybe what I need most of all, to howl. A pure howl, without any more words between me and it! "This is the police speaking. You're surrounded, Portnoy. You better come on out and pay your debt to society." Up Society's ass, Copper! "Three to come out with those hands of yours up in the air, Mad Dog, or else we come in after you, guns blazing. One." Blaze, you bastard cop, what do I give a shit? I tore the tag off my mattress—"Two."—But at least while I lived, *I lived big!*

Is there a finale to any Roth novel grander than that? Is there a conclusion to any novel that scales such heights of farce and terror more hysterically? After such fiction, what commentary? How does the critic, the reviewer, even the therapist put the straight face back on, adjust the mask of authority, and claim not to be disarmed, when in fact what he really wants to do is just to revel in the comedy, maybe even let out a cheer for Alex Portnoy. What is there to say? This guy is in dreadful shape; he has descended into the coal mines of his own heart and come back improbably with diamonds: a story of the last humiliation—impotent in Israel—and a farcical daydream of social retribution for mattress abuse. Meanwhile, the analyst, Spielvogel, who has been silently taking this all in, and hopefully keeping awake, has other patients in the waiting room nervously flipping pages while Alex Portnoy, still on the couch, is flipping out. Time *is* up.

Yet, like Spielvogel, those of us who take up our pens, or our Pentiums, to have a go at this book are professional explainers. We are licensed to produce explanations, and sometimes we get away clean with an analysis or two, but here we find ourselves on the hook. As they say in the old labor song, "Which side are you on, boy?" If there is a note of ambivalence, of self-doubt, that runs through this entire book it can be traced back to that single question: which side am I on? That of Mad Dog Portnoy, holed up in his own imagination, crying "Up society's ass, Copper!"? Or that of the woolgathering Spielvogel, desperately buying time, fumbling for clarity, hoping the hour is about ended, and able to muster only his lame "Now vee may perhaps to begin. Yes?"?

You can see where this might go. "Up Society's Ass" has been almost as much a theme song for Roth as "Sweet Georgia Brown" has been for the Harlem Globetrotters, and if I were writing this for tenure I might well trace the "motif" through Roth's career and put the whole anal megillah up in lights. But nobody is looking over my shoulder and nothing obliges me to adopt and defend a point of view and to keep everything that is surprising and mercurial about Roth at arm's length. Proclaiming that one has struck pay dirt too quickly distracts us from the detours, anecdotes, impersonations, punch lines, send ups, pratfalls, visions, mutterings, and trash talk that are the purest distillations of Roth's art.

Rather I want to conclude differently and to look at Roth through the eyes of two other writers who have chosen sides and allow them the last words. They are Alan Lelchuk and Mark Krupnick, both of whom have lately written about Roth after a long acquaintance, either with his books or, in Lelchuk's case, with Roth himself. Although the two have little in common save the euphonious rhythms and final k's of their names, they share a deep history. For a brief time in the early 1970s they were associate editors of the journal *Modern Occasions,* which was founded by Philip Rahv after he had broken with his coeditor, Williams

Phillips, at *Partisan Review* over that magazine's surrender to the "new sensibility": its going mod with Susan Sontag on Camp and Against Interpretation, McLuhan on media, William Burroughs, Charles Reich on the Greening of America. The best account I know of *Modern Occasions*, its rise and its collapse, was written by Krupnick in Ian Hamilton's *The New Review* in England in 1976, and what follows here is taken from Krupnick's account.[1]

Roth, Lelchuk, Krupnick, and Rahv were brought together briefly in the summer of 1970 by Rahv, who had been teaching at Brandeis since 1958 while editing *Partisan Review*. In Krupnick's recollection, "We lived in separate houses about ten miles apart from each other and got together a few times a week for dinner to plan the first issue, which was to come out in the fall. Lelchuk had met Philip Roth at a writer's colony and was now his protégé. Alan treated Roth like the king of the mountain, and, in return, when Alan's first novel, *American Mischief*, was about to appear, Roth puffed it in print as 'the greatest New England love story since *The Scarlet Letter*.'"[2] These were high times indeed for all of them. Roth had the usual lovely woman with him while Lelchuk had his then girlfriend, Frances Fitzgerald, who was at work on her book about the Vietnam War, *Fire in the Lake*. "Roth's friend," Krupnick remembers, "was silent and beautiful the whole time, and except for a little mugging and a big brother–little brother routine Roth and Lelchuk had worked up, the two Philips did almost all the talking as the rest of us sat in attendance. The incongruities were wonderful in the meeting of the quick and voluble laureate of masturbation with the heavy-lidded, somnolent-looking old Trotskyite. It was like Lenny Bruce meeting Doctor Johnson."

Modern Occasions was launched with high hopes. It brimmed with essays and stories by Saul Bellow and Philip Roth, John Gardner, Juliet Mitchell, Jean-Paul Sartre, Isaac Deutscher, William Styron, Mary McCarthy, Elizabeth Hardwick, César Vallejo, Robert Bly, and Albert Moravia, as well as some younger writers, like Krupnick himself and Eugene Goodheart. For a journal that was university based and dealt solely in literature and ideas, it was remarkably chrome plated and high end. But it ran through material and contributors in record time without cultivating a new generation of writers. In the end, *Modern Occasions* produced just six issues, from 1970 through 1972, and then succumbed to the chaos of Rahv's own personal life: his drinking, his rages, his depression and instability. He would die a year later.

Such gatherings as Krupnick recalls and the events to follow were sure to leave an impression, and no one was more impressed than Lelchuk. Alan Lelchuk in the early 1970s was a young writer with a gamy imagination and an insurrectionary sense of fun. To cite the most infamous example, the lead character in his *American Mischief,* having just read Norman Mailer's famous essay "The White Negro," meets the great writer in his room after a lecture at Harvard. Taking cues from Mailer's own apocalyptic sermon about creating a new nervous system and encouraging the psychopath in oneself, he pulls a gun on Mailer and shoots him in the anus, leaving the author in a pool of blood. Up society's ass had become up Mailer's ass, and the fundament was beginning to seem fundamental to literature. To the real-life Mailer, that was taking the psychopath business too literally, and he sicced his lawyers on Lelchuk, hoping to frighten him out of publishing that scene. Lelchuk brought Roth to the meeting, and Mailer promptly vowed to "get" Roth for his role in the matter. Had Roth egged Lelchuk on in this? I like to think so.

Back then, Roth saw in Lelchuk the feral and socially unaccommodated side of himself and wrote him into two of his novels: as the poet Ralph Baumgarten in *The Professor of Desire,* a figure of naked appetite known to his colleagues as the "abomination in residence," and as the novelist Ivan Felt in *The Anatomy Lesson,* author of a book about the "insolent anarchy and gleeful debauchery" of the sixties, whose message was to cultivate anger as a principle of writing: "Point it and fire it and just keep firing until they [enemies, pains, troubles] disappear." That was Lelchuk, all right, as Roth describes Felt, "the brash, presumptuous, overconfident, and ostentatious egotist" and something more: a writer who did with brio what most writers harrow their souls to do at all: fill the page with the pure force of his being.

Lelchuk would go on over the years to write five more novels, but none of them occasioned the notoriety of *American Mischief,* and his career went into decline while Roth's ripened, not only into critical acclaim but something even stranger and unpredictable: stardom on an international scale. Perhaps as a prelude to the Nobel Prize or in a national mood of apology, one hears Roth spoken of now and again as a national treasure, no matter what he writes or how obstinately he shrouds himself in isolation. As he has elected not to rally 'round the flag, the flag seems disposed to rally 'round him.

Lelchuk recalls the early days glowingly in his new novel, *Ziff: A Life?*, in which Roth reappears, more or less, as the famed novelist Arthur Ziff, Lelchuk as his biographer, Danny Levitan, and Mailer for a Hitchcockian instant as "the old punch-drunk writer/journalist L. Postman," though otherwise the shooting scene with "the blood pouring out torrentially" is airbrushed out.[3] Enough is enough. We are set up from the very beginning for a gossip fest and a titillating roman à clef, in which Levitan/Lelchuk, a novelist whose career has been sliding toward oblivion, embarks on a biography of his mentor and friend, Ziff/Roth, who has rocketed into some far galaxy of stardom light years away. He comes across as a magnetic force, a gravitational field, a raffish war god. In books of this sort, we eagerly expect revelations, betrayals, paybacks, brushbacks, sucker punches, and the usual mayhem that accompanies writers writing about writers who have previously written about them. Since Lelchuk is, after all, a tactician, a jokester, and a Brooklyn brawler, we anticipate a stormy ride and a therapeutic disburdening of his own resentments. What we actually get is lighter fare, an homage, a grungy fanfare for a writer who turns out at the end to be a hidden saint who has been filmed in the act of cultivating his public image as a barbarian.

Reading *Ziff: A Life?* is rather like reading Shakespeare's *Henry IV,* with Ziff/Roth as Prince Hal and Levitan/Lelchuk as Falstaff. One moment they are prowling the streets of Cambridge together, hot young men on the make, and the next Prince Hal has grown up to be King Henry and is no longer returning Falstaff's calls. That is by far the most affecting part of the book; the disciple agonizing over the cost of his discipleship and deciding that it was worth it after all, though the blows he has taken are grievous. That is a story all its own. What biographer of a living figure hasn't faced the confounding choice of whether to write *about* his subject or *to* him instead, forsaking independent judgment for being loved? What punches do you throw and which do you pull? What face do you show? What price do you pay for your sins of commission and your sins of omission? Which side are you on? That may be the deeper issue of this book, but it is not relevant here. It is the

portrait of Roth we are after, and while Arthur Ziff is a fictional creation, he isn't all *that* fictional, the whole point of the roman à clef being
the transparency of the alias to everyone but the legal system.

Danny Levitan is portrayed as a distinctly tyro biographer, un-
trained for the task and forever beginning afresh with new ideas. For
starters, he imagines Arthur Ziff as the Erwin Rommel of literature.
(Erwin Rommel?! Well, no one ever said that Lelchuk was one to
shrink from absurdity.) Ziff cuts a rakish figure, is smart, has a playboy
style, has been "a master strategist of his books and career," and is "a
purposeful, shrewd hawk, searching here, scrutinizing there for prey." It
is hard to know when reading such prose whether Lelchuk is exposing
his alter ego to ridicule as an infatuated disciple who is in over his head
as a biographer or if he stands squarely behind such hagiography as his
own slant on Philip Roth. "Yes, there was a life to lead, but one in accordance with a true literary superstar. Here, too, as in literature, it was
Rommel directing and planning with a sly masterly hand."

Levitan will triangulate these excited imaginings with the testimony
of others. The ex-wife, French actress Jeanne Lemaire, will fork over
the diary of her marriage, which discloses such inventive polymorphism
and perversity in their conjugal doings that you might well wonder why
either of them would ever want to flee from that particular house of
bondage. A Brandeis professor testifies that he always thought Ziff had
RRD, or "Relentless Retention Disorder." Voices chime in from the far
corners of the earth and the dim recesses of the past. "He was a great
mimic" and "would have made a great D.A." and "To us in Budapest he
was a god" and "The age of Hemingway is over. And Mailer or Capote.
We're living in the era of Ziff." A rabbi confides that he reads Torah and
Talmud with Ziff. A school principal writes in, "Irving Howe said it
all." A woman from Budapest reveals Ziff's secret life as a student of
Holocaust testimonies and a quiet supporter of Eastern European
friends and causes. Ziff himself nervously kibitzes the project and does
everything to dissuade Levitan. He threatens, he cajoles, he offers hush
money, he publishes withering stories about his biographer in *The New
Yorker* and counsels him, "Stick to fiction."

Nothing in the book is stranger than the presence for long stretches
of a Hungarian woman named Éva Kertész, who meets Levitan in
Rome and Budapest and plies him with stories of Arthur Ziff's secret

life in Hungary. Transposing Roth's actual Prague to an imagined Budapest, Lelchuk makes of Éva Kertész an emissary from this concealed life and gives her the entire center of the book to disburden herself to Levitan. What, we might ask, would take us deeper into the heart of Arthur Ziff than his Rommellian dash, his tactical brilliance, his survivalist tenacity, his masturbatory heroics, his sexual inventiveness, his postmodern elusiveness, his Jamesean cunning, his tonal delicacy and professional aplomb, his relentless retention disorder, his psychological adventurism, his dark-eyed stare of determination, his balls, his clout, his weaknesses for soft flesh and High Art, all of which Danny Levitan dutifully notes in his running commentary on Ziff. What could this Éva have to disclose that should occasion Levitan's multiple flights to Europe and would weigh more than the ex-wife's revelations about her novelist husband's proclivity for bondage theater. Only this: that Arthur Ziff is more serious about the Jews and himself as one of them than he will ever let on in public.

If this is about the Roth behind the Ziff, it is hardly a bombshell. It is old news. Roth's Jewishness, as a catalyst of his being, however resistant, inflamed, and unstable, has been there from the start, and in books like *The Counterlife* and *Operation Shylock* it has been the basic premise. It hasn't been everyone's Jewishness—neither was I. B. Singer's or Nahman of Bratslav's—but there is little doubt that when biographers eventually pry their way into Roth's life, as Levitan tries to do into Ziff's, they will be obliged to treat Roth the Jew more seriously than, say, James Atlas had to treat Saul Bellow the Jew or future biographers will have to treat Bernard Malamud the Jew. And this is not simply because Roth's Jewishness is more tormented or antinomian or schismatic or aggrieved than theirs, but because it is closer to the place of injury in him and to the fire that burns day and night to cauterize it: to whatever it is that troubles him into words, day in and day out. It needn't be anything more than the brand of Jewishness that Nathan Zuckerman identifies in himself at the end of *The Counterlife:* "A Jew without Jews, without Judaism, without Zionism, without Jewishness . . . a Jew clearly without a home, just the object itself, like a glass or an apple." But then, as the great Russian poet Osip Mandelstam had said, "As a little bit of musk fills an entire house, so the least influence of Judaism overflows all of one's life."

In *Ziff: A Life?* we find a Ziff who has been in Europe secretly re-
searching a novel on the life of Raoul Wallenberg, the Swedish diplo-
mat who saved hundreds of Hungarian Jews during the Holocaust
and then mysteriously disappeared into Soviet territory after the war.
Titled *The Wallenberg Wars*, it is described by Levitan/Lelchuk as "a
vast, sprawling canvas filled with harrowing scenes and memorable
characters—especially the dashing Swede and his doomed Budapest
Jewess—marred perhaps by high melodrama and postmodern trickery.
A richly mixed bag, with the riches sounding a Nobel resonance."
(Style alert. Avoid using "rich" twice in the same sentence.) Surely here
is where the fictional Ziff and the actual Roth part company, as Ziff becomes Leon Uris and writes the brand of historical romance that Alexander Portnoy once called "that stupid saga shit." One doesn't know
what to make of Ziff's means of research, a "Jewish Healing Program"
in Budapest that collects stories of Holocaust trauma by e-mail and offers "grants, fellowships, and/or other financial aid" to people with "un-
usual or noteworthy tales pertaining to the Holocaust." We can be certain that this isn't Roth, not because of the largesse of the pay-for-pain
offer but because of the utter callousness of it. It is one thing to collect
testimony for the Yale Holocaust Project and quite another thing to buy
it for your next novel, which is going to be your bid for international celebrity. These are stories to be collected as material for a novel of Ziff's
own to catapult him into Nobel Prize contention by—of all things—
exploiting survivors and pandering to Swedish vanity. Of all the vulgar-
ities that Roth is reputed to have committed, nothing compares to this,
and Lelchuk imagines it not as a vulgarity but as a sign of Arthur Ziff's
unspoken covenant with his people and his eminent nobility—not to
say his imminent Nobelity! Toward the end of the *Ziff: A Life?*, after
Levitan's biography has appeared to mixed reviews, Levitan and Ziff sit
down and have a good chuckle. Levitan tells Ziff, "If the Jews believe
you've turned over a new leaf, or always had another secret leaf, who
knows what the Gentiles will think, especially the Swedish ones, huh?"
Ziff replies, "Very cute. Who knows? Stranger things have occurred."
But seldom, one thinks, more indecent ones.

Granted this picture of Arthur Ziff is not intended to be more than
a cartoon of a writer, and though it is based on Philip Roth, that's no
more significant than saying that Superman is a cartoon based on

Nietzsche's Übermensch. Whatever the source of this portrait of the artist as a satyr-prince, it is dimensionless, lacking, among other things, any hint that the novelist might possess common human frailties: that he could be vulnerable; that he might suffer failure or desperation or the black dog of depression; that he could be shattered by love or by death or by divorce; that wealth and fame beyond dreams might be poor ano-dynes for a case of the blues; that he could be injured to the quick by book reviews. So, finally, it can't be Roth at all, lacking entirely the sul-len undertones of Roth's writing and his life or any serious account of the blows he has sustained and the notes of grief that have dominated his novels over the past decade or so. "Yes, there was a life to lead," writes Danny Levitan, "but one in accordance with a true literary super-star." Where Roth is concerned, there was more to it than that.

We know that by reading Roth himself, recalling, for example David Alan Kepesh's excruciating confessions about love in *The Dying Animal:* "People think that in falling in love they make themselves whole? The Platonic union of Souls? I think otherwise. I think you're whole before you begin. And the love fractures you. You're whole and then you're cracked open." This isn't a voice from the firmament. We'd know too by reading another recent commentary on Roth by the other of Philip Rahv's Brandeis student assistants in the 1970s, Mark Krupnick. What I will be quoting from is not in print as I write though it will be before long, and it merits attention in advance.[4] Krupnick's early involvement with Rahv and *Modern Occasions* inaugurated him into life-long in-volvement with New York intellectual culture that resulted in his writ-ing a definitive book on Lionel Trilling in 1986, *Lionel Trilling and the Fate of Cultural Criticism.*[5] In the intervening years, as a professor of English first at the University of Illinois at Chicago Circle and later at the Divinity School and Committee on Jewish Studies of the University of Chicago, he has been refining his insights in essays on what he calls, taking a phrase from Trilling, the "deep places of the imagination," looking, among Jewish writers and intellectuals, for those deep places and a writer's capacity to access and write out of them. Among the book's key chapters is one on Roth titled "A Shit-Filled Life: *Sabbath's Theater.*" It could not be more different from Alan Lelchuk's portrait of Ziff/Roth as the Erwin Rommel of his own life and career. Or if it is Rommel, it is Rommel after El Alamein. It begins this way:

In his writing during the past fifteen years or so, Philip Roth has continued to be a writer with little interest in dreams or traditional ideas of beauty, except if represented in the shape of the female breast. He has increasingly found loss, humiliation, and death at the heart of things. And increasingly reductive in his sense of reality, he has found the most basic, most elemental principle of things in excrement. The protagonists of his most recent books have been in the end overcome by storms of shit. It might seem excessive to say that Roth was invoking shit more than as a metaphor, but it is an important literal fact in the doomed careers in some of his main characters.

Yes, Krupnick's is a focused literary study with an emphasis on a single book: *Sabbath's Theater*, but his broader message is plain: something—many things—happened to Roth from the late 1980s and after, and his books throughout the 1990s record, with seismographic precision, a collapse of morale. We need only reflect on what we do know—the death of his father, the collapse of his marriage, his episode with Halcion, his cardiac surgery—and wonder if that was all, or if it was not indeed more than we expect a man to bear. *Sabbath's Theater* in 1995 gives us the deepest penetration into that collapse, not by describing it frontally but by working through a metaphor for how it felt to Roth.

Krupnick regards *Sabbath's Theater* as the best of Roth's novels to come out during the 1990s, a judgment that, as I read Krupnick, comes in two parts. One, that the book's own narrative is more consistent with itself than those novels that followed it: *American Pastoral, I Married a Communist,* and *The Human Stain.* It is not so vitiated by sidetracks, subplots, evasions, clunky narrative strategies, pasteboard characterizations (Merry Levov, Faunia Farley), and in particular by the "irrepressible zest for sermonizing" by which Roth is increasingly overcome. More significant, the book appears to be closer to the bone than the others; it appears to be hot-wired directly into Roth's moral and psychological core, in which Krupnick finds humiliation and defeat. He finds in *Sabbath,* a novel built on "increments of excrement," a sequel to Roth's memoir about the death of his father in *Patrimony.* He cites in particular the scene in which Roth's father visits his rural Connecticut home. At one point the father slips away from the company and goes upstairs. "When he does not reappear, Philip mounts the stairs himself and discovers his father in a state of shock. Repeatedly moaning 'I beshat myself,' the old man stands in his son's bathroom surrounded by the effects of the volcanic eruption of his bowels: 'The shit was everywhere.' Philip ends his inventory of stain with striking detail: 'It was even on the tips of the bristles of my toothbrush hanging in the holder over the sink.'"

The father is ashamed. "Don't tell the children. . . . Don't tell Claire." Krupnick writes: "To honor his father's wish, the son seeks no help in cleaning up the mess. He even gets down on his hands and knees, and with a bucket of hot water and Spic and Span goes to work with that toothbrush trying to clean flecks of shit from where they have lodged in the crevices between the planks of the floor." Roth goes to work meticulously cleaning up after his father and reflects upon what has happened. "Why this was right and as it should be couldn't have been plainer to me, now that the job was done. So that was the patrimony. And not because cleaning it up was symbolic of something else but because it wasn't, because it was nothing less or more than the lived reality that it was. There was my patrimony: not the money, not the tefillin, not the shaving mug, but the shit."

I earlier observed that the publication of *Patrimony* in 1991 ushered in a decade of robust publishing for Roth, being followed in assembly-line succession by *Operation Shylock* (1993), *Sabbath's Theater* (1995), *American Pastoral* (1997), *I Married a Communist* (1998), and *The Human Stain* (2000). Krupnick sees it differently, seeing everything colored by Roth's personal crisis, which encouraged in him "an extremism of subject-matter and style that goes far beyond the artistic self-liberation he achieved in *Portnoy's Complaint.*" Part of that extremism is an openness, as never before, to the reality of the "shit-filled life," which pervades all the novels of the 1990s, and even lends a title to *The Human Stain.* In the words of that novel's Faunia Farley, who is so terribly familiar with defeat, "We leave a stain, we leave a trail, we leave our imprint. Impurity, cruelty, abuse, error, excrement, semen—there's no other way to be here."

Krupnick concludes: "*Sabbath's Theater* will someday receive the honor it deserves. It is not didactic fiction propelled by argument like [Saul Bellow's] *Herzog* and is free of Roth's own tendency in recent novels to preach cultural jeremiads. Also, its nihilism is not doctrinal. Rather, it is a triumph of fantasy, emotion, instinct. Roth was able to reach down far into the deep places of imagination. In this unique novel, Roth reached down within himself to the deepest springs of his being, which freed his imagination as never before or since. The result, as with Mickey Sabbath himself, was a giant surge of energy, but, unlike in the case of Sabbath, energy not so anarchical that it ran away with itself and turned the book into a mess."

⌐⌐

It may seem clumsy to conclude a book with the words of others, but as the idea of this epilogue was forming, both Lelchuk's novel and Krupnick's chapter came into my hands within days of each other. Given the coincidence of their history, to have been briefly involved together on *Modern Occasions,* which Roth himself helped midwife into existence, it seemed to me inevitable to bring them together, something that they themselves, no doubt, would never dream of. Moreover, I've been well aware of both during much the same span of time that I've been reading Roth. Both have been, each in his own way, voices inside my own head. They are radically different voices, and it does not surprise me that in the end I find Krupnick a more trustworthy authority on Roth, even though Lelchuk has had far closer relations and more consistent access. (Yes, of course Lelchuk has written a fiction, but that cannot be used as an excuse for a character so unburdened that no novelist would wish to be mistaken for him.) It may be the paralyzing effect of friendship itself that Lelchuk can't venture too far from the sunny myth of Roth: the satyr-king, the flowing energy, the voltage, the "hard rock mimetic voice," the "tonal delicacy and professional aplomb," the "Spirit of Inauthenticity in modern letters" who has "debunked the myth of the self" (all phrases from Lelchuk), while the man who has kept his distance, attended solely to the written word and dedicated himself to finding the deep places of the imagination, finds a Roth who has harrowed his soul, bravely disassembled the delicate machinery of his personality, and come up with shit.

If Freud remains relevant to this picture it is not the Freud-in-Spielvogel who is clearing his throat and choosing his words ever so carefully in preparation for ushering his anguished patient to the door, but the young Freud of the latency years before he became "Freud," looking intrepidly into his own dreams after his father's death, hoping

234 — *Epilogue*

to find there clues to what he was made of. Freud came up with Oedipus Rex; Roth comes up with Mickey Sabbath. To see that is not at all to disparage Roth but rather to celebrate his own labors to break through to the subterranean self—the old psychoanalytic program recycled as a perilous exercise of imagination—and to call attention to that book in which Roth presents all that is most wretched, sly, sybaritic, lonely, contemptuous, comedic, unsociable, villainous, excremental, manipulative, and above all despairing in himself and offers it to us without palliatives, except the one palliative that the reader has every right to demand: an artist's mastery, through which we are reassured that he is in full awareness of his mission and his materials and unafraid to wrestle into full view whatever he requires to show us in thrilling and indecent detail precisely how his heart and soul—call them if you will ego, id, and superego—are stitched together.

Notes

Roth and His Readers: Notes toward a Bibliography

Notes

Introduction

1. As the mystique of Soviet Communism began to unravel for American intellectuals, the phrase "I had my Kronstadt when . . ." took on a certain currency. It signaled the moment when a member of the Communist Party or a fellow traveler woke up to the reality of Soviet Communism. The first awakenings hit as early as 1921, when a revolt by Russian sailors at the port of Kronstadt was brutally put down by the Bolsheviks under the generalship of Leon Trotsky. Kronstadt was a Kronstadt for some, the famine in the Ukraine was another, the Moscow Trials still another, and for laggards there was the 1956 invasion of Hungary and Khrushchev's de-Stalinization speech that same year. Maybe the most famous Kronstadt of all was Mikhail Gorbachev's in the 1980s, which brought down the entire Soviet empire.

2. Frederick Crews, "Uplift," review of Roth's *The Breast, New York Review of Books*, November 16, 1972.

Chapter 1. The Facts and *The Facts*

1. Philip Roth, "A Talk with Aharon Appelfeld," *New York Times Book Review*, February 28, 1988. It is reprinted in Roth, *Shop Talk*.

2. Claire Bloom, *Leaving a Doll's House: A Memoir* (New York: Little Brown, 1996).

Chapter 2. The Road of Excess

1. Philip Roth, "'I Always Wanted You to Admire My Fasting'; or, Looking at Kafka," *American Review* 17 (May 1973). Reprinted in Roth, *Reading Myself and Others.*

2. Philip Roth, "On the Air," *New American Review* 10 (1970).

3. Géza Róheim (1891–1953) was one of the first anthropologists to import psychoanalytic theory into the analysis of cultures, in such books as *Australian Totemism* (1925), *Animism, Magic, and the Divine King* (1930), *The Eternal Ones of the Dream* (1945), *Psychoanalysis and Anthropology* (1950), and *The Gates of Dream* (1952).

4. That particular notion, which Roth was familiar with, comes from a remarkable essay by Isaac Rosenfeld titled "Adam and Eve on Delancey Street."

It can be found in Mark Shechner, ed., *Preserving the Hunger: An Isaac Rosen-feld Reader* (Detroit: Wayne State University Press, 1988).

5. I'd be hard put to write a sentence like that now, but since Roth was for a while working out of the same frame of reference, it worked well enough where it was.

Chapter 3. Only a *Weltanschauung*

1. Irving Howe, "Philip Roth Reconsidered," *Commentary* 54 (December 1972), reprinted in Howe, *The Critical Point* (New York: Delta, 1973). See also Norman Podhoretz, "Laureate of the New Class," *Commentary* 54 (December 1972); Marie Syrkin, "The Fun of Self-Abuse," *Midstream* 15 (April 1969); and Bruno Bettelheim, "Portnoy Psychoanalyzed," *Midstream* 15 (June–July 1969). See also Syrkin's letter to the editor of *Commentary* in March 1973, complaining that Howe had let Roth off too easily and accusing Roth of reveling in *Rassenschande* (racial defilement) "right out of the Goebbels-Streicher script." The diminished echo, the dying fall, to such carpet-bombing was Joseph Epstein, "What Does Roth Want?" *Commentary* 77 (January 1984). For an instructive contrast, see also Robert Alter's more considered, ambivalent, and finally more illuminating discussion of anti-Semitism in Ernest Lehman's filmed version of *Portnoy's Complaint,* "Defaming the Jews," *Commentary* 55 (January 1973).

2. Howe's essay, "The Lost Young Intellectual," appeared in *Commentary* 2 (October 1946), though I first encountered it in the anthology *Mid-Century,* edited by Harold U. Ribalow (New York: Beechhurst Press, 1955). In the Ribalow volume, Howe's essay is flanked by supporting documents with titles like "A Parable of Alienation" by Daniel Bell, "Plight of the Jewish Intellectual" by Leslie Fiedler, and "Troubled Intellectuals" by Charles Angoff. Is it any wonder that a young Philip Roth might have imagined that in *Portnoy's Complaint* he was working in an established tradition, but extending it into new territory: the territory of sex?

3. Irving Howe, "The New York Intellectuals," *Commentary* 46 (October 1968), reprinted in Howe, *Decline of the New* (New York: Horizon Press, 1970).

Chapter 6. This Is How I Will Live

1. "'I Always Wanted You to Admire My Fasting'; or, Looking at Kafka," *American Review* 17 (May 1973). Reprinted in Roth, *Reading Myself and Others.*

2. John Leonard, "Fathers and Ghosts," *New York Review of Books,* October 25, 1979.

3. Anatole Broyard, "Listener with a Voice," review of *Zuckerman Unbound, New York Times,* February 22, 1981.

4. Joseph Epstein, "What Does Philip Roth Want?" *Commentary* 77 (January 1984).

5. Quote is from Babel's story "Guy de Maupassant," which can be found in almost any Babel collection, the most recent of which is *The Complete Works*

of Isaac Babel, edited by Nathalie Babel, translated by Peter Constantine (New York: W. W. Norton and Company, 2001).

Chapter 7. The Jersey Bounce

1. The background to this novel is the story of Herbert Stempel, whose reign on the popular quiz show *Twenty One* in 1956 was ended when the producers found a more photogenic and bankable contestant in Charles Van Doren and fed him the right answers while ordering Stempel to take a dive. In exchange for promises that were never kept, Stempel blew an easy question, "What motion picture won the Academy Award for 1955?" Stempel knew the answer was *Marty,* but kept his part of the bargain and answered *On the Waterfront,* handing the victory to Van Doren. According to one account, backstage after the show, Stempel overheard someone say, "Now we have a clean-cut intellectual as champion instead of a freak with a sponge memory." Robert Redford's 1994 film, *Quiz Show,* is a docudrama about the rigging of *Twenty One* and Stempel's public grievances afterward, which eventually led to the congressional investigation that brought the curtain down on the show.

2. "Jersey Bounce," copyright Johnson/Bradshaw/Plater/Feyne, Lewis Music Publishing Company.

> They call it the Jersey Bounce
> A rhythm that really counts
> The temperature always mounts
> Whenever they play the funny rhythm they play
>
> It started in Journal Square
> And somebody heard it there
> They put it right on the air
> And now you hear it everywhere
>
> Uptown gave it some licks
> Downtown added some tricks
> No town made it sound the same
> As where it came from
>
> So if you don't feel so hot
> Come down to some Jersey spot
> And whether you're hep or not
> The Jersey Bounce will make you swing.

Chapter 8. The Jawbone of an Ass

1. See chapter 3 for a summary of the real-life backgrounds to Milton Appel and his attack on Nathan Zuckerman.

2. Richard Gilman, review of *Zuckerman Unbound, The Nation,* June 13, 1981.

3. There was for a while a sizable literature of Roth at home that was designed no doubt to expand his reader base to include women. It included James Atlas, "A Visit with Philip Roth," *New York Times Book Review,* September 2, 1979; Richard Stern, "Roth Unbound," *Saturday Review,* June 1981; David Plante, "Conversations with Philip," *New York Times Book Review,* May 4, 1981; Cathleen Medwick, "A Meeting of Arts and Minds," *Vogue,* October 1983; Jesse Kornbluth, "Zuckerman Found? Philip Roth's One-Man Art Colony," *House and Garden,* December 1983.

4. From Isaac Rosenfeld's journals, *Preserving the Hunger: An Isaac Rosenfeld Reader,* with an introduction and edited by Mark Shechner (Detroit: Wayne State University Press, 1988).

5. We needn't read *The Anatomy Lesson* as Harold Bloom does, as moral prophesy, to agree with his own notion of progression here: "One of the many esthetic gains of binding together the entire Zuckerman ordeal (it cannot be called a saga) is to let the reader experience the gradual acceleration of wit from the gentle Chekhovian wistfulness of *The Ghost Writer* on to the Gogolian sense of the ridiculous in *Zuckerman Unbound* and then to the boisterous Westian farce of *The Anatomy Lesson,* only to end in the merciless Kafkan irrealism of 'The Prague Orgy.'" Harold Bloom, "His Long Ordeal by Laughter," *New York Times Book Review,* May 19, 1985.

Chapter 9. "The Prague Orgy" and the Other Europe

1. See Roth's account of this in his introduction to Milan Kundera's *Laughable Loves* (New York: Penguin, 1974). Reprinted in Roth, *Reading Myself and Others.*

2. From the interview with Ivan Klíma published in *Shop Talk.*

3. The following titles in the Writers from the Other Europe series are published by Penguin Books. George Konrad, *The Case Worker* (1974); Milan Kundera, *Laughable Loves* (1975) and *The Book of Laughter and Forgetting* (1980); Ludvík Vaculík, *The Guinea Pigs* (1975); Tadeusz Borowski, *This Way for the Gas, Ladies and Gentlemen* (1976); Bruno Schulz, *The Street of Crocodiles* (1977) and *Sanatorium under the Sign of the Hourglass* (1979); Tadeusz Konwicki, *A Dreambook for Our Time* (1983); Witold Gombrowicz, *Ferdyduke* (1983); Géza Csáth, *Magician's Garden and Other Stories* (1983).

4. See Roth's introduction to Kundera's *Laughable Loves.*

5. George Steiner, "The Archives of Eden," *Salmagundi* 50/51 (Fall 1980/Winter 1981).

6. Mervyn Rothstein, "The Unbounded Spirit of Philip Roth," *New York Times,* August 1, 1985.

Chapter 10. The Five Books of Nathan

1. Robert Alter, "Defenders of the Faith," *Commentary* 84 (July 1987).

Chapter 13. Let Your Jewish Conscience Be Your Guide

1. Of course, this is dated and could easily be updated to 2003. But the original examples carry their own weight. They'll do.

2. From Roth's interview with Dan Cryer in *Newsday*, March 28, 1993.

3. It should be clear that Roth/Pipik's manifesto calling for the Jews to return to their European roots owes its title only to Kitaj (*First Diasporist Manifesto* [New York and London: Thames and Hudson, 1989]), nothing of its content. Kitaj's book is a meditation on his own art as a product of diaspora culture and psychology as well as a general rumination on diaspora as a condition of creativity. As Kitaj's book takes its prologue from Philip Roth, Roth's in turn does this ironic homage to Kitaj.

4. The drum roll for *Operation Shylock* was unprecedented. You'd have thought Roth was starting quarterback in the Super Bowl. Roth's publisher at the time, Simon and Schuster, had invested heavily in him, and the previous novel, *Deception*, had given them a poor return on its investment. *Operation Shylock* had to be a smash hit for them, and they put out what was in effect an all points bulletin on the book. Below are just some of the reviews that appeared.

John Updike, "Recruiting Raw Nerves," *The New Yorker*, March 15, 1993; Robert Alter, "The Spritzer," *New Republic*, April 5, 1993; Ted Solotaroff, Review, *The Nation*, June 7, 1993; Harold Bloom, "Operation Roth," *The New York Review of Books*, April 23, 1993; D. M. Thomas, "Face to Face with His Double," *New York Times*, May 7, 1993; Richard Eder, "Roth Contemplates His Pipik," *Los Angeles Times*, March 7, 1993; Hillel Halkin, "The Traipse of Roth," *Jerusalem Report*, April 1993; and S. T. Meravi, "Roth Meets Roth," *Jerusalem Post*, July 23, 1993. There were a good many others in prominent places. Roth also made himself available for interviews in the *New York Times* and *Newsday*.

Operation Shylock was a bust in the bookstores, which probably proves that you can't tell a book by its coverage. Roth had lost his audience, whatever there was of it to lose by 1993, and he soon afterwards left Simon and Schuster for Houghton, Mifflin, which has remained his publisher ever since. There were rumors in the popular press that Roth's depression over the popular reception of *Operation Shylock* contributed to the breakup of his marriage with Claire Bloom, but who knows about that? Like most celebrities, Roth has always had a shadowy other self—a real world Pipik—who is the subject of titillating rumors and provocative press releases.

Chapter 14. *Sabbath's Theater*

1. *New York Times*, August 22, 1995.
2. *Boston Globe*, August 20, 1995.
3. *Baltimore Sun*, August 10, 1995.

4. McGuane was quoted in the *San Francisco Chronicle,* November 29, 1995. The National Book Award ceremony that night had elements of farce and fiasco. Pleading illness, Roth did not attend to pick up his award, which was accepted instead by his friend Joel Connarroe. The newspaper account continues: "The crowd was divided on whether Roth was behaving like a prima donna because that's what he always does or whether he 'was merely afraid that his controversial and critically unpopular book wasn't going to win,' said the *New York Observer.*

"His official excuse was illness. His friend Joel Connarroe, who read an acceptance speech written by Roth, said the novelist's doctor had diagnosed bronchial flu and hadn't allowed him to attend, 'although he sounded better' the next morning. 'There's nothing like winning a prize to improve things.'

"Fiction committee chairman Thomas McGuane told the *Observer:* 'The book is beyond abrasive, it's insulting to everybody represented in it, but I think it's brilliant, and really challenges people to weigh what art is in literature. . . . My wife hated it so much she threw it across the room after the first sixty pages.'"

5. Frank Kermode, *Pleasing Myself: From Beowulf to Philip Roth.*

6. James Wood, "My Death as a Man," *New Republic,* November 23, 1995.

7. See for example, Anthony Quinn's review in the *Observer,* October 8, 1995. "With this new book, something in the prose has been released, uncorked: Sabbath explodes like some mad genie out of his bottle, rampantly egotistical, exuberantly perverse, demonically cunning. He has dedicated himself to violating taboos, to going a step beyond 'the pale, therapy, good and evil.'"

8. James Wolcott, "The Last Swinger," *New Criterion,* September 1995.

Chapter 16. Take a Bow, Little Guy

1. Norman Corwin, *On a Note of Triumph* (New York: Simon and Schuster, 1945).

2. What Nathan actually heard on the Red Army Chorus record was this:

Mnogo pesen slyhal ya v rodnoj storone,
V nih o gore i radosti peli,
No iz vsex lish' odna v pamyat' vrezalas' mne -
E'to pesnya rabochej arteli:

Ex, dubinushka, uhnem!
Ex, zelyonaya, sama pojdyot, sama poydot!
Podyornem, podyornem,
Da uhnem! *Etcetera.*

Chapter 17. The Psychopathology of Everyday Life

1. Read in particular Anatole Broyard, *Kafka Was the Rage* (New York: C. Southern Books, 1993). About Broyard's "inauthenticity," see Broyard, "Portrait of the Inauthentic Negro," *Commentary* (July 1950). The contributor's

note says of Broyard: "Here Anatole Broyard attempts a similar analysis [to Jean-Paul Sartre's *Anti-Semite and Jew*] to the situation of the American Negro, which he knows at first hand."

2. Henry Louis Gates, "The Passing of Anatole Broyard," initially published as "White Like Me" in *The New Yorker* (June 17, 1996) and reprinted in Gates's *Thirteen Ways of Looking at a Black Man* (New York: Random House, 1997).

3. See the article that appeared in the *New Orleans Times-Picayune*, titled "Writer Explores Hidden Black Heritage Famous Father Kept Secret until His Death," which interviews Broyard's daughter, Bliss (February 5, 2001). Now that she knows, Bliss Broyard says, "You can't be part black. You either are or you aren't. So I call myself an ex-white girl from Connecticut."

Chapter 18. Death and the Maiden

1. Michiko Kakutani, "A Man Adrift, Living on Sexual Memories," *New York Times*, May 8, 2001.

2. Gail Caldwell, "Love and Death: These Are What Preoccupy David Kepesh, the Intellectual Crank at the Center of *The Dying Animal,*" *Boston Globe*, June 11, 2001.

3. Ronald Bush, "My Life as an Old Man," *Tikkun*, January–February 2002.

4. Franz Schubert took the text for the song "Death and the Maiden" from the poet Matthias Claudius (1740–1815) and set it to music in his D. 531, published in 1821. In the later string quartet of 1824, the melody of the second movement, the mournful andante, carries echoes of the original song.

Chapter 19. Third Thoughts

1. S. T. Meravi, "Roth Meets Roth," *Jerusalem Post*, July 23, 1993.

2. R. B. Kitaj, *First Diasporist Manifesto*.

3. Robert Alter, "The Jewish Voice: Jewish Intellectual Life," *Commentary* 100 (October 1995).

Chapter 20. Epilogue

1. Mark Krupnick, "He Never Learned to Swim," *The New Review* 2:22 (January 1976). Whatever I say here about Rahv and *Modern Occasions* is drawn from that article.

2. Alan Lelchuk's novel *American Mischief* was published in New York by Farrar, Straus & Giroux in 1973. The passage quoted in the chapter epigraph can be found on pages 291–92.

3. Alan Lelchuk, *Ziff: A Life?* (New York: Carroll & Graf, 2003).

4. Mark Krupnick, *Deep Places of the Imagination* (Madison: University of Wisconsin Press, forthcoming). The book was completed shortly before Krupnick's death in March 2003.

5. Mark Krupnick, *Lionel Trilling and the Fate of Cultural Criticism* (Evanston: Northwestern University Press, 1986).

Roth and His Readers: Notes toward a Bibliography

In compiling a bibliography of Philip Roth, you have to protect yourself or risk being swamped. Once he started, Roth never stopped writing, and there are uncollected stories whose titles at least are known dating all the way back to the Bucknell University literary magazine, *Et Cetera*, in 1952. Moreover, some of the uncollected fiction is Roth at the peak of his game and will, hopefully, find its way into a collection one day. A particular favorite of mine is "On the Air," which appeared in Ted Solotaroff's magazine, *New American Review* 10, in 1970. Still, you have to set limits, and a comprehensive bibliography of Roth's writing and writing about him will have to await a publication of a different kind with more comprehensive ambitions. What follows of Roth's own writing limits itself to books only.

By Philip Roth

Fiction

Goodbye, Columbus and Five Short Stories. Boston: Houghton Mifflin, 1959.
Letting Go. New York: Random House, 1962.
When She Was Good. New York: Random House, 1967.
Portnoy's Complaint. New York: Random House, 1969.
Our Gang (Starring Tricky and His Friends). New York: Random House, 1971.
The Breast. New York: Holt, Rinehart and Winston, 1972.
The Great American Novel. New York: Holt, Rinehart and Winston, 1973.
My Life as a Man. New York: Holt, Rinehart and Winston, 1974.
The Professor of Desire. New York: Farrar, Straus and Giroux, 1977.
The Ghost Writer. New York: Farrar, Straus and Giroux, 1979.
A Philip Roth Reader. New York: Farrar, Straus and Giroux, 1980.
Zuckerman Unbound. New York: Farrar, Straus and Giroux, 1981.
The Anatomy Lesson. New York: Farrar, Straus and Giroux, 1983.
Zuckerman Bound: A Trilogy and Epilogue. New York: Farrar, Straus and Giroux, 1985.
The Counterlife. New York: Farrar, Straus and Giroux, 1986.
Deception: A Novel. New York: Simon and Schuster, 1990.
Operation Shylock: A Confession. New York: Simon and Schuster, 1993.
Sabbath's Theater. Boston: Houghton, Mifflin, 1995.
American Pastoral. Boston: Houghton, Mifflin, 1997.

I Married a Communist. Boston: Houghton, Mifflin, 1998.
The Human Stain. Boston: Houghton, Mifflin, 2000.
The Dying Animal. Boston: Houghton, Mifflin, 2001.

Nonfiction

Reading Myself and Others. New York: Farrar, Straus and Giroux, 1975.
The Facts: A Novelist's Autobiography. New York: Farrar, Straus and Giroux, 1988.
Patrimony: A True Story. New York: Simon and Schuster, 1991.
Shop Talk. Boston: Houghton, Mifflin, 2001.

Secondary Reading

You can drown in Roth criticism. By 2003, the sheer tsunami of it stupefies. If by the mid-1970s we might have spoken of a Roth industry, what about the 1990s? A Rothmart? A Roth outlet mall? The effort to compile a usable list of reviews, essays, and books, let alone read and make sense of it, will send the most sedentary scholar out to paint the house. Roth criticism makes Borges's Library of Babel look like the bookmobile. To cite a simple example, the best monitoring posts for book reviews of any American writer are the Gale Research series' *Contemporary Authors, Contemporary Authors New Revision,* and *Contemporary Literary Criticism (CA, CANR,* and *CLC),* and a recent check shows synoptic essays on Roth in *CA* 1-4R, *CANR*-1, and *CA* 46, as well as *CLC,* volumes 1, 2, 3, 4, 6, 9, 15, 22, 31, 47, 66, and 86. Some of these entries are gargantuan, including one in *CLC* 66 that runs to thirty-nine pages on *Portnoy's Complaint* alone. Literary research is not for the faint-hearted. If the sheer tonnage of Roth criticism, reviews, and commentary alone tells us anything, it is that Roth possesses a far-flung readership to whom he matters, and that to read him is to have an opinion about him. There are approximately fifteen books on Roth alone and perhaps three times that many with chapters devoted to him. Virtually all of this writing belongs to one of two categories: disinterested scholarship, in which Roth is examined and dissected as entomologists go about examining and dissecting fruit flies, and raging polemic, in which Roth is badgered and cross-examined as prosecutors and FBI investigators might cross-examine a serial killer or a terrorist. The trial transcripts are more absorbing and entertaining than the scholarly monographs, reflecting as they do the schismatic cultural environment into which his books were published and in which they have had their most telling impact. Also, book reviewers and cultural polemicists write better than the academics. They have to: besides knowing that they are in the entertainment business, they also have to come out on top. Thus their vehemence, their ebullience, their parti pris, their will-to-spin, their posture of fatigue and savvy, their can-you-top-this phrasing. By contrast, the academics seem to be following the plow from furrow to furrow. Without attempting to distinguish one sort from the other, I've come up with a selection that I hope will be usable.

Books Either about Roth or Significantly Devoted to Him

Appelfeld, Aharon. *Beyond Despair: Three Lectures and a Conversation with Philip Roth.* Translated by Jeffrey M. Green. New York: Fromm International, 1994.

Baumgarten, Murray, and Barbara Gottfried. *Understanding Philip Roth.* Columbia: University of South Carolina Press, 1990.

Bloom, Claire. *Leaving a Doll's House: A Memoir.* Boston; Little, Brown, 1996.

Bloom, Harold, ed. *Philip Roth.* New York: Chelsea House, 1986.

Cooper, Alan. *Philip Roth and the Jews.* Albany: SUNY Press, 1996.

Finkielkraut, Alain. *Le juif imaginaire.* Paris: Editions du Seuil, 1980. Reprinted as *The Imaginary Jew,* translated by Kevin O'Neill and David Suchoff. Lincoln: University of Nebraska Press, 1984.

Halio, Jay L. *Philip Roth Revisited.* New York: Twayne, 1992.

Jones, Judith Paterson, and Guinevera A. Nance. *Philip Roth.* New York: Ungar, 1981.

Krupnick, Mark. *Deep Places of the Imagination.* Madison: University of Wisconsin Press, forthcoming.

Lee, Hermione. *Philip Roth.* New York: Methuen, 1982.

Lelchuk, Alan. *Ziff: A Life?* New York: Caroll and Graf, 2003.

McDaniel, John. N. *The Fiction of Philip Roth.* Haddonfield, N.J.: Haddonfield House, 1974.

Meeter, Glenn. *Bernard Malamud and Philip Roth: A Critical Essay.* Grand Rapids, Mich.: Eerdsmans, 1968.

Milbauer, Asher, and Donald G. Watson, eds. *Reading Philip Roth.* New York: St. Martin's Press, 1988.

Pinsker, Sanford. *The Comedy that "Hoits": An Essay on the Fiction of Philip Roth.* Columbia: University of Missouri Press, 1975.

Pinsker, Sanford, ed. *Critical Essays on Philip Roth.* Boston: Hall, 1982.

Rodgers, Bernard F., Jr. *Philip Roth.* Boston: Twayne, 1978.

———. *Philip Roth: A Bibliography.* Metuchen, N.J.: Scarecrow Press, 1974.

Searles, George J. *The Fiction of Philip Roth and John Updike.* Carbondale: Southern Illinois University Press, 1985.

Shechner, Mark. *After the Revolution: Studies in the Contemporary Jewish-American Imagination.* Bloomington: Indiana University Press, 1987.

Wade, Stephen. *The Imagination in Transit.* Sheffield, England: Academic Press, 1996.

Articles, Reviews, or Book Chapters about Roth

This section is so vast that all you can do is put on blinders, cast out whole categories, and then throw darts at the remaining items and hope to hit a few bulls-eyes. It is highly selective about book reviews from metropolitan newspapers and popular weeklies, though a good deal of that writing is as incisive and penetrating as anything to be found in the scholarly journals, maybe even more so. One takes informed guesses based on intuition and already-existing collections of citations, like those in *Contemporary Authors* or *Contemporary Literary Criticism,* to which I refer readers desiring more material. There is a bias here toward recent writing, from the late 1980s through 2002, on the principle that it is likely to contain citations to earlier essays and studies, thus leading scholars and students back through a chain of references to prior commentary. Moreover, since much of my research of this sort is done by computer search, magazines that provide online indices to their archives and, even better, access to full-text articles, are more likely to wind up here than those that do not.

Abramovitch, Alex. "The Smutty Professor." Review of *The Dying Animal. Village Voice,* May 16–22, 2001.
Adams, Robert M. "The Reality Game." Review of *Patrimony. The New York Review of Books,* May 16, 1991.
Adams, Tim. "Miss America Turns Bomber. Do You Still Blame the Parents?" Review of *American Pastoral. The Observer,* May 25, 1997.
Alexander, Edward. "Philip Roth at Century's End." *New England Review–Middlebury Series* 20:2 (spring 1999).
Alter, Robert. "Defenders of the Faith." *Commentary* 84 (July 1987).
―――. "The Spritzer." Review of *Operation Shylock. New Republic* 208:14 (April 5, 1993).
―――. "The Jewish Voice: Jewish Intellectual Life." *Commentary* 100 (October 1995).
Annan, Gabrielle. "Theme and Variations." Review of *Deception. The New York Review of Books,* May 31, 1990.
[Anon.] "Roth's Writer and His Stumbling Block." Review of *The Anatomy Lesson. New York Times,* October 30, 1983.
Atlas, James. "The Laureates of Lewd: P. Roth, G. Vidal and J. Updike." *Gentlemen's Quarterly* 63 (April 1993).
Bailey, Peter J. "'Why Not Tell the Truth?': The Autobiographies of Three Fiction Writers." *Critique* 32 (1991).
Beatty, Jack. "The Crooked Timber of Humanity." A triple review of *American Pastoral, I Married a Communist,* and *The Human Stain. Atlantic Monthly* (March 8, 2001).
Berman, Jeffrey. "Philip Roth's Psychoanalysts." In *The Talking Cure: Literary Representations of Psychoanalysis.* New York: New York University Press, 1985.
Bernstein, M. A. Review of *The Dying Animal. Times Literary Supplement,* May 26, 2000.
Bernstein, Richard. "Thinking Man's Talk with Thinkers." Review of *Shop Talk. New York Times,* September 26, 2001.

Berryman, Charles. "Philip Roth and Nathan Zuckerman: A Portrait of the Artist as a Young Prometheus." *Contemporary Literature* 31 (1990).

Bertens, J. W. "'The Measured Self vs. the Insatiable Self': Some Notes on Philip Roth." In *From Cooper to Philip Roth: Essays on American Literature,* edited by J. Bakker and D. R. Wilkinson. Amsterdam: Rodopi, 1980.

Bettelheim, Bruno. "Portnoy Psychoanalyzed." *Midstream* 15 (1969).

Birkerts, Sven. "Old Dog, New Tricks." Review of *The Human Stain. Esquire,* June 2000.

Birnbaum, Milton. "Philip Roth: The Artist in Search of Self." *Modern Age* 36 (Fall 1993): 82.

Bloom, Harold. "His Long Ordeal by Laughter." Review of *Zuckerman Bound. New York Times,* May 19, 1985.

———. "Operation Roth." Review of *Operation Shylock. The New York Review of Books,* April 23, 1993.

Bourjailly, Vance. "A Cool Book on a Warm Topic." Review of *The Professor of Desire. New York Times,* September 18, 1975.

Boyers, Robert. "The Indigenous Berserk." Review of *American Pastoral. New Republic,* July 7, 1997.

Brown, Russell E. "Philip Roth and Bruno Schulz." *ANQ* 6 (1993).

Broyard, Anatole. "Listener with a Voice." Review of *Zuckerman Unbound. New York Times,* February 22, 1981.

Brauner, David. "Fiction as Self-Accusation: Philip Roth and the Jewish Other." *Studies in American Jewish Literature* 17 (1998).

Bush, Ronald. "My Life as an Old Man." Review of *The Dying Animal. Tikkun,* January–February 2002.

Caldwell, Gail. "Roth Redux: The Wicked Ironist Is Back." Review of *American Pastoral. Boston Globe,* April 20, 1997.

———. "Philip's Follies." Review of *Sabbath's Theater. Boston Globe,* April 20, 1995.

———. "The Intellectual Crank at the Center of *The Dying Animal.*" Review of *The Dying Animal. Boston Globe,* June 11, 2001.

Cohen, Robert. "The Indigenous American Berserk." Review of *American Pastoral. The New Leader,* May 19, 1997.

Cohen, Joseph. "Paradise Lost, Paradise Regained: Reflections on Philip Roth's Recent Fiction." *Studies in American Jewish Literature* 8 (1989).

Cowley, Jason. "The Nihilist." Review of *The Dying Animal. Atlantic Monthly* (May 2001).

Crews, Frederick. "Uplift." *The New York Review of Books,* November 16, 1972. Reprinted in Crews, *Skeptical Engagements.* New York: Oxford University Press, 1986.

Dickstein, Morris. "Now Vee May Perhaps Have Begun." Review of *My Life as a Man. New York Times,* June 2, 1974.

————. "Black Humor and History: The Early Sixties." In *Gates of Eden: American Culture in the Sixties*. New York: Basic Books, 1977.

Eder, Richard. "Raging Roth." Review of *American Pastoral*. *Los Angeles Times*, May 4, 1997.

————. "Roth Contemplates His Pipik." Review of *Operation Shylock*. *Los Angeles Times*, March 7, 1993.

————. "Zuckerman Leashed." Review of *The Human Stain*. *Newsday*, October 11, 1998.

Edwards, Thomas. "Vita Nuova." Review of *The Facts*. *The New York Review of Books*, October 13, 1988.

Epstein, Joseph. "What Does Philip Roth Want?" *Commentary* 77 (January 1984).

Ezrahi, Sidra DeKoven, Daniel Lazare, Daphne Merkin, Morris Dickstein, and Anita Norich. "Philip Roth Symposium." *Tikkun* 8:3 (May 1993).

Finney, Brian. "Roth's *Counterlife*: Destabilizing the Facts." *Biography* 16 (1993).

Fredericksen, Brooke. "Home Is Where the Text Is: Exile, Homeland, and Jewish American Writing." *Studies in American Jewish Literature* 11 (Spring 1992).

Furman, Andrew. "The Ineluctable Holocaust in the Fiction of Philip Roth." *Studies in American Jewish Literature* 12 (1993).

————. "A New 'Other' Emerges in American Jewish Literature: Philip Roth's Israel Fiction." *Contemporary Literature* 36 (1995).

Gass, William. "Deciding to Do the Impossible." Review of *The Counterlife*. *New York Times*, January 4, 1987.

Gates, David. "Celebrating an Unholy Sabbath." Review of *Sabbath's Theater*. *Newsweek*, August 21, 1995.

Gilman, Richard. Review of *Zuckerman Unbound*. *The Nation*, June 13, 1981.

Girgus, Sam. "'The New Covenant' and the Dilemma of Dissensus: Bercovitch, Roth, and Doctorow." In *Summoning: Ideas of the Covenant and Interpretive Theory*, edited by Ellen Spolsky. Albany: SUNY Press, 1993.

Gitlin, Todd. "Weather Girl." Review of *American Pastoral*. *The Nation*, May 12, 1997.

Goodheart, Eugene. "'Postmodern' Meditations on the Self: The Work of Philip Roth and Don DeLillo." In *Desire and Its Discontents*. New York: Columbia University Press, 1991.

————. "Writing and the Unmaking of the Self." *Contemporary Literature* 29 (1988).

Green, Geoffrey. "Metamorphosing Kafka: The Example of Philip Roth." In *The Dove and the Mole: Kafka's Journey into Darkness and Creativity*, edited by Ronald Gottesman and Moshe Lazar. Malibu, Calif.: Undena, 1987.

Greenberg, Robert M. "Transgression in the Fiction of Philip Roth." *Twentieth Century Literature* 43:4 (winter 1997).

Greenstein, Michael. "Ozick, Roth, and Postmodernism." *Studies in American Jewish Literature* 10:1 (1991).

———. "Secular Sermons and American Accents: The Nonfiction of Bellow, Ozick, and Roth." *Shofar: An Interdisciplinary Journal of Jewish Studies* 2:1 (2001).

Gross, Kenneth. "Love among the Puppets." *Raritan* 17:1 (summer 1997).

Halio, Jay L., ed. *Philip Roth. Shofar: An Interdisciplinary Journal of Jewish Studies* 19:1 (2000).

Halkin, Hillel. "The Traipse of Roth." Review of *Operation Shylock. Jerusalem Report*, April, 1993.

———. "How to Read Philip Roth." *Commentary* 97 (February 1994).

Hardwick, Elizabeth. "Paradise Lost." Review of *American Pastoral. The New York Review of Books*, June 12, 1997.

Harris, Roger. "Brilliant Prose Stained by a Strained Plot." Review of *The Human Stain. Newark Star-Ledger,* May 5, 2000.

Heller, Zöe. "The Ghost Rutter." Review of *The Dying Animal. New Republic,* June 21, 2001.

Henscher, Philip. "Terrorism: The Perfect Choice." Review of *American Pastoral. The Spectator,* May 31, 1997.

Hoberman, J. "Dangerous Liaisons." Review of *I Married a Communist. Village Voice*, October 20, 1998.

Howe, Irving. "Philip Roth Reconsidered." *Commentary* 54 (December 1972).

Iannone, Carol. "An American Tragedy." *Commentary* 104 (August 1997).

Kakutani, Michiko. "A Postwar Paradise Shattered from Within." Review of *American Pastoral. New York Times*, April 15, 1997.

———. "Manly Giant vs. Zealots and Scheming Women." Review of *I Married a Communist. New York Times*, October 6, 1998.

———. "Confronting the Failures of a Professor Who Passes." Review of *The Human Stain. New York Times*, May 2, 2000.

Kamenetz, Rodger. "'The Hocker, Misnomer . . . Love/Dad': Philip Roth's *Patrimony.*" *The Southern Review* 27 (1991).

Kaplan, Justin. "Play It Again Nathan." Review of *The Facts. New York Times*, October 25, 1988.

Kauvar, Elaine M. "This Doubly Reflected Communication: Philip Roth's Autobiographies." *Contemporary Literature* 36 (1995).

Kazin, Alfred "The Earthly City of Jews." In *Bright Book of Life*. Boston: Atlantic, Little, Brown and Co., 1973.

Kellman, Steven G. "Philip Roth's Ghost Writer." *Comparative Literature Studies* 21 (1984).

Kermode, Frank. "Philip Roth." In *Pleasing Myself: From Beowulf to Philip Roth*. London: Allen Lane; The Penguin Press, 2001. Reprinted from *The New York Review of Books*, November 16, 1995.

Koenig, Rhoda. "Torah de Force?" *New York* 26:10 (March 8, 1993).

Krupnick, Mark. "Jewish Autobiographies and the Counter-Example of Philip Roth." In *American Literary Dimensions: Poems and Essays in Honor of Melvin J. Friedman.* Edited by Jay Halio. Newark: University of Delaware Press; London: Associated University Presses, 1999.

Leavey, Ann. "Philip Roth: A Bibliographic Essay (1984–1988)." *Studies in American Jewish Literature* 8 (1989).

Leonard, John. "Fathers and Ghosts." Review of *The Ghost Writer. The New York Review of Books,* October 25, 1979.

———. "Bedtime for Bolsheviks." Review of *I Married a Communist. The Nation,* December 28, 1998.

———. "A Child of the Age." Review of *The Human Stain. The New York Review of Books,* June 15, 2000.

Levi, Jonathan. "Reading Lessons." Review of *Shop Talk. Los Angeles Times,* November 25, 2001.

Lodge, David. "Sick with Desire." Review of *The Dying Animal. The New York Review of Books,* July 5, 2001.

Lombreglia, Ralph. "The Life of Job in Suburbia." Review of *American Pastoral. Atlantic Monthly,* June 1997.

McLemee, Scott. Review of *I Married a Communist. Salon.com,* September 28, 1998.

Mendelsohn, Daniel. "Roth's Cause." Review of *The Human Stain. New York,* May 29, 2000.

Meravi, S. T. "Roth Meets Roth." Review of *Operation Shylock. The Jerusalem Post,* July 23, 1993.

Moore, Lorrie. "The Wrath of Athena." Review of *The Human Stain. New York Times,* May 7, 2000.

O'Donnell, Patrick. "The Disappearing Text: Philip Roth's *The Ghost Writer.*" *Contemporary Literature* 24 (1983).

Olcott, Anthony. "Philip Roth and His Hall of Mirrors." Review of *Zuckerman Bound. Washington Post,* June 16, 1985.

Pinsker, Sanford. "Imagination on the Ropes." *The Georgia Review* 37 (1983).

———. "Jewish-American Literature's Lost-and-Found Department: How Philip Roth and Cynthia Ozick Reimagine Their Significant Dead." *Modern Fiction Studies* 35 (1989).

———. "Deconstruction as Apology: The Counterfictions of Philip Roth." *Bearing the Bad News.* Iowa City: University of Iowa Press, 1990.

———. "The Facts, the 'Unvarnished Truth,' and the Fictions of Philip Roth." *Studies in American Jewish Literature* 11 (1992).

———. "Imagining American Reality." *The Southern Review* 29 (1993).

———. "Art as Excess: The 'Voices' of Charlie Parker and Philip Roth." *Partisan Review* 69:1 (2002).

Pinsky, Robert. "Letting Go." Review of *Patrimony. New York Times,* January 16, 1991.

Pritchard, William. "Roth Unbound." Review of *Sabbath's Theater*. *New York Times*, September 10, 1995.

Podhoretz, Norman. "Laureate of the New Class." *Commentary* 54 (December 1972).

———. "The Adventures of Philip Roth." *Commentary* 106 (October 1998).

———. "Bellow at 85, Roth at 67." *Commentary* 110 (July–August 2000).

Quinn, Anthony. "Connoisseur of Whoring." Review of *Sabbath's Theater*. *The Observer*, October 8, 1995.

Ravvin, Norman. "Strange Presences on the Family Tree: The Unacknowledged Literary Father in Philip Roth's 'The Prague Orgy.'" *English Studies in Canada* 17 (1991).

Rifkind, Donna. "The End of Innocence." Review of *American Pastoral*. *Washington Post*, June 8, 1997.

Rubin-Dorsky, Jeffrey. "Honor Thy Father." *Raritan* 11 (1992).

———. "Philip Roth's *The Ghost Writer:* Literary Heritage and Jewish Irreverence." *Studies in American Jewish Literature* 8 (1989).

Safer, Elaine. "Tragedy and Farce in Roth's *The Human Stain*." *Critique: Studies in Contemporary Fiction* 49:3 (spring 2002).

Sale, Roger. "Reading Myself and Others." Review of *Reading Myself and Others*. *New York Times*, May 25, 1975.

Scott, A. O. "Alter Alter Ego." Review of *The Dying Animal*. *New York Times*, May 27, 2001.

Senior, Jennifer. "Roth Blows Up." *New York*, May 1, 2000.

Shechner, Mark. "Philip Roth." *Partisan Review* 41 (1974).

———. "Philip Roth: The Road of Excess." In *After the Revolution: Studies in the Contemporary Jewish-American Imagination*. Bloomington: Indiana University Press, 1987.

———. "Zuckerman's Travels." *American Literary History* 1 (1989). Reprinted in *The Conversion of the Jews and Other Essays*. New York: St. Martin's, 1990.

Sheed, Wilfred. "Howe's Complaint." *New York Times*, May 6, 1973.

Showalter, Elaine. "Tedium of the Gropes of Roth." Review of *The Dying Animal*. *Times of London*, June 27, 2001.

Sokoloff, Naomi. "Imagining Israel in American Jewish Fiction: Anne Roiphe's *Lovingkindness* and Philip Roth's *The Counterlife*." *Studies in American Jewish Literature* 10 (1991).

Solotaroff, Theodore. "The Journey of Philip Roth." *Atlantic Monthly*, April 1969.

———. Review of *Operation Shylock*. *The Nation*, June 7, 1993.

Spargo, R. Clifton. "To Invent as Presumptuously as Real Life: Parody and the Cultural Memory of Anne Frank in Roth's *The Ghost Writer*." *Representations* 76 (2001).

Stade, George. "Roth's Complaint." Review of *Zuckerman Unbound*. *New York Times*, May 24, 1981.

Stone, Robert. "Waiting for Lefty." Review of *I Married a Communist. The New York Review of Books*, November 5, 1998.

Taylor, Charles. Review of *The Dying Animal. Salon.com*, May 18, 2001.

Thomas, D. M. "Face to Face with His Double." Review of *Operation Shylock. New York Times*, May 7, 1993.

Towers, Robert. "The Lesson of the Master." Review of *The Ghost Writer. New York Times*, September 2, 1979.

Trachtenberg, Stanley. "In the Egosphere: Philip Roth's Anti-Bildungsroman." *Papers on Language and Literature* 25 (1989).

Updike, John. "Recruiting Raw Nerves." Review of *Operation Shylock. The New Yorker*, March 15, 1993.

Wallace, James D. "'This Nation of Narrators': Transgression, Revenge and Desire in *Zuckerman Bound*." *Modern Language Studies* 21 (1991).

Webb, Igor. "Born Again." Review of *The Human Stain. Partisan Review* 68:4 (2000).

Weldon, Fay. "Talk before Sex and after Sex." Review of *Deception. New York Times*, March 11, 1990.

Whitfield, Stephen J. "Comic Echoes of Kafka." *American Humor* 9 (1982).

———. "Laughter in the Dark: Notes on American-Jewish Humor." *Midstream* (February 1978).

Wilson, Matthew. "Fathers and Sons in History: Philip Roth's *The Counterlife*." *Prooftexts* 11 (1991).

———. "The Ghost Writer: Kafka, Het Achterhuis, and History." *Studies in American Jewish Literature* 10 (1991).

Wirth-Nesher, Hana. "The Artist Tales of Philip Roth." *Prooftexts* 3 (1983).

Wolcott, James. "The Last Swinger." *New Criterion* 14:1 (September 1995).

Wood, James. "My Death as a Man." Review of *Sabbath's Theater. New Republic*, October 23, 1995.

———. "The Sentimentalist." Review of *I Married a Communist. New Republic*, October 12, 1998.

———. Review of *The Human Stain. New Republic*, April 17–24, 2000.

Wood, Michael. "The Trouble with Swede Levov." Review of *American Pastoral. New York Times*, April 20, 1997.

Interviews with Roth, Including Self-Interviews and Comments on His Own Books, Excluding Interviews Collected in *Reading Myself and Others*.

Elusive as he is famed for being, and usually is, Roth has in fact been uncommonly available to talk about his writing and occasionally his life. As if D. H. Lawrence had never admonished us to trust the tale, not the teller, Roth has been constantly at our elbow, chauffeuring us through his books, for which I have been consistently grateful. Especially in the early years when he felt obliged to explain himself and then explain the explanation, Roth has been, in interviews and sometimes self-interviews, a consistently illuminating commentator on the writing of Roth. His self-commentary—strange to say for a writer who specializes in compulsive characters—invariably comes across as measured and sensible. Recall that the first 112 pages of his *Reading Myself and Others* consists of Roth's explanations, exculpations, and interpretations of himself. And while he is not always quick to point out the obsessions, vulnerabilities, denials, self-indulgences, and flat spots in his own writing—who is?—he has, at least once, assigned that task to his understudy and hand puppet, Nathan Zuckerman, in *The Facts*, letting Zuckerman have the last word.

The following list of interviews and visits with Roth and fireside chats is undoubtedly far from exhaustive. These were simply the easiest to find. They are arranged by date of publication.

Davidson, Sara. "Talk with Philip Roth." *New York Times,* September 18, 1977.

Atlas, James. "A Visit with Philip Roth." *New York Times,* September 2, 1979.

Kakutani, Michiko. "Is Roth Really Writing about Roth?" *New York Times,* May 11, 1981.

Stern, Richard. "Roth Unbound." *Saturday Review,* June 1981.

Finkelkraut, Alain. "The Ghosts of Roth." *Esquire,* September 1981.

Roth, Philip. "The Book that I'm Writing." On *The Anatomy Lesson. New York Times,* June 12, 1983.

Medwick, Kathleen. "A Meeting of Arts and Minds." *Vogue,* October 1983.

Kornbluth, Jesse. "Zuckerman Found? Philip Roth's One-Man Art Colony." *House and Garden,* December 1983.

Plante, David. "Conversation with Philip Roth." *New York Times,* January 1, 1984.

Lee, Hermione. The Art of Fiction LXXXIV: Philip Roth Interview. *Paris Review* 26 (fall 1984).

Hamilton, Ian. "A Confusion of Realms." *The Nation,* June 1, 1985.

Rothstein, Mervyn. "The Unbounded Spirit of Philip Roth." *New York Times,* August 1, 1985.

Rothstein, Mervyn. "Philip Roth and the World of 'What If.'" *New York Times,* December 17, 1986.

Span, Paula. "Roth's Zuckerman Redux: For *The Counterlife,* Leading His Altered Ego through Life, Death and Renewal." *Washington Post,* January 6, 1987.

Rothstein, Mervyn. "From Philip Roth, 'The Facts' as He Remembers Them." *New York Times,* September 6, 1988.

Adachi, Ken. "Is Anyone Out There Actually Reading?" *Toronto Star,* September 17, 1988.

Roth, Philip. "Goodbye Newark: Roth Remembers His Beginnings." *New York Times,* October 1, 1989. Reprinted as the preface to the thirtieth anniversary edition of *Goodbye, Columbus.*

Brent, Jonathan. "What Facts? A Talk with Roth." *New York Times*, September 25, 1988.

Darling, Lynn. "His Father's Son." *Newsday*, January 28, 1991.

Rothstein, Mervyn. "To Newark, with Love. Philip Roth." *New York Times*, March 29, 1991.

Keyishian, Marjorie. "Roth Returning to Newark to Get History Award." *New York Times*, October 4, 1992.

Roth, Philip. "A Bit of Jewish Mischief." *New York Times*, March 7, 1993.

Fein, Esther B. "Philip Roth Sees Double. And Maybe Triple, Too." *New York Times*, March 9, 1993.

Cryer, Dan. "Talking with Philip Roth: Author Meets the Critics." *Newsday*, March 28, 1993.

McGrath, Charles. "Zuckerman's Alter Brain." *New York Times*, May 7, 2000.

Remnick, David. "Into the Clear." *The New Yorker*, May 8, 2000.